The Ghosts of Berlin

The University of Chicago Press

The Ghosts of Berlin

Confronting German History in the Urban Landscape

Brian Ladd

Chicago and London

Brian Ladd teaches history at Rensselaer Polytechnic Institute. He is the author of *Urban Planning and Civic Order in Germany, 1860–1914*.

The University of Chicago Press, Chicago 60637
The University of Chicago Press, Ltd., London

Printed in the United States of America
06 05 04 03 02 01 00 99 98 97 5 4 3 2 1

ISBN (cloth): 0-226-46761-9

Frontispiece: Berlin Wall and Potsdamer Platz, 1966, looking east. Photo courtesy of Landesbildstelle. The map facing page 1 is by Ellen Cesarski. Uncredited photographs are by the author.

Library of Congress Cataloging-in-Publication Data

Ladd, Brian, 1957–
The ghosts of Berlin : confronting German history in the urban landscape / Brian Ladd.
p. cm.
Includes bibliographical references and index.
ISBN 0-226-46761-9 (alk. paper)
1. City planning—Germany—Berlin. 2. Urbanization—Germany—Berlin—History. 3. City and town life—Germany—Berlin—History. 4. Urban ecology—Germany—Berlin. I. Title.
HT169.G32B4127 1997
307.1′216′0943155—dc20 96-28562
CIP

The paper used in this publication meets the minimum requirements of the American National Standard for Information Sciences—Permanence of Paper for Printed Library Materials, ANSI Z39.48-1984.

Contents

Illustrations

Illustrations

Acknowledgments

Berliners—especially those typical Berliners who come from somewhere else—love to talk about their city. I have borrowed ideas from friends and strangers alike and in many cases have conveniently forgotten whom to credit. For assistance offered in their particular areas of expertise, however, I would like to thank Michael S. Cullen, Frank Dingel, Eberhard Elfert, Alfred Kernd'l, Annette Tietenberg, Helmut Trotnow, Johannes Tuchel, James J. Ward, and Horst Weiss.

The Free University's Berlin Program for Advanced German and European Studies brought me to Berlin to do another project—but it brought me to Berlin. The American Council of Learned Societies supported a summer research trip to study the Wall. I profited from the use of newspaper archives at the Free University's Otto-Suhr-Institut, the Humboldt University, the *Tageszeitung,* the Aktives Museum Faschismus und Widerstand, and the Gedenkstätte Deutscher Widerstand.

I am especially grateful to those who read and commented on all or part of the manuscript: Richard Bodek, Donna Harsch, Claus Käpplinger, Daniel Mattern, Dan Sherman, Ray Stokes, Sam Tanenhaus, and the Press's anonymous reviewers. Karen Wilson and the staff of the University of Chicago Press guided the manuscript through a lengthy but useful review process. Finally, Louise Burkhart was my most careful and relentless critic and supporter. This book is for her and for Clare, whose imminent arrival spurred me to completion of the manuscript and whose presence keeps me from brooding about faraway cities.

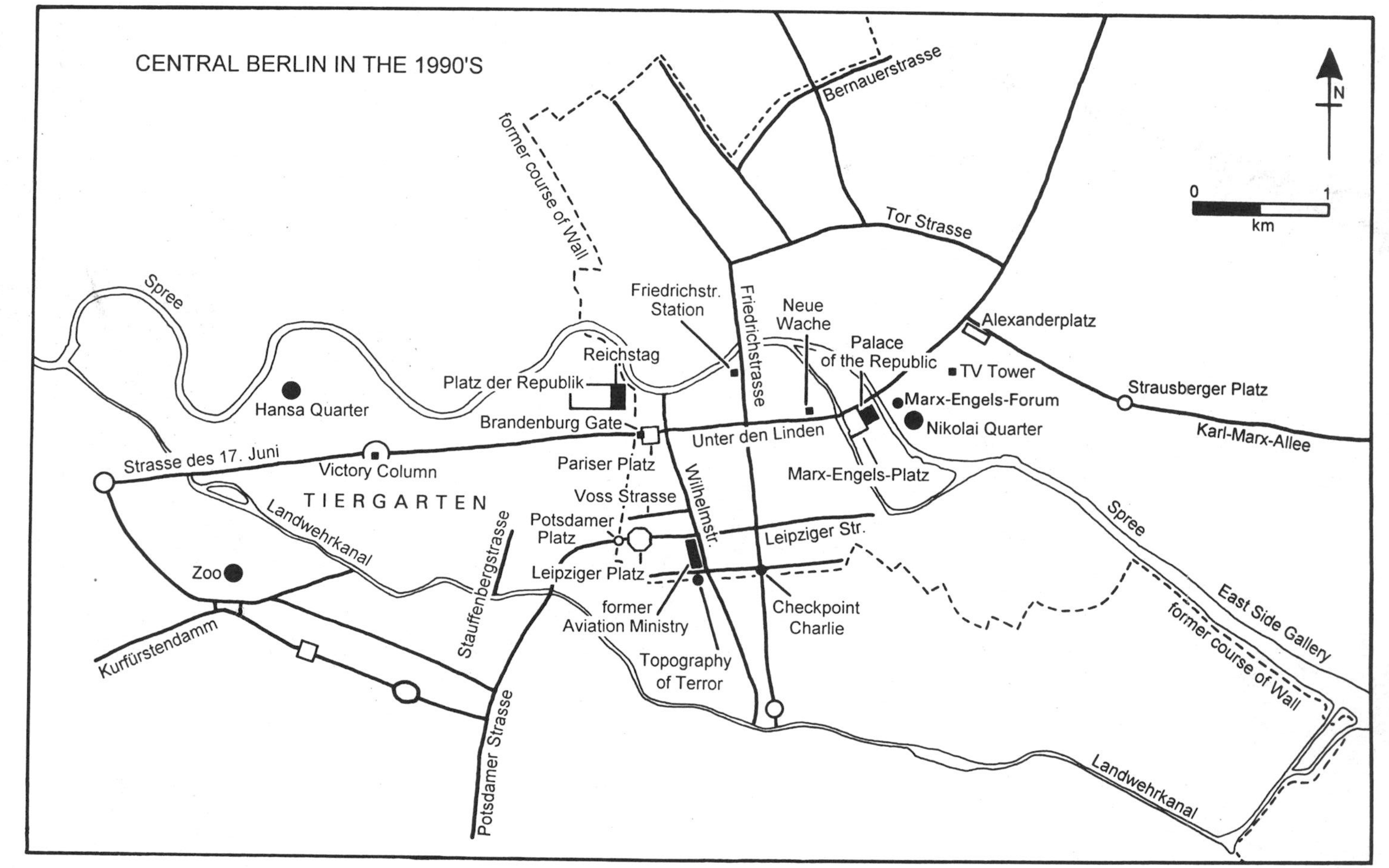
CENTRAL BERLIN IN THE 1990'S
N
0
1
km
Bernauerstrasse
former course of Wall
Tor Strasse
Spree
Friedrichstr.
Station
Friedrichstrasse
Neue
Wache
Palace
of the Republic
Alexanderplatz
TV Tower
Strausberger Platz
Reichstag
Platz der Republik
Hansa Quarter
Marx-Engels-Forum
Nikolai Quarter
Brandenburg Gate
Unter den Linden
Karl-Marx-Allee
Strasse des 17. Juni
Victory Column
Pariser Platz
Marx-Engels-Platz
TIERGARTEN
Voss Strasse
Wilhelmstr.
Spree
Landwehrkanal
Potsdamer
Platz
Leipziger Str.
Stauffenbergstrasse
Zoo
Leipziger Platz
former
Aviation Ministry
Checkpoint
Charlie
East Side Gallery
former course of Wall
Kurfürstendamm
Topography
of Terror
Potsdamer Strasse
Landwehrkanal

Introduction

Berlin is a haunted city. By the middle of this century, people living in Berlin could look back on a host of troubles: the last ruler of an ancient dynasty driven to abdication and exile by a lost war; a new republic that failed; a dictatorship that ruled by terror; and that terror unleashed on the rest of Europe, bringing retribution in the form of devastation, defeat, and division. Now that division, and the regime that ruled East Berlin, are also memories. But memories can be a potent force. There are, of course, Berliners who would like to forget. They think they hear far too much about Hitler and vanished Jews and alleged crimes of their parents and grandparents—not to mention Erich Honecker and the Stasi and their own previous lives. Probably most Germans and most Berliners feel this way, but at every step they find they must defend their wish to forget against fellow citizens who insist on remembering. The calls for remembrance—and the calls for silence and forgetting—make all silence and all forgetting impossible, and they also make remembrance difficult.

Memories often cleave to the physical settings of events. That is why buildings and places have so many stories to tell. They give form to a city's history and identity. There are other ways to tell a city's history; the most common focuses on the famous leaders of high politics or high culture, and on the events that bound them together. In both politics and culture, Berlin richly deserves attention, whether one associates Berlin politics with Frederick the Great, Bismarck, Hitler, Brandt, or Honecker, and whether Berlin culture is seen through the eyes of Kaiser Wilhelm, Hegel, Einstein, Brecht, or Goebbels. Other historians look at the lives of the common people: how they lived, worked, loved, and amused themselves. A book about buildings and places, by contrast, might be seen as history with the people left out. But the haunts of Berlin's famous ghosts have provoked, and continue to provoke, impassioned and sometimes thoughtful discussion. Berlin is the city of the Berlin Wall, the Reichstag, Prussian palaces, Hitler's chancellery, and some of the grand experiments of modern architecture. People's responses to these buildings, ruins, and vacant sites reveal a great deal about Berlin as a collection of people and as a place. The controversies over their disposition are what this book is about.

Buildings matter. So do statues, ruins, and even stretches of vacant land. Buildings provide shelter for human activities, but it is the activities, not the shelter, that make structures and spaces important to human beings trying to define their place on this earth. Buildings and monuments are also the visible remnants of the past: they often outlast the human beings who created them. How these structures are seen, treated, and remembered sheds light on a collective identity that is more felt than articulated.

Civilizations have always erected buildings and monuments to stake their claims on the land and in the cosmos. But more striking in recent years have been the battles over existing buildings and even over vanished ones. In Bosnia, Christian Serbs blow up mosques in order to build churches where, they say, churches stood centuries ago. Hindus in India destroy a mosque for similar reasons. The president of South Korea decrees the destruction of Seoul's most prominent buildings because they are products of Japanese imperialism. Moscow rebuilds a cathedral destroyed by Stalin sixty years before. North Americans and Western Europeans tend to think that people in Eastern Europe and Asia are weighed down by the past and need to free themselves from its yoke. Yet at the same time, the West is filled with yearning for attachment to history. And we often look to buildings and places to provide that attachment. Berlin is a typical Western city in that its citizens and leaders now take historical preservation very seriously. Any decision to destroy an old building is likely to be controversial, as are questions of what and how and whether to build on blood-stained ground. But not every old structure and site can be preserved; cities are not museums. Hard decisions must be made, and bitter debates often precede them. How does a city or a nation decide which buildings or places matter enough to be worth preserving? In what form should they be preserved? What kind of development properly respects tradition? Sometimes the fierce debates over these questions seem to engage only a few querulous intellectuals. The intellectuals, however, often give voice to a widely felt sense of place.

Every city and every country must weigh development against preservation. Why is Berlin special? Certainly not for its beauty or its state of preservation. Berlin is fascinating, rather, as a city of bold gestures and startling incongruities, of ferment and destruction. It is a city whose buildings, ruins, and voids groan under the burden of painful memories. Tourists in Berlin can take regularly scheduled English-language tours of "infamous Third Reich sites." The fate of these and other infamous places is hotly disputed, making Berlin's landscape uniquely politicized. Planners and developers at work in the new Berlin come to grief again and again when they try to treat the city's streets and buildings and lots as mere real estate. In this historical minefield, dangers not apparent to the eye are revealed by memory.

An uncertain national identity also fuels Berlin's debate about monuments and ruins. Two related facts—Berlin's status as a national capital and its division—have made the civic identity of Berlin inseparable from the national identity of Germany since World War II. Since 1871 Berlin has been Germany's capital—a status interpreted in different ways by different regimes, but one nonetheless acknowledged by the Hohenzollern monarchy, the Weimar Republic, the Third Reich, the four Allied occupiers, the two postwar German states, and the unified Germany of the 1990s.

The reunification of Berlin and of Germany in 1990 has forced Berliners to make many decisions about what to build and what to preserve. The impulse to preserve or to destroy—whether motivated by nostalgia, desire for prestige or for legitimacy, or even economics—reflects deep-seated beliefs about historical identity. The work of historians may help to shape these beliefs, but more often it just describes them. Is Berlin above all the city of Prussian militarism? Or the city of bureaucratically directed genocide? Or is it rather the city of Prussian rationality and order? Or the quintessential modern city, the place of the most outrageous experimentation—in architecture, the visual and performing arts, popular entertainment, political activity, and sexual behavior? These often contradictory images shape contemporary decisions about architecture, planning, and preservation.

Architecture and urban design are not the least of the fields in which Berlin is attracting attention, talent, and money. Architects find that they and their work receive more attention in Berlin than almost anywhere else, although not all that attention is welcome or flattering. This book is not, however, an architectural history of Berlin in any conventional sense. Nor is it a book about preservation as such. Buildings matter for me here not because of any intrinsic beauty or value, but because they are the symbols and the repositories of memory. Surveys of architectural history typically turn to Berlin at three points: the early-nineteenth-century work of Karl Friedrich Schinkel, Peter Behrens's industrial buildings around 1910, and the modernist achievements of the 1920s. As icons of Berlin, those fine buildings are relevant my story, but they do not stand at the center of it. My focus is instead on buildings and sites that have attracted recent attention and controversy, places whose beauty or ugliness is more political than aesthetic.

In attempting to give form to the German capital, Berliners are seeking to come to terms with the troubled course of German history in this century. Since World War II, German history has been an intellectual war zone. Educated Germans, most of them insecure in their national identity, have sought to salvage some meaning or lessons from their recent past. We non-Germans who study Germany tend to take a certain comfort in these battles: *our* identity is not at stake. At some point, however, we recognize that the national traditions we carry more lightly have their dark sides, too. Even many Germans might agree that German history carries with it a heavier moral burden than, say, American history. But perhaps it is also true that the Germans, more than the rest of us, are facing up to the moral dilemmas inherent in a national identity.

This is one reason why the attempts to understand Berlin's history and identity deserve international attention. The concentration of troubling memories, physical destruction, and renewal has made Berliners, however reluctantly, international leaders in exploring the links between urban form, historical preservation, and national identity.

Each era in Berlin's history has left its monuments—visible

and remembered, planned and accidental. Although this book is not a history of Berlin from its beginnings to the present, chapters 2 through 6 are arranged chronologically. That is, each chapter deals with recent controversies, but at issue in those disputes is the interpretation of a particular era of Berlin's history. Each of these eras gave the city a distinct identity: as royal residence, as industrial and imperial powerhouse, as Nazi capital, as Cold War battleground, and as newly reunified capital. Nevertheless, particularly where buildings and places are concerned, the years flow together in the memory. This kind of living history cannot be bracketed between particular dates. (Readers who want a more systematic array of dates will find a chronological table at the end of the book.) For example, as chapter 2 shows, the fate of the royal palace is yoked to that of the East German parliament building. More generally, many (if not all) pre-1933 structures in Berlin are indelibly marked as witnesses to or participants in the events of the Third Reich. And in chapter 1 we begin with the Berlin Wall, which cast its shadow on much of Berlin's historic landscape.

In good and in evil, Berlin is the trustee of German history, which has left its scars here as nowhere else.[1]

—Richard von Weizsäcker, 1983

For me the visits to this city over the past twenty years have been the only genuine experiences of Germany. History is still physically and emotionally present here. . . . Berlin is divided just like our world, our time, and each of our experiences.[2]

—Wim Wenders, 1987

To put it crudely, the American foot in Europe had a sore blister on it. That was West Berlin. . . . We decided the time had come to lance the blister of West Berlin.[3]

—Nikita Khrushchev, recalling 1961

When flowers bloom on concrete, life has triumphed.

—Berlin Wall graffiti

Greatest artwork of all time.

—Berlin Wall graffiti

What are you staring at? Never seen a wall before?

—Berlin Wall graffiti

One

Berlin Walls

The Monument

In a rarely visited corner of northern Berlin, piles of concrete debris fill a vast lot. This is not an unusual sight in what geographers call the "gray zones" of a city, those tracts of land somehow disqualified from more valued uses. Here, where the district of Pankow meets neighboring Wedding, machines are grinding the huge slabs of mangled concrete into smaller pieces, freeing up the land for some other use and turning the concrete into usable gravel. This ordinary industrial scene turns extraordinary when a closer look at the concrete reveals an unexpected sight: the famous spray-painted graffiti of the Berlin Wall. In 1991, this lot is a graveyard for a few of the one hundred miles of Wall that had enclosed West Berlin two years before. It is indeed located in a "gray zone" of Berlin, one of many fringe areas created by the presence of the Wall that is now reduced to rubble (fig. 1).

The Berlin Wall had been one of the city's premier tourist attractions. More than that, it was probably the most famous structure that will ever stand in Berlin. The Pankow lot, and a few others, contained what was left of it (with a few exceptions, as we shall see). Yet such boneyards were not tourist attractions. Indeed, they were scarcely known at all. If a monument can be decommissioned, that is apparently what has happened with the Berlin Wall. Did the concrete lose its aura when it was removed from its original location? Or did that happen earlier, when it lost its power to kill, so to speak—that is, when the guards stepped aside and let the crowds through on November 9, 1989?

1
Pieces of Berlin Wall, Brehmestrasse, Berlin-Pankow, 1991

The Wall retained a strange kind of magic in the days and months that followed, as Berliners and tourists hacked away at the concrete. Pieces of the Wall did indeed have a special aura: they were treated as holy relics that bespoke our deliverance from the Cold War. For that brief moment, the Wall was in demand precisely because it was disappearing. Detached pieces of it were valued as evidence of an apparently spontaneous will to destroy the Wall. The cold night air during that winter of 1989–90 was filled with the sound of *pik-pik-pik.* First Berliners, then tourists hacked away at the Wall. They contributed in a minuscule way to the removal of the concrete, but more significant was their ritual participation in the removal of the symbolic barrier. It was in this carnival atmosphere that the concrete was divested of its murderous aura and invested with magical properties (its high asbestos content aside) that made visitors take it home to display on mantels around the world.

These magical properties translated into its market value. The Wall, symbol of the epic confrontation between capitalism and communism, became a capitalist commodity. Enterprising locals sold hacked-off pieces of concrete from tables set up at Checkpoint Charlie and the Brandenburg Gate (fig. 2). Others would rent you a hammer and chisel so that you could chop your own. Still other entrepreneurs, more ambitious and better capitalized, filled crates and trucks with this East German state property and supplied genuine Wall fragments to American department stores

2
Vendor selling pieces of Berlin Wall at Brandenburg Gate, 1991

in time for the Christmas shopping season. The result in Berlin was a cat-and-mouse game as East German authorities tried for a short time to enforce their ownership of the concrete, making a few arrests in the process.

As it stepped gingerly into a market economy, East Germany's brief post-Wall regime recognized that the Wall had become a commodity. It sought to assert its rights of ownership and to sell pieces of the Wall in order to raise badly needed funds for health care and historical preservation. A state-owned firm that specialized in the export of building materials was given the job of marketing the defaced concrete, now separated into its prefabricated segments. An auction in Monte Carlo in June 1990 attracted wealthy collectors and drove prices for painted segments of Wall into the tens of thousands of dollars. As East Germany passed into history, though, the Wall's aura faded and its price fell. A final auction in Fort Lee, New Jersey, in 1993 attracted only three buyers.

What does it mean to buy a monument? A brochure prepared for the Fort Lee auction described the segments of Wall as the perfect way to "decorate the entrance hall of your corporate headquarters, museum, or estate."[4] Some pieces were re-erected as works of art—or were they just souvenirs? Others stood as victory monuments or Cold War booty, such as the piece ("hated symbol of, yes, an evil empire") proudly unveiled by former president Ronald Reagan at the dedication of his presidential library.[5]

It was difficult enough to define the meaning of Wall fragments removed to sites where they stood alone. The idea of leaving pieces on their original site made no sense at all to most Berliners. Proposals to preserve parts of the Wall, and to create a Wall memorial in Berlin, faced organized and unorganized opposition. Every suggestion to preserve one section or another was met with a chorus of objections, particularly from neighbors. The overwhelming desire, it seemed, was to be rid of the hated obstruction. Before reunification, the East Berlin office for historical preservation identified stretches of the Wall worthy of possible preservation. But the signs identifying them as historical monuments were promptly stolen, and the chopping continued unabated. The assaults with hammer and chisel preempted attempts to save pieces of particular artistic merit, such as that painted by the American artist Keith Haring, who had died of AIDS early in 1990. Haring's section stood at the most popular pilgrimage site, next to Checkpoint Charlie, and it was quickly destroyed.

Even in its comical afterlife, the Wall continued to divide Berliners. After November 9, 1989, at least the non-German press routinely referred to the Wall in the past tense. Yet only at a few tourist sites, such as Checkpoint Charlie, did the popular onslaught come close to obliterating the concrete wall. Most of the hundred miles of border fortifications remained largely intact for months. What had disappeared, rather, was the symbolic Wall—which meant that the concrete and the symbol were no longer the same thing. To understand the Wall, then, we must understand what it meant. Symbols and monuments are invested with their meaning through human action, so we can best understand the Wall (and its physical and metaphoric demise) by looking at the way it has been treated.

Wherever human beings live, they endow the things around

them with cultural meaning. Places and objects become resonant symbols that embody hopes, fears, and value. That is, they become monuments, as the Wall did. Often a monument defines a group's identity, marking a place honored by, say, all adherents of a religious faith or all members of a community. Such monuments are rarely controversial. In Berlin, by contrast, the landscape is politicized in the extreme, and undisputed monuments are the exception. The Wall and other Berlin monuments recall controversial deeds, mostly of the recent past, deeds that prevent any consensus about the sort of things monuments are supposed to embody, such as a national identity or a common ideal. It is this deep uncertainty that makes Berlin such a contested landscape, and creates a charged atmosphere that foreigners find hard to grasp. One controversy in recent U.S. history that approached the intensity of feeling in Berlin was the design proposed for the Vietnam Veterans Memorial in Washington, which reopened wounds in the nation's sense of itself. In Berlin, Germany's wounds still lie open everywhere.

More than a century ago, the young Friedrich Nietzsche lamented his fellow Germans' overdeveloped sense of history. Only by selective forgetting, according to Nietzsche, can we overcome a sense of helplessness in the face of historical destiny. He argued that only the ability to forget makes creative action possible.[6] In short, if I cannot select certain facts from history and discard others, I will never have any beliefs firm enough to act on. In the wake of Bismarck's unification of Germany in 1871, Nietzsche was appalled by Germans' blind Hegelian confidence that the forces of history were on their side. But the events of twentieth-century German history have given a new coloration to his thoughts. Today's historical paralysis is a product not of complacency but of fatalistic angst. Some Germans fear that the weight of past misdeeds has made their fellow Germans uncertain what it means to be German and afraid to act in the name of Germany. The Germans thus accused see things differently: they say that any move to discard the burdens of the past will return Germany to blind confidence and thus to disaster.

Monuments are nothing if not selective aids to memory: they encourage us to remember some things and to forget others. The process of creating monuments, especially where it is openly contested, as in Berlin, shapes public memory and collective identity. That process can take very different forms, however.

There is an obvious difference between the Berlin Wall and a monument like the Lincoln Memorial in Washington, D.C.: the builders of the former did not intend to create a monument; they had other purposes in mind. But the Wall, too, became an important monument because it took on a meaning of its own. Both kinds of monuments, the "intentional" and the "unintentional," give form to the collective memory of a city.[7]

The Wall became an unintentional monument to the remarkable era in which two rival states simultaneously claimed Berlin. The division marked by the Wall, in turn, grew out of the shattering era of German history that culminated in World War II. Thus the Wall was built—literally and figuratively—atop the ruins of war, terror, and division. And it, too, is now among the ruins and memories of Berlin. The Wall—from concrete, to monument, to rubble—gives form to the story of Berlin and of Germany in our time.

The Barrier

When East German border troops and construction workers sealed the border with West Berlin on August 13, 1961, they put an end to a peculiar episode in the history of the Cold War. During the 1950s, Berlin had been the one place in Germany where East and West truly met. Families and friends scattered across the two German states could rendezvous in Berlin. Berliners lived astride the Iron Curtain that divided the rest of Europe. Two currencies and two political systems coexisted awkwardly, with people and goods passing frequently, if not always smoothly, between them. On August 13, that changed abruptly. Sixty thousand people who lived on one side and worked on the other lost their jobs. After 1961 people and vehicles in Berlin circulated within one half of the city or the other. Neighbors who could no longer see one another grew apart.

West Berliners, now walled off from their poor cousins in East Germany, began to share in the prosperity of West Germany's postwar "economic miracle," thanks in part to enormous subsidies from the Bonn government. West Berlin never became quite like West Germany, however: its subsidized economy, peculiar legal status, and frontier allure meant that artists, draft dodgers, and nonconformists (but also pensioners) were overrepresented, businessmen and factory workers underrepresented in its population. Nevertheless, the city displayed the neon signs, shop windows, new cars, and most of the other trappings of postwar Western prosperity.

East Berlin certainly looked different. Its gray buildings did not merely lack a coat of paint that their Western counterparts had; there were fewer new buildings, and fewer of the old ones were being renovated. Fewer cars, fewer shops, less advertising, and less bustle gave most Western visitors the impression of a dreary and lifeless place. The colors were more drab, the sounds were more muted—and the smells were different too. Two distinctive aromas pervaded the streets of East Berlin. One was the exhaust of the Trabant (or Trabbi), the tiny standard-issue East German car, whose two-stroke engine burned an acrid mixture of gasoline and oil. Trabbis were not as numerous as Volkswagens and Opels in the West, but many were about, despite a typical wait of ten years before a citizen could become the proud owner of one. The other familiar smell came from the burning of soft coal, East Germany's only domestic source of energy and hence the main fuel both for industry and for home heating. It turned the winter sky brown in both Berlins, but its aroma was most pungent in the quiet residential streets of the East's older neighborhoods, where (as in much of West Berlin) most apartments were still heated by coal-burning tile ovens.

Berlin had been divided into twenty districts in 1920 (fig. 3). The four occupying powers apportioned them in 1945: eight to the Soviets, six to the Americans, four to the British, and two to the French. The zigzag course of the Wall across the city was thus largely determined by arbitrary administrative decisions in 1920 and 1945. The district of Mitte (Middle), the historical center, lay in the Soviet sector, but after 1961 it bordered the Wall on its southern, western, and most of its northern side. Across the Wall to its south, the tenements of Kreuzberg were cut off not only from the city center but also from the parks in Treptow, to the east. East Berliners who lived just north of the center could no longer walk across the sectoral boundary to Wedding's many small shops and cinemas. Those businesses, in turn, lost their customers in 1961 and many soon closed.

By severing long-established paths of inner-city circulation, the Wall created peculiar urban backwaters in the center of Berlin, devoid of the usual bustle of pedestrians and—what was often more noticeable—of automobiles. This was true, in different ways, on both sides. The crucial difference was that the

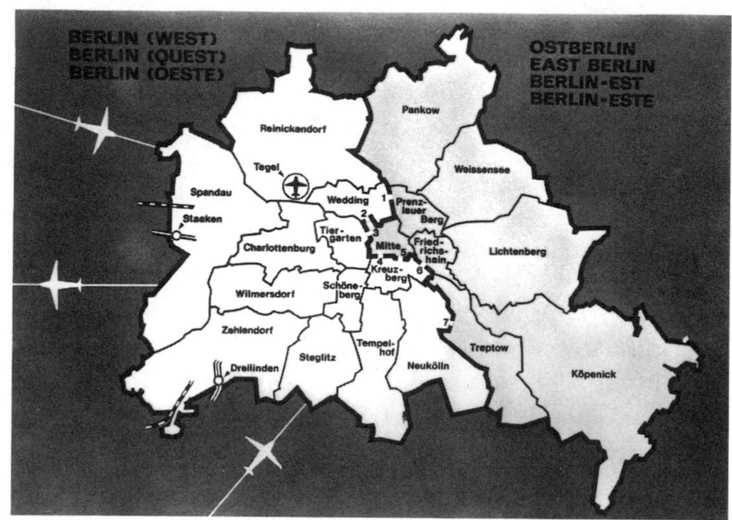

3
Berlin's districts.
Courtesy of German
Information Center.

approaches to the Wall's Eastern side were carefully controlled. Apart from official ceremonies, Easterners were discouraged from approaching the Wall and even taking note of its existence. Those East Berliners who lived in the streets next to the Wall had to adjust to special restrictions, intrusions, and inconveniences. Friends from outside the neighborhood could never just drop by, for example: permission had to be obtained from the police.

Unlike Easterners, West Berliners were free to heap scorn upon the Wall, or to gaze over it, but in the end they, too, mostly sought peace of mind by accepting the Wall or ignoring it, by coming to think of their city as an island connected by causeways and air corridors to a Western mainland. The commonly used "island" metaphor is an apt one, since the Wall created quiet recreational spaces on the newly established edge and, more generally, came to be seen—or rather not seen—as the edge of the world.

In contrast to the East, the Western side of the Wall was a notably disordered space. Neglect of the streets, bridges, and other structures abutting the border was apparent to anyone coming from other parts of West Berlin or West Germany. The proximity of the Wall devalued old neighborhoods, particularly in Kreuzberg, and their working-class populations were increasingly supplanted by an odd mix of Turkish immigrant workers and the growing West Berlin alternative society of self-styled dropouts, artists, musicians, punks, anarchists, and squatters in abandoned buildings. The marginal location of West Berlin in general and eastern Kreuzberg in particular nurtured the Kreuzberg "scene." (When the Wall disappeared, Kreuzberg became centrally located, and real estate speculation doomed the "scene.")

The act of crossing the forbidden border naturally became wrapped in its own aura of liminality. The ordeal of a legal border crossing was experienced at least once by many people, even, by the 1980s, many East Germans. Within days of closing the border in 1961, the East German authorities had reduced the number of checkpoints within the city to seven, most of which they designated for exclusive use either by West Berliners, West Germans, or foreigners. The most famous was the crossing for foreigners, Checkpoint Charlie—as the Americans (and everyone else) had named their official gateway to the Soviet sector.[8] Because crossing into East Berlin represented a journey far greater than the short distance across the street, Checkpoint Charlie became associated with mystery and intrigue, a reputation enhanced by dozens of spy novels. So, too, did the Glienecke Bridge, which connected West Berlin with Potsdam, the place where East and West exchanged spies.

Westerners could also travel by subway or elevated train to the Friedrichstrasse rail station in East Berlin and formally cross the border there. Friedrichstrasse was the typical departure point for the fortunate East Germans who received permission to travel to the West, and for Westerners ending family visits. Departing travelers were processed through a new annex to the station. The building, a place of painful leave-taking, acquired the nickname "Palace of Tears."

This suitably depressed-looking building stood on a triangular lot whose fate had long been in limbo. For a 1922 architectural competition for the site, Ludwig Mies van der Rohe had sketched a revolutionary glass skyscraper. His sketch has found a place in every history of modern architecture, but neither it nor anything else was built on the site for decades. In 1992 a group of investors proposed to tear down the empty Palace of Tears and finally to build Mies's glass tower. Ironically, they shared the same motivation as the sponsors of the 1922 competition, who had spurned Mies's design in favor of another. In both cases, an attention-getting design was supposed to bring an exemption from municipal height limits for the construction of a more profitable office building. But the authorities proved unwilling on both occasions. Instead, the Palace of Tears was left standing for the time being and converted into a nightclub, which kept the notorious name.

One of the oddest incidents in the Wall's history was the only mass flight from West to East. It was the unwanted result of a minor diplomatic bargain intended to smooth East-West relations. In 1988 the two sides agreed to exchange several tiny parcels of land in order to regularize their borders. One parcel transferred from East to West lay in the city center, between Potsdamer Platz and the Tiergarten. This "Lenné triangle" protruded so awkwardly into West Berlin that the East had left it on the west side of the Wall in 1961 rather than bother to enclose it. As a result, these ten acres had sat completely neglected for years. But the West wanted the land for a long-planned expressway. During the summer of 1988, Green-minded West Berliners began protesting the expressway and counting rare plant and butterfly species in the wild growth of the triangle. Joined by anarchists for whom this ungoverned place was a utopia and an adventure, they set up tents to occupy the land. The annoyed West Berlin authorities were helpless to intervene on this foreign territory, the relevant Allied powers (British and Soviet) chose not to interfere, and the East Germans loudly denounced the "inhuman police terror" and the violations of their sovereignty as Western police and protesters clashed repeatedly along the border between West Berlin and the temporarily autonomous enclave. When the territory was officially transferred to the West on July 1, the West Berlin police seized it by force. The protesters thereupon scaled the Wall to the East to escape arrest. Eastern border guards escorted them away, served them breakfast, asked them to use a regular border crossing for their next visit to the German Democratic Republic, and sent them home on the subway.

The Symbol

The story of divided Berlin is more than a story of concrete and construction workers. But the Berlin Wall remains at the center of that story because it was more than mere concrete. After all, the Wall that ceased to exist one night in 1989 was not the concrete but rather the system of East German border security.

In other words, the "Berlin Wall" came to signify all the consequences of the division of Berlin and of Europe.

It is a well-known fact that the Wall was put up in a single day. Virtually the entire perimeter of West Berlin—a hundred miles—was indeed sealed on August 13, 1961, but with barbed wire. The first pieces of concrete wall were put up two days later (fig. 4). Over the years the first, hastily erected block-and-mortar wall was in turn replaced, more than once, by taller and stronger barriers built with prefabricated concrete forms. And the wall itself was only part of the border fortifications. By gradually removing structures and hindrances on their side, the East German authorities established a security zone accessible only to guards. Here was the so-called death strip, of varying width, punctuated by observation towers; enclosed by walls or

4
The Wall being built, Harzerstrasse, August 16, 1961. Courtesy of German Information Center.

fences on either side; and secured with bright lights, barbed wire, tank barriers, dog runs, and carefully raked sand. Contrary to its name and reputation, then, the security system was in its essence less a wall than a controlled sequence of empty, visible *spaces.* More than that, "the Wall" signified a set of activities—searches, patrols, observation, and identification checks at the crossing points—that protected the border.

The name stuck, however. From the Western side it was the concrete wall that marked the border's menacing presence. And only on that side was it officially a "wall." Eastern officials dubbed their new edifice the "antifascist protective rampart." By the 1980s, they rarely referred to any physical structure, speaking rather of "the border" or of "border security." Use of the word "wall" *(Mauer)* was strictly forbidden in the East. This rule has usually been interpreted as an Orwellian denial of reality, but we must also consider it as an attempt—perhaps equally Orwellian—to control the dangerous implications of figurative language.

Why was the name "Wall" embraced by some and eschewed by others? The notion of a wall carries historical baggage: through many centuries of European history, walls were basic to the identity as well as the security of European cities. Berlin itself was a walled town for most of its history, until the 1860s. Both East and West Berlin honored this tradition. A remnant of Berlin's medieval wall was excavated and displayed in East Berlin's Waisenstrasse, and during the 1980s West Berlin's archaeological office excavated a segment of the city's eighteenth-century customs wall in Stresemannstrasse. The fact that the course of the latter wall coincided for a distance with the border between East and West Berlin, and hence with the 1961 wall, offered the new Berlin Wall a historical pedigree. The official Eastern name, "antifascist protective rampart," also invoked the traditional wall, if not the traditional enemy, by alluding to the kind of fortification that had protected earlier towns. The same went for each side's descriptions of West Berlin: "imperialist bridgehead" for some, "bastion of freedom" and "bulwark of the Western world" for others.

But a yawning historical caesura divided the wall of 1961 from its antecedents. The nineteenth and twentieth centuries have been an age of mobility, communication, and integration. Modernity has tended to free cities from all traditional fetters.

Walls fell or were riddled with openings for roads, canals, and railroads. In other words, in an earlier age, with much less human mobility, rulers would not have needed and subjects would not have noticed this barrier to mobility. But that is precisely the sense in which the Berlin Wall of 1961 connoted an attempt, by political fiat, to reverse the growing economic and social mobility of the modern world.[9] The name "Wall," shunned by its builders, called attention to this anachronism and came to signify a crime against history as well as humanity: a "wall of shame" *(Schandmauer).* The competing description "antifascist protective rampart" became farcical and fell into disrepute.

It was immediately obvious that the Wall was antithetical to the mobility and circulation characteristic of a modern city. In Berlin a political decision had disrupted invisible forms of modern circulation usually taken for granted—gas and water mains, for example. More visibly, it blocked streets, and streetcar tracks led straight into the Wall (see fig. 4). Most of Berlin's intercity rail stations became useless and were abandoned. The elevated rail stations above Nollendorfplatz and Bülowstrasse, on a line that went nowhere, became flea markets. And how was a subway system supposed to work in a walled city? Two subway lines connected northern and southern parts of West Berlin by passing under central East Berlin, gliding through ghostly stations where no train had stopped since 1961.

Meanwhile, other products of modern technology passed effortlessly over the Wall: air pollution and broadcast signals. So, for shorter distances, did the amplified sounds of internationally famous rock musicians who played at outdoor concerts by the Reichstag. East German youths gathered behind the Wall to hear the stars they were unable to see; altercations ensued when the police drove them away.

Heightening the poignancy of the Wall's limits on mobility was the importance of travel in the minds of East German citizens. Their education and relative prosperity made them especially eager travelers even by the standards of the late twentieth century, and their government knew (and acknowledged) that otherwise obedient citizens demanded the "right to travel." Many became obsessed with the Wall that visibly barred them from West Berlin, West Germany, and beyond.[10] East German leaders knew that their citizens were tempted by—and had to be protected from—the fruits of capitalism. The Wall held back

5
Postcard: "Greetings from Berlin." Courtesy of Claudia Katz-Palme.

the seductive bustle and mobility that accompanied free trade and bourgeois society.

When we think of the Wall, then, we think of the shocking division of Berlin in all its ramifications. And because we knew Cold War Berlin above all as a divided city, the Wall became inseparable from the city's identity. Clear evidence of this link is a popular postcard sold in Berlin since the 1980s. A picture of the Great Wall of China, it reads simply, "Greetings from Berlin"—Berlin being the place with the Wall (fig. 5). In the language of semiotics, the Wall is the signifier; Berlin, the signified. The postcard also served as an ironic commentary on the relative insignificance of the Wall as a physical structure. Tourists were often disappointed not to find a more imposing structure: it was, on its Western side, a plain concrete wall thirteen feet high, not at all like its Chinese namesake.

The plain concrete wall brimmed with meaning. Not only did it signify the carefully maintained division of Berlin, it also came to connote the division of a German nation, or of Europe, as otherwise known by Churchill's metaphor of the "iron curtain." The Wall became most famous as the preeminent Cold War symbol. That symbolic linkage is itself ironic, since the Wall could be said to mark the end of Berlin as a Cold War battlefield. Berlin became an international problem as the division of Germany hardened after 1945, since the Western allies' sectors of the city lay in the middle of the Soviet occupation zone (fig. 6). The city then became a flashpoint of international conflict during

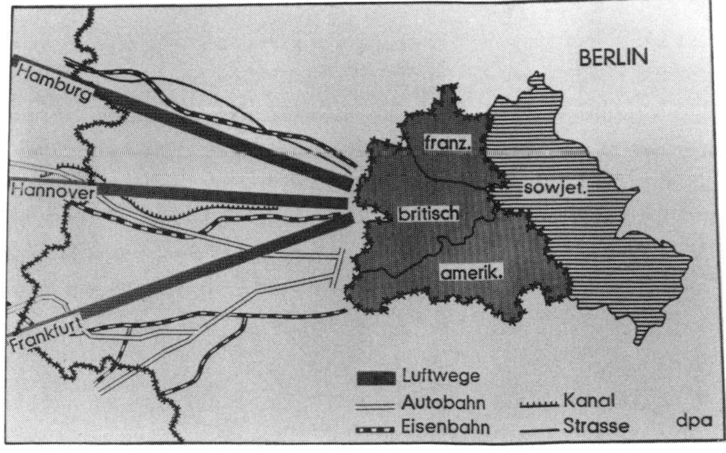

6
The four Allied sectors of Berlin. Courtesy of German Information Center.

the Berlin blockade of 1948–49, when American and British planes foiled a Soviet attempt to detach Berlin from the sphere of the Western powers. More than any other event, the triumphant Berlin Airlift made the city a symbol of Western resolve in the Cold War. As a practical matter, however, the airlift reinforced rather than resolved the Berlin anomaly. It hastened the creation, in 1949, of two separate German states, leaving only Berlin's status in limbo. The United States and its allies were determined to hold West Berlin, despite its vulnerability, while the Soviet bloc wished to remove a painful embarrassment. During the late 1950s, the Soviet Union under Khrushchev again sought to force the Berlin issue. Its East German ally pressed for urgent action because the virtually unrestricted freedom of movement within the city was enabling thousands of its most skilled workers and professionals to flee west. The Western powers would not back down from the commitment to Berlin they had made at the time of the airlift, despite fears that the Berlin crisis could not be solved by any means short of war.

Hence Western leaders breathed a secret sigh of relief on August 13, 1961, when a midnight action by the East German army sealed off the sectoral lines in Berlin and began the construction of a barrier all the way around West Berlin, ostensibly to foil an imminent Western invasion. Because the West did not intervene, this sudden move effectively resolved the conflicting claims to the entire city: the West implicitly accepted division and the East surrendered its claim to West Berlin. It could thus be said that the Wall, by removing Berlin from center stage in the Cold War, marked the city's irrelevance. But it also gave divided Berlin a visible signifier.

The political rituals of Cold War leaders added important new connotations to the Wall's meaning. Immediately after the Wall's construction, Berlin represented something of a political embarrassment, a place to avoid, since Western leaders—Adenauer of West Germany, Macmillan of Britain, Kennedy of the United States—were criticized for their failure to respond to it, and since they could scarcely admit to being relieved at its construction. Before long, however, West Germany and its allies began to exploit the propaganda value of the Wall as a symbol of Communism's failure.[11] By the time of Kennedy's triumphal visit in June of 1963, a pilgrimage to the safely fortified forward post had become a favorite photo opportunity. Every state visitor in Bonn was if possible brought to Berlin to view the infamous Wall. President Ronald Reagan's visit in 1987, for example, sounded the metaphor of mobility and connectedness. He stood before the walled-off Brandenburg Gate and demanded, "Mr. Gorbachev, open this gate. Mr. Gorbachev, tear down this wall."

The East could respond in kind: it declared the statements of Western politicians at the Wall to be a provocation showing the necessity and the efficacy of the border fortifications, which they, too, proudly displayed to guests—at least to carefully selected ones. One of the old guardhouses flanking the Brandenburg Gate housed an exhibition justifying the "modern border." An occasional Western journalist was admitted, as were delegations and dignitaries from friendly countries.[12] Some of the latter left their words of praise in a guest book now preserved in a Berlin archive. East Germany ritually commemorated the heroic defense of the border every August 13, granted the border guards an annual day of honor, and taught all schoolchildren the correct interpretation of the events of 1961, when alert security measures had staved off war.[13]

In this battle to define a symbol, each side was trying to make the Berlin Wall comprehensible in ways that would justify its cause. Each side knew it had to redefine what a wall meant. Traditionally, a wall has an inside and an outside; it protects the people on one side from those on the other. But which was the outside of the wall that encircled West Berlin? Who was being walled in, and who kept out? West Berliners, physically surrounded by the Wall, felt they were the ones penned in. But so did most East Germans.

In the end, both sides came to think of the Wall as a temporal more than a spatial barrier. Western leaders denounced the Wall as anachronistic: a relic from an earlier age, it was built to keep progress out, and people in. Meanwhile, the Wall's builders justified their work as a necessary defense against the atavistic forces of the West. According to this view, informed by Marxist theories of historical development, the proletariat was defending itself against lingering influences of the bourgeoisie. Specifically, it was "fascism" that threatened the march of socialist progress. Marxists usually defined fascism as a degenerate form of late bourgeois capitalism. The "antifascist protective rampart" shielded the triumphant proletariat from the remnants of pre-1945 German fascism (that is, from Nazism). The Western view was different, of course, but there is a striking parallel: according to it, too, the Wall's necessity arose from a historical discrepancy between the two systems. Liberal narratives of history, like Marxist ones, describe a progressive development: the unfolding of an individualistic and democratic order. Part of that development is the growing freedom of movement mentioned above. Thus the construction of a wall turned back the clock to a constricted and authoritarian age. The West has often defined that age as "totalitarian." Theories of "totalitarianism," a word connoting a fundamental similarity between Nazism and Communism, portrayed the Cold War as a continuation of the West's struggle in World War II and, in the German context, East German Communist leader Walter Ulbricht as Hitler's successor. Again, the implication was that enemies from the past hid behind the Wall. Thus East and West agreed that the Wall was a temporal barrier, dividing past from present, and that the other side harbored the unredeemed heirs of Hitler.

On an official level, the ideological interpretation of the Wall thus became part of the Cold War's propaganda battle: "antifascist protective rampart" versus "wall of shame." It is difficult to gauge the extent to which popular views affirmed official positions, particularly in the East. In the West, however, official and popular views certainly converged in treating the Wall as a place of death. The attention of the mass media and their proven ideas about newsworthy topics explain the attention given to unsuccessful escape attempts, most of which ended in capture and imprisonment, some in death. The first fatal shooting came within days of the border closing. The most famous death occurred a year later, when eighteen-year-old Peter Fechter, shot just short of the final obstacle, bled to death while crying for help just beyond the reach of American soldiers and West Berlin policemen. Just as newsworthy, though, were those who successfully defied death. A privately run but officially sanctioned museum on the Western side of Checkpoint Charlie drew crowds of visitors by displaying the paraphernalia of imaginative escapes: hot-air balloons, cars with secret hiding places, homemade Red Army uniforms, and debris from tunnels dug under the Wall and trucks that crashed through it. The museum's founder, Rainer Hildebrandt, a human-rights campaigner, sought to draw public attention to the plight of those trapped behind the Iron Curtain.

At least seventy-eight people died in confrontations at the Wall during its twenty-eight-year existence. The Wall was not among the leading causes of mortality in East or West Berlin, but the political context of the suffering of families and neighbors lent the Wall its aura of brutality and inhumanity. West Berliners put up crosses and simple markers to commemorate many of the dead, whether their identities were known or not. These became a part of the landscape of the Wall, and clearly marked its Western side as a memorial (fig. 7). Western politicians could key their visits to the Wall to the tone set by the crosses, exhibiting an appropriate combination of solemnity and outrage.

Much less known in the West was the corresponding process

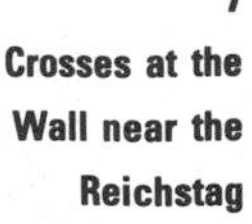

7
Crosses at the Wall near the Reichstag

8
Memorial to slain border guards, East Berlin

of commemoration on the Eastern side, although the officially controlled Eastern media gave similar prominence to its stories of heroism and suffering. Several East German border guards died in confrontations at the inner-city border, and they were officially honored as martyrs to the defense of the socialist state. Four stone monuments in East Berlin commemorated their deaths (fig. 8).[14] Despite the regime's lack of credibility with its own people, the pathos of victimhood could sway their emotions. Ordinary East Germans found it plausible that "bandits" in the West took potshots at border guards doing their duty, a story not corroborated by Western accounts of any of the incidents. And not only ordinary citizens: even as he awaited trial for murders at the Wall, Erich Honecker, when asked if he regretted the deaths there, would only reply that he was sorry for the murders of twenty-five East German border guards.

Graffiti added a different dimension to the Western side of the Wall. Kreuzberg boasted the most impressive display of Wall

9
The Wall in Niederkirchnerstrasse, 1983. Behind it is the former Third Reich aviation ministry. Courtesy of Landesbildstelle.

graffiti, if that word may be used to encompass the personal outbursts, political slogans, posters, painting, attachments, and occasional destruction wrought upon the Western side of the Wall. The Wall attracted painted expressions of defiance in its early years, but it began to flourish as a mural only in the 1970s, when it (that is, the original, western perimeter of the fortifications) was rebuilt with huge prefabricated concrete slabs that created a smooth canvas (fig. 9). The entire West Berlin side of the Wall, actually within East Berlin territory but effectively free of anyone's political control, served as an all-purpose bulletin board as well as an experimental studio for art with political overtones. The Western wall of the death strip thus became a showcase of spontaneity and a tourist attraction. The sharp contrast with the purposes of the Wall's builders became part of the Wall's fascination and meaning. A small element of risk added a further tinge of excitement: on rare occasions East German border guards slipped through concealed doors in the Wall and nabbed graffiti artists defacing the border fortifications.

By making the Wall *visible,* the colorful graffiti (or art) also counteracted West Berliners' inclinations to ignore it. Much of the graffiti underscored the efforts of Western political leaders to heap scorn on the Wall. That was obvious in the case of the many pictorial and verbal denunciations of the Wall itself and the regime behind it. More subtly, one recurring theme of the Wall paintings highlighted the sense of historical anomaly described above. This was the attempt to disrupt the solidity and continuity of the Wall by suggesting the existence of openings in it or the process of breaking through it. Many artists painted climbing or jumping figures; others employed trompe l'oeil (fig. 10). The effect of this graffiti was to call attention to the injustice, anomaly, or artificiality of the barrier.

At the same time, however, the levity of much Wall art threatened to blur the Western message. The sculptor Joseph Beuys, enfant terrible of postwar West German art, aimed to confound official opinion when he declared that it would be best to increase the Wall's height by five centimeters to give it more aesthetically pleasing proportions.[15] This set the tone for many of the more sophisticated graffiti artists, whose work, while giving scant comfort to the builders of the "antifascist defensive rampart," subverted the categories of Western as well as Eastern political posturing. Did lovers, angels, or bathroom fixtures have anything to do with the Cold War? The very process of appropriating the Wall as art made it, arguably, less ugly, less obscene, less criminal. The kaleidoscopic Western side of the Wall became either a showcase of Western freedom or embarrassing evidence of Western decadence. Whereas in earlier years the East periodi-

10
Wall graffiti, 1983. Courtesy of Landesbildstelle.

cally whitewashed the Western side of the Wall, in 1987 it was the Western authorities who hurriedly obliterated anti-American and anti-Reagan slogans before the president's visit to the Brandenburg Gate.

The German Democratic Republic (GDR) knew how to prevent graffiti and other spontaneous displays of private sentiment at home. Apart from officially sponsored commemorations, this side of the Wall—of the border, that is—was not available for contemplation. Easterners were compelled to turn their backs on it and build their lives within "Berlin, capital of the German Democratic Republic," as the city was officially known. Official Eastern parlance knew no "East Berlin," only a remote and infrequently mentioned "Westberlin," which appeared as a blank space on the GDR's city maps. On Western maps, by contrast, it was the Wall that was often inconspicuous, indicated only by a stripe barely distinguishable from those dividing the districts within East or West Berlin. The maps on each side serve as evidence of denial and wishful thinking.

Although we cannot look at any Eastern equivalent of Wall graffiti, we can learn something about Easterners' reactions to the Wall from a book published in 1973 by a prominent East German psychiatrist who had fled to the West two years before. The title of his book, wrote Dr. Dietfried Müller-Hegemann, was a term already in common use in Berlin.[16] *The Berlin Wall Disease (Die Berliner Mauerkrankheit)* is a collection of case studies of patients suffering from depression and other psychological ills, often expressed in physical ailments and, according to the author, attributable to the border closing in 1961. These case studies of divided families and of pressures for ideological conformity clearly reflect the stresses of life in a police state, in which the Wall had become established as the paramount symbol of control. But Müller-Hegemann saw a more direct connection between the Wall and "wall disease." He found that patients reacted directly to the shock of the Wall's appearance—that is, to the sudden imposition of strict limits on mobility that left them no possibility of leaving the country or even, in many cases, seeing children, parents, spouses, or lovers. Without trivializing these people's symptoms, we can see "wall disease" as an extreme version of the widely shared sense that the Wall violated normal and accepted possibilities. Müller-Hegemann links the pain of the Wall more closely to its violation of expectations when he contrasts the 1960s, an era of peace and growing prosperity in the GDR, with times of war and mass suffering. Indeed, many of his patients had suffered similar setbacks during and after World War II without the psychological consequences, precisely because their expectations and hopes were appropriately modest then.[17] "Wall disease" thus takes to pathological extremes the more general sense of historical inappropriateness stirred by the Wall.

The Zipper

The concrete barrier in Berlin stood as a signifier in many discourses: psychopathology, families' grief, political ideology, urban identity, and modern art. And it loomed large in the debates over German national identity that raged throughout the decades of division and still persist today. Since both German regimes claimed Berlin as their city and their capital, it was inevitable that the Wall, Berlin's preeminent structure and symbol, would be drawn into these debates. In divided Germany, Berlin (especially West Berlin) was always the front line. The citizens of the divided city were the most prominent victims of division.

The suffering of these victims redeemed all Germans. Since the airlift of 1948–49, Berliners, more than other Germans, had been able to claim the hearts of their former enemies in the west. In a famous speech during the airlift, West Berlin's mayor, Ernst Reuter, demanded, "Peoples of the world, look upon this city!" At least in the West, they looked, and they saw freedom-loving heroes where only a few years before they had seen Hitler's minions. It was a thrilling moment for Germans who, like Reuter, had opposed the Nazis. They had been sustained through the years of the Third Reich by a belief in a better Germany; now the Western world endorsed their cause. But former Nazis also basked in their redemption: all anticommunist Berliners stood together, and bygones could be bygones. West Berlin celebrated its new identity with its first major postwar monument, the Airlift Memorial dedicated by Reuter at Tempelhof airport in 1951.

The Wall later supplanted the airlift as the symbol of Berlin's role as Cold War victim. The most celebrated visit to the walled city was probably that of President John F. Kennedy on June 26, 1963. After reviewing the Wall, he proceeded to the Schöneberg Town Hall, home of the West Berlin government, where he gave a speech famous for the German phrase with which he concluded. His words underscored the political symbolism of Berlin: "All free men, wherever they may live, are citizens of Berlin. And therefore, as a free man, I take pride in the words, 'Ich bin ein Berliner.'" What did it mean for Kennedy to call himself a Berliner? Certainly he was not about to pronounce himself a German. "Berliners" were victims of Communist tyranny and virtuous exemplars of a noble steadfastness, and they were portrayed as such in American Cold War propaganda.

The adoption of the victim's perspective made it possible to turn the shame of the Wall into a position of moral superiority. For Western opponents of the division of Germany, the Wall came to represent the justice rather than the futility of their cause. West Berliners first saw the Wall as a defeat, driving a wedge between them and their allied protectors, who had not acted to stop its construction. But the Wall could become a Western political symbol when its existence was interpreted as proof that only force could keep Germany divided. Incidents like the death of Peter Fechter convinced most Westerners that the Wall was both cruel and absurd. The Wall, then, showed the division of Germany to be "unnatural," meaning that Germany was "naturally" and properly a single nation.

In the peculiar state of German nationalism after World War II, the Berlin Wall—the looming obstacle to national unity—became the West's favorite nationalist symbol. The ritual denunciations of the Wall—speeches, demonstrations, graffiti, crosses—were the most acceptable expressions of German national feeling in the West. At the same time, the very existence of the Wall served to displace any anxieties about German identity onto it. It was "a zipper," observed the East Berlin writer Lutz Rathenow, linking Germans even as it divided them.[18] The separation enforced by the Wall made it easy to explain away any apparent disunity among Germans and to render harmless the whole idea of German identity. This is the point made recently by the West Berlin writer Peter Schneider: "it was the Wall alone that preserved the illusion that the Wall was the only thing separating the Germans."[19]

The Wall, then, signified both division and unity. Under the circumstances it was an ideal national symbol, affirming a divided German self as well as an underlying unity. The Wall seemed to explain the existence of apparently irreconcilable characteristics of "Germans"—not only in the form of the simplistic but persistent categories of "good" and "bad" Germans. Many analyses of German national character—a favorite topic for decades—resort to images of dualism, division, exclusion, and separation. The existence of the Wall at once confirmed these beliefs and offered a way to account for them without denying an essential bond between all Germans. The East-West division embodied by the Wall permitted Germans themselves to project "otherness" onto their fellows. On the one hand, Germans could interpret official propaganda as implying that the people on the other side of the Wall monopolized the prejudiced, predatory, or authoritarian traits of the bad old days. On the other hand, it was common in both Germanies to characterize the East as the "old" Germany or the "real" Germany, implying that the GDR was the repository of traditional German virtues, unspoiled by foreign (especially American) influences.

As a counterpoint to assertions of German unity, the GDR offered its official ideology of German antifascism—looking not to the old Germany or the whole Germany, but to the better Germany. Obviously, antifascism was also (like anticommunism and opposition to Germany's division) defined by what it was not. The "antifascist protective rampart" became its most famous symbol, but since hardly anyone in East or West long took seriously its "antifascist" purpose, the Wall also did much to discredit the entire notion. In other words, as the idea of an "antifascist protective rampart" became an embarrassment, the state that built such a "rampart" (or "wall," or "modern border") lost its legitimacy. In 1961, Communist leaders saw the Wall as crucial to the survival of the "antifascist" German state; by 1989, the Wall had failed—and so, apparently, had the state. With the demise of the Wall, the imagined unity of Germany yielded to a real embrace of East and West Germans.

The Relic

East Germany is now gone, and most Germans seem to want to forget it. The same holds true of the Wall. Since 1989 the former death strip has bit by bit been reintegrated into the city. Within two years it was difficult to tell where the Wall had stood. That was only natural and proper, in the view of most Berliners: with the Wall would vanish the painful memory of division. An early proposal to mark the Wall's former course across the city received little support. (By 1995, however, the Wall had become sufficiently historical for the plan to be revived.)

Most people who hated the Wall as an obstacle to German unity wanted to see all traces of it disappear as quickly as possible. Their sense of triumph expressed itself in the spontaneous destruction of the Wall. But others could concede the necessity of preserving a little piece of it. For example, the *Berliner Morgenpost,* of the conservative and nationalist Axel Springer newspaper chain, editorialized:

> A few meters of Wall should remain standing as a memorial. That may be painful to some, but this decision is unavoidable. This structure of concrete and barbed wire has caused too much inhumanity and too much suffering, too many people striving for freedom were murdered at it, for its complete removal to be warranted. The small remnant of the Wall—at whichever location it may stand—must forever admonish that a people may never again be arbitrarily divided.[20]

The reason for preservation was thus to protect a place of national memory and to keep alive the lesson of the Wall: the unbreakable unity of the German people.

This was a remarkably rare position. Most citizens in East and West who called for preservation of part of the Wall certainly were not motivated by conventional patriotism. Indeed, they were likely to be seen as disgruntled opponents of unification seeking to spoil the triumphant moment. Instead of a victory monument, they had in mind a place of solemn remembrance. Although the *Morgenpost* was not really proposing a victory monument either, the attempt to enshrine the Wall as a symbol of national strength was bound to leave that impression. And any proclamation of German strength remains a touchy subject at home and abroad. A Wall memorial that proclaimed the message the *Morgenpost* wanted would be enormously controversial. Nationalists thus found it easier to think of the Wall as a symbol of division than as a symbol of unity. Typically they wished not to preserve the Wall, but to destroy it—that is, to forget it.

It was not easily forgotten, however. The Wall, now invisible, became the symbol of Germany's identity crisis in the 1990s as well. In his novella of divided Berlin, *The Wall Jumper* (1982), Peter Schneider had prophesied that "tearing down the Wall inside our heads will take longer than any demolition job on the visible Wall."[21] After 1989 the "wall inside our heads" became the way Germans described post-Wall problems of German national identity—specifically, the growing sense of difference between Easterners and Westerners ("Ossis" and "Wessis"). In another use of the same metaphor, the slogan "I want my wall back" on lips and T-shirts in 1990 expressed some West Berliners' quixotic flight from the specter of unification. In the fairy-tale version of unification, the disappearance of the murderous system of border security was supposed to lead to the happily-ever-after marriage of East and West. But the joyful embrace at the Wall soon gave way to grumbling about overbearing and exploitative Wessis and shiftless and uncouth Ossis. Berlin without a Wall in the 1990s was not a coherent whole, which meant that the Wall had betrayed the hopes invested in it. Its disappearance raised new questions about Berlin's identity.

What, then, to do with the Wall? Which of its meanings deserved preservation or remembrance? Proponents of a Wall memorial faced serious problems: securing the physical remains, overcoming the desire to forget, and somehow presenting an interpretation of the Wall that satisfied a sufficiently large or influential constituency. The German Historical Museum (Berlin's new national museum) proposed to preserve a block-long section of the border fortifications as part of a Wall memorial. So that the very possibility of a memorial would not be precluded, in 1990 the museum fenced off the hacked-up stretch of Wall. In addition, it dismantled and stored the fences, lights, tripwires, and watchtowers that had separated East from West Berlin. Museum officials planned to reconstruct the entire border on a third of the block. This was the key to the entire project, they argued: the famous Wall alone could not give future visitors a sense of the way the border functioned. The rest of the site would then be devoted to a solemn memorial to victims of the Wall.

The museum had chosen one of the most famous points in the Wall, despite its location outside central Berlin. Pictures from Bernauer Strasse had captured the world's attention in 1961. The street divided the district of Mitte from the West

Berlin district of Wedding, and by historical accident the actual border was the East Berlin side of the street. Here the front windows of hundreds of Easterners' apartments faced a West Berlin street. In the days after August 13, as the border troops sealed doors and ground-floor windows, many residents on upper floors climbed or jumped into the street, aided by West Berliners and hindered by Eastern guards. With the improvements in border security, the street's fame faded, although one of the most famous tunnels under the wall, through which fifty-seven people escaped in 1964, passed under Bernauer Strasse. Long before that, the famous windows were bricked up and the residents relocated, and in the mid-1960s the buildings were torn down (except for the front facades up to a height of twelve feet) to clear the way for the border security zone. Until their replacement in the 1980s, the bricked-up first-floor facades continued to serve as the Wall in Bernauer Strasse, and the neo-Gothic Church of the Reconciliation stood inaccessible in no-man's-land until it was blown up in 1985. West Berlin tourist buses could be counted on to drive down the street.

The desire to forget the Wall manifested itself in several different forms of opposition to the memorial proposed here. Some local officials pronounced the wide swath of open land an ideal site for new inner-city housing. The city's traffic planners quickly designated it as the site for a multilane thoroughfare—also badly needed, in their view. Across Bernauer Strasse, on the West Berlin side of the proposed memorial, stands the Lazarus home for the chronically ill. Its director announced that to preserve the Wall outside their front windows would damage the health of the patients by causing depression and anguish. His prognosis seemed to imply that "wall disease" would persist until its visible cause was eradicated. Further obstacles arose from the fact that the death strip included land the GDR had expropriated from private owners. Among those who came forward with claims after 1989 was the church of St. Sophia, whose cemetery had included part of the proposed memorial's site. The church's pastor declared that the Wall memorial would represent a second desecration of the cemetery.

The local and federal governments nevertheless approved the memorial. But property claims as well as financing and design long remained unsettled, and the fenced-in piece of Wall sat untouched for years. Neither popular nor commercial pressures created a sense of urgency. This Wall memorial would not offer the same kind of tourist attraction as either the functioning Wall or the crumbling Wall. The drama of unresolved conflict, the sense of active participation, and (if the museum had its way) the overt commerciality would be lacking.

Meanwhile, Wall tourism did find a place to thrive into the 1990s, thanks to a private initiative. During 1990, tourists seeking to relive the Wall experience wandered through the derelict death strip and sprayed graffiti on interior sections of Wall previously inaccessible. Greetings from and to America were common: "Tammy, Mike, John, and everyone else from New Jersey, you are now on the Wall." But soon those walls were gone. What is now the longest intact piece of the Wall stands along Mühlenstrasse, a busy six-lane street connecting central Berlin with southeastern districts. The street parallels a stretch of the Spree River that had marked the border. The concrete wall along Mühlenstrasse was thus the inner wall that kept Easterners out of the security zone, a blank, invisible, desolate space a world away from the colorful graffiti on the Western side. Its out-of-the-way location made possible the "East Side Gallery" (the name is in English, a Scottish gallerist, Christine MacLean, having been instrumental in its creation) (fig. 11). In the course of 1990, the "gallery" took shape in a mural. First a few artists came, then others followed, each claiming a section of the nearly mile-long stretch of wall. In the end 118 artists from around the world produced 106 paintings while breathing the fumes from thousands of East German cars and trucks and negotiating the cars parked or even junked on the sidewalk. Much of the work features widely recognized motifs. Many of the artists were from the former Soviet bloc, and their paintings proclaim the messages of Eastern European political dissidence. Others recall traumas of German history, especially Kristallnacht and other events in the Nazi persecution of Jews. Many paintings, like much of the old Wall graffiti, illustrate events or fantasies of breaking through or leaping over the Wall itself. Gradually this mural came to wider public attention, and Mühlenstrasse joined the short list of Wall segments slated for possible preservation.

By 1993, when the East Side Gallery's preservation was officially decreed, word had spread that this was the place to experi-

11
East Side Gallery, 1991

ence the historic Wall. Tourists (mostly Americans, at least in the summer) dodged traffic to photograph themselves and their friends in front of the painted wall. At a kiosk they could buy postcards and T-shirts of the paintings. Some could not resist the temptation to inscribe some traditional Wall graffiti—much to the dismay of the gallery's creators and their new municipal backers, who wished to *preserve* the site and its art. Unlike the Bernauer Strasse memorial, hardly anything here was an authentic remnant of divided Berlin. The concrete was real enough, but for the tourists it illustrated something that had happened on the Western side of the Wall. The artists' sentiments and images, interesting as they were, belonged to the post-Wall era. As a historical site, this was a welter of confusion; but as a popular attraction, it worked—briefly. By 1995, the artists' paint was peeling or was disappearing under uninspired graffiti. Removed from a politically liminal space and a sense of transitory creation, the Wall became a mere ghost of its former self.

Thus one might argue that the best way to reproduce the experience of the Wall would be a theme-park reenactment, such as has been offered or proposed by entrepreneurs in Manchester,

England, Fort Lauderdale, Florida, and in the Brandenburg countryside outside Berlin. Tourists could visit a rebuilt Wall and be interrogated by actors in border-guard uniforms. However, the director of the German Historical Museum, Christoph Stölzl, argued that the Bernauer Strasse memorial retained the authenticity of the original site and thus was superior to a "Disneyland" project that could be built anywhere.[22]

Authenticity is, after all, what Berlin has to offer. At the height of the Berlin crisis, in 1960, a British journalist proposed that West Berlin be abandoned and a new Berlin be built in West Germany on the empty land of Lüneburg Heath. Of course the idea of moving West Berlin lock, stock, and barrel was too absurd to deserve serious thought (although the GDR's official party newspaper chimed in with the suggestion that all problems would be solved if only a handful of spies, Nazis, and Cold Warriors were packed up and sent to Berlin, Wisconsin).[23] A historic city is not Disneyland, and it is indeed as an authentic site that Berlin fascinates visitors: here stood the Wall; here walked Hitler; here spoke Bismarck; here rolled the tanks. Berlin will long remain the city of the Wall, even if the concrete ends up in Florida, because the Wall, as an unintentional monument, came to define the urban space of Berlin. It was thus an exemplary, if by no means typical, case of a monument giving form to collective identity.

The fate of the Wall since 1989 dramatizes a different link between place and identity, as it is caught in a struggle between destruction, or forgetting, on one hand, and preservation, or the establishment of an intentional monument, on the other. In a sense it is fitting that Berlin's most famous structure has now been demolished. Berlin is a city associated with destruction, mainly but not exclusively because of the horrors unleashed from here by Hitler. In happier times as well, before and after the Third Reich, Berlin has practiced the destruction that is supposed to bring renewal. Many of the buildings that survived the war did not survive the peace: by the 1960s, preservationists were charging that the "second destruction" of Berlin had exceeded that of the war. And even before the Allied bombers came, Berlin, like New York, had a reputation as a city that quickly consumed its own past, a city of great buildings that no longer exist. Europeans believe—not without reason—that U.S.

cities are showcases of the American practice of planned obsolescence. But whereas New York supposedly casts off the shackles of the past in order to forget them and to live in a dynamic present, Berlin since World War II has ceased to be a city that forgets.

For half a century, Berlin has struggled in vain to purge itself of the ghost of Hitler. At times the will to forget has manifested itself in acts of destruction: when the Soviet authorities quickly leveled Hitler's chancellery after the war, for example, and when the West Berlin government razed SS and Gestapo headquarters. In 1989 a similar fate loomed for the Wall, symbol of the division that came in Hitler's wake. Berlin also offers many examples of the less radical act of forgetting that takes place when new rulers appropriate a building for their own use. In post-Wall Berlin, however, painful memories often impede any smooth disposal of the detritus of history. The desire to forget Hitler or Honecker, the SS or the Stasi, struggles in vain against a determination to remember.

Structures and sites are preserved for all kinds of practical reasons. In some places where the Wall followed a street, and the street has since been reopened, it was simply practical to keep the lights of the death strip as streetlights. This is a decision rich with irony for the few who notice it, but it implies no wish to commemorate the Wall. Similarly, a Toyota dealer who set up shop behind the Reichstag used remnants of the border fortifications to enclose a sales lot—a fascinating snapshot of East Berlin's urban space in transition, but an act devoid of any judgment about the Wall. Preservation becomes an act of remembrance through some further gesture, such as the staging of ceremonies, the establishment of a memorial, or at least the erection of an explanatory or hortatory plaque. In 1945, no one in Germany thought of preserving the memory of most Nazi sites in this way. But after 1989, nearly every proposal to sweep away a relic of the East German state was met with opposition in the form of calls for remembrance. This should not have been a surprise. As we shall see, attitudes toward the Nazi past, and toward Nazi sites, had in the meantime undergone a long and painful transformation. The cumulative effects of two world wars plus a cold war have made German historical memory excruciatingly sensitive, at least in Berlin. Either a Nietzschean paralysis has destroyed the national will to act, or a healthy skepticism has developed about the deeds of nations and human beings, particularly Germans. Although the late-twentieth-century crisis of historical confidence is not unique to Germans, they may lead the world in agonized self-examination.

There is nothing in Berlin to captivate the foreign visitor, except a few museums, palaces and the army.[1]

—Emperor Wilhelm II, 1892

I've never loved this place. Here on the Palace Bridge, we schoolchildren were lined up in the cold on the Emperor's birthday, January 27. . . . On the hot August days of 1914 I stood here wedged in the crowd in front of the palace that is now in ruins. The crowd sang one song after another. Then they pushed down Unter den Linden in the delirium of war. After four years I saw revolutionary workers marching behind red flags in the same streets. . . . Nothing of that can be seen or heard any more, nothing of the people, nothing of the buildings. This place is a parcel of land through which the Spree flows. This is what history looks like.[2]

—Alfred Döblin, 1947

The Eastern zone regime will surely center its headquarters on the site of the old Hohenzollern palace, now "Marx-Engels Platz." The chief government building will dominate the scene just as its prototypes do in Warsaw, Moscow, and other capitals in the East. Even if the government of a reunited Germany never moves into that building at all, it will nevertheless be standing there in case unification is long delayed and we shall have to wrestle with the problem of what to do with it.[3]

—Friedrich Fürlinger,
West Berlin city planner, 1960

We should rebuild the palace as a sign that we are at least trying to forget forty years of socialism.

—from a comment book
for the 1993 exhibition "The Palace?"

Without the palace—at least its exterior—I lack part of my identity as a Berliner.

—from the comment book
for "The Palace?"

Two

Old Berlin

Europe used to be ruled by kings, and its capital cities still have palaces to remind us of their days of glory. So, in a sense, what visitors to Berlin encountered in the summer of 1993 would have been a familiar sight in any other European capital. Walking or driving from the Brandenburg Gate down the grand old boulevard Unter den Linden, they approached an ornate yellow facade shimmering in the distance. Here, where the boulevard reached the banks of the Spree, resided the Hohenzollerns for four hundred years.

For Berliners, too, it was an impressive sight, but one that elicited a different response. They knew that the ruins of the palace had been dynamited in 1950—or at least they knew that the huge space at the end of Unter den Linden had been a parking lot for years. The palace they saw in 1993 and 1994 was made of painted canvas hung from an enormous scaffold in the exact dimensions of the vanished building (fig. 12). It was an extraordinary apparition of something long forgotten, or something never seen—or perhaps of something that might be. For the mockup had a purpose: it was erected by a group dedicated to seeing the palace rebuilt. The decorated scaffold brought to the general public what was already a heated debate among intellectuals.

In Berlin even the remote past cannot escape controversy. Many cities proudly display their historical pedigrees in the form of ancient buildings and monuments. But in Berlin, these buildings must be restored from ruins, if not re-created entirely. And each choice of building and of identity is freighted with all the burdens of German history.

Medieval Berlin: The Nikolai Quarter

The demise of the Wall restored to Berlin its historical center. Both the politics and the geography of division had forced East and West Berlin into peculiar compromises with the historical city. Now the imaginary unity long projected onto the Wall could give way to a real focal point. Or so Berlin's political and cultural leaders thought, naturally enough. For most ordinary citizens, orbits of home, work, and leisure remained entirely on one side or the other of the now invisible Wall. Their habits would be slow to change—especially since the historical center was largely empty of homes, shops, corporate headquarters, and (temporarily) a central government as well. A physical void at

12
Scaffolding and canvas facade on site of royal palace, 1993

the center had to be filled, but so did a psychological void left by political, economic, and cultural forces pulling East and West apart. To re-create a sense of wholeness, leaders looked for points of orientation.

The oldest part of Berlin, since 1920 defined as the district of Mitte (Middle), belonged to the East. Despite its name, after 1945 it lay on the edge of East Berlin, surrounded on two and a half sides by West Berlin and thus by the Wall. Mitte had encompassed the central institutions of government, finance, and culture for successive Prussian and German regimes, including the German Democratic Republic. All had established themselves within the narrow confines of medieval and early modern Berlin. This process of continuous redevelopment has ensured that little remains of old Berlin. The bombers of World War II reshaped the city, of course, but even before the war, Berlin was busy reinventing itself. In the boom years around the turn of the century, many narrow streets of ancient houses gave way to massive new structures for government and business, and the Nazis continued the process on a few enormous sites. Speculation and redevelopment even claimed most buildings from the eighteenth and early nineteenth centuries, replacing them with bigger, taller, more ornate and impressive ones. After 1945, once the rubble had been cleared, the heart of East Berlin was a windswept district of vacant spaces, which were only slowly covered with new buildings. The sense of desolation was hardly countered by the row of high-rise apartment houses built along the southern edge of Mitte around 1970 as a symbolic and visual barrier reinforcing the Wall.

Of course, Berlin never amounted to much as a medieval city. Its identity in later times (unlike Cologne's or Nuremberg's) was thus rarely linked to its medieval past, permitting that past to be neglected. The major cities of medieval Germany lay mainly to the south and west. The vast plain of northeastern Germany was on the margins of the Roman-influenced Christian civilization defined by Charlemagne's empire. Only in the twelfth century did most of the territory of the later GDR forge permanent links to Germany and the West. Under the sponsorship of various princes, ethnic German colonists began settling the area. They founded towns and conquered, assimilated, or drove out the Slavic inhabitants of the area, who were for the most part neither

Christians nor town-dwellers. Although there may have been an earlier settlement on the site, Berlin's poorly documented origins can probably be placed in the late twelfth century. Sometime in the early thirteenth century, town charters were granted to two settlements on opposite sides of a fordable crossing of the Spree River. The larger town on the right bank was named Berlin; the other, an island enclosed by an arm of the river, was Cölln. Each was protected by walls. The two towns would remain closely allied, and soon the name Berlin was customarily applied to both together.

Documents that could give these events precise dates are lost. An exact date is furnished only by the oldest document that clearly identifies either town, one from 1237 that mentions Cölln. In 1937, Berlin's Nazi leaders decided that was occasion enough to stage a celebration of the city's 700th anniversary. In 1987, neither East nor West Berlin found this precedent too tainted to stop them from two ambitious and competing celebrations of Berlin's 750th anniversary.

Churches, fragments of churches, and one small piece of a restored town wall are all that remain of the buildings of medieval Berlin. Even the street pattern and scale of the medieval town has been virtually obliterated. The northern half of the Cölln island was appropriated long ago for royal use; the southern tip of the island has been rebuilt with high-rises; in between is next to nothing. On the Berlin side, after wartime rubble had been cleared, there remained one lonely church to the north and a few streets to the south in which one can still find the ruins of a monastery church as well as a sense of the old scale of the town.

But amid the multilane thoroughfares and windswept plazas, the visitor can find refuge in the winding lanes and intact rows of traditional houses around the church of St. Nikolai (St. Nicholas). St. Nikolai is the oldest medieval church of Berlin, and the Nikolai Quarter was the heart of the medieval town. Here is a concentration of cafés and craft shops clearly aimed at tourists. Visitors to German cities are used to finding the "Altstadt," the ancient city center, restored as a place for pedestrian strolls, nightlife, and tourists' deutschmarks. West Berlin had no such Altstadt, except in the remote suburb (and once-independent town) of Spandau. With reunification, all Berliners could again embrace their city's historical center (fig. 13).

13
Nikolai Quarter, 1995. At left is the apse of the St. Nikolai Church.

One peculiar fact about this ancient neighborhood should be noted, however: it is brand new. In 1979, it was mostly empty land. The ruins of the church and a few scattered buildings were all that stood in one of the more desolate patches of central Berlin. It was at this time that the East German authorities authorized a plan by the architect Günter Stahn to re-create the neighborhood. In addition to restoration of the church, the project entailed the careful re-creation of entire rows of long-destroyed houses. Some of these could lay claim to particular historical significance—the home of the eighteenth-century writer Gotthold Ephraim Lessing, for example—but most were simply typical examples of merchants' houses from the seventeenth and eighteenth centuries.

The new-old Nikolai Quarter, finished in 1987 for the East's 750th anniversary celebration, contributed to the German Democratic Republic's rediscovery of history during the 1980s. During these years, the German workers' state sought to place itself at the end of a line of progressive development that passed through German history. Anniversaries, exhibitions, books, and (not least) urban restorations commemorated worthy predecessors, some of whom had been deemed entirely unworthy not long before. Frederick the Great, heretofore a militarist aggressor, was rehabilitated as promoter of the Enlightenment, and in 1980 his equestrian statue was returned to its prominent spot on Unter den Linden. The rediscovery of Prussia as something other than a fount of militarism also transformed Bismarck from reactionary oppressor of German socialism into incubator of the progressive historical forces of bourgeois revolution.

Where did the Nikolai Quarter fit in? This neighborhood of merchants testified to the vigor of the new middle class at the end of the Middle Ages, rising to power in a feudal society and thus illustrating (in the most basic Marxist theory) the bourgeois revolution that was the prerequisite for the proletarian revolution that the Red Army brought to Germany in 1945.[4] As inner-city redevelopment, the Nikolai Quarter also contributed in a more tangible way to the GDR's search for urban identity. It was one of several projects East Berlin undertook during the 1980s to revive its inner city. Planners hoped that the Nikolai Quarter would encourage tourists to linger after visiting the scattered historical sites nearby, but it also contained apartments for two thousand privileged residents in a part of town long uninhabited.

The visitor to the Nikolai Quarter first encounters large buildings with uninviting concrete facades. They are intended to shield the interior of the quarter from the traffic and noise on the wide streets outside. Unlike the typical East German high-rise slabs, the mass and form of these buildings are oriented to the streets of the quarter. Some of them also mimic Renaissance gables in their concrete rooflines. Only after passing these buildings does the pedestrian arrive in the quiet lanes of new houses that try to imitate their vanished predecessors in every detail. For many people familiar with the old GDR, this painstaking effort was a galling sight. The Communist state had inherited many of the least bombed German cities after 1945; forty years later, complete neglect had doomed many blocks of intact buildings in the centers of cities such as Halle, Erfurt, and Potsdam. Money and attention that might have saved them had instead gone to Berlin. For that matter, even in Berlin the so-called Fishermen's Island, the southern tip of old Cölln, had survived fairly intact into the 1960s, when it was leveled to make way for high-rise apartment buildings. For somewhat different reasons, the Nikolai Quarter's architecture was poorly received in the West. The concrete buildings were seen as ugly, the re-creations as an offense against proper historical preservation, the entire design as unalloyed kitsch. The quality of the food and drink served in the many cafés and restaurants offered Western critics a final confirmation of their established belief in the aesthetic bankruptcy of East German Communism.

Little about this historical stage set is uniquely Communist, however. In it, rather, we see a longing for urban tradition found far beyond Berlin and Germany. Indeed, the Nikolai Quarter's transition to capitalism has been relatively smooth. Not painless, of course: the privatization of businesses and the setting of market rents is never easy, and the summer of 1993 saw a heated conflict between café owners seeking to expand the seasonal beer-garden trade and residents who discovered that order, quiet, and early closing hours were East German customs they were loath to surrender. They will probably have to adapt or move, later if not sooner, since this socialist project is a perfect haven for free-enterprise tourism. West German intellectuals generally scorn the kitschy Altstädte built out of the ruins of cities like Cologne and Düsseldorf, but tourists and business travelers continue to patronize their bars. With the Nikolai Quarter, reunified Berlin came with a ready-made Altstadt that quickly began to absorb visitors from the West. The intellectuals will have to accept that visitors in search of authentic old Berlin will find it in the counterfeit form created by the East German government during its final years.

A Tale of Two Palaces

Once we leave behind the Middle Ages, we find that historical nostalgia in Berlin becomes politically explosive in ways that might dumbfound planners and preservationists elsewhere. The identifiable building blocks of German unity and identity can be traced back to the princes and dynasties of the early modern era. And all national symbols, including palaces, are prized by some Germans and feared by others.

The early fifteenth century marked the beginning of a new era that would leave more lasting traces in the sandy soil of the twin towns. The Holy Roman Emperor granted the territory of Brandenburg to Burgrave Friedrich of the south German family of Hohenzollern, and gave Friedrich and his heirs the title of elector of Brandenburg. Although the territory was named after an older town to the west, Berlin-Cölln had meanwhile emerged as the leading commercial center of the sparsely settled region. The following years were marked by tensions and disputes as the citizens of Berlin and Cölln fought to protect their legal rights against Friedrich and his successors, who sought to establish a firmer hold over their subjects. In 1442, the elector compelled Cölln to hand over land on the northern part of the island for construction of a castle from which he could assert his authority. By the end of the century, the castle had become the permanent residence of the electors of Brandenburg. Berlin and Cölln had lost the independence prized by medieval townspeople, and had become entirely subject to the ruler's will. That was a great blow to their prosperity as well as their pride; in this feudal era of German history, it was not the capital cities but the free cities—Frankfurt, Nuremberg, Augsburg—that flourished.

In the seventeenth century, however, the electorate of Brandenburg emerged as one of the most powerful German principalities. It was in this age, which we associate with the principles and practices of absolutism, that princes strove to make their residences into capital cities. Berlin was no exception, despite the devastation it (along with much of Germany) suffered during the Thirty Years' War (1618–48). The elector Friedrich Wilhelm, who came to the throne of Brandenburg in 1640, has been known since his lifetime as the Great Elector. Through diplomacy and military posturing, more than through conquest, he enlarged his territorial holdings while strengthening his control over them. As part of his mercantilist policies of promoting domestic trade and industry, he also sponsored the expansion of Berlin. To the two walled towns of Berlin and Cölln he added a third and a fourth: in 1662, Friedrichswerder, just west of Cölln, and in

1674 a larger planned grid, Dorotheenstadt, centered on a grand western boulevard, Unter den Linden, which led from the castle to the prince's game park, the Tiergarten.

Meanwhile, he settled disputes between Lutherans and Calvinists in 1664 by issuing an edict of religious toleration—a rare practice at the time. This edict proved valuable in attracting skilled merchants, craftsmen, and farmers to populate the expanded Berlin and neighboring villages. Friedrich Wilhelm actively recruited persecuted Protestants, notably French Huguenots, and, with somewhat less open arms, Jews expelled from Vienna.

The Great Elector was succeeded in 1688 by his son, Elector Friedrich III, who immediately founded a fifth town, Friedrichstadt, larger than the others and laid out in blocks extending south from Unter den Linden. In 1709, he officially united these five towns into a single city of Berlin (fig. 14).

Friedrich failed to match his father's successes in diplomacy

14
Berlin, 1737. South is at the top of this map; thus the tree-lined boulevard Unter den Linden extends from the vicinity of the royal palace (center) west to the Brandenburg Gate (right). Courtesy of Landesbildstelle.

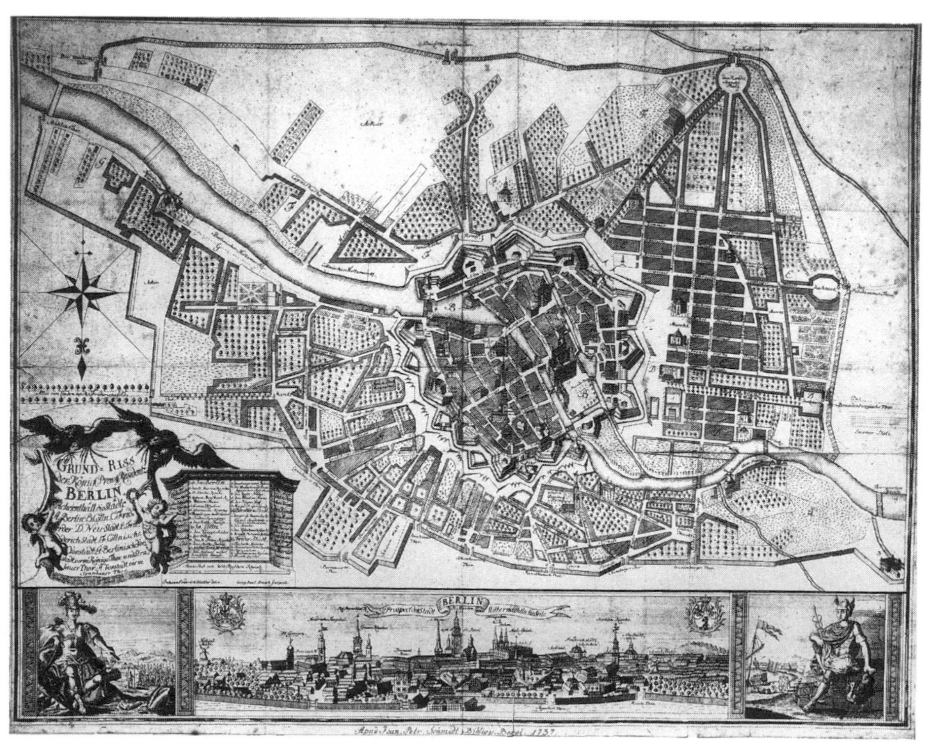

and expansion. More interested in establishing a grand court, he did manage to score one important success: he acquired the title of king. He obtained his crown through complicated diplomatic maneuvers. German sovereign princes were electors, grand dukes, counts, and many other things, but not kings, because they were nominally subordinate to the Holy Roman Emperor. Friedrich, however, took advantage of the fact that Brandenburg had acquired the duchy of Prussia, which lay to the east, outside the Holy Roman Empire's borders. After currying favor with the emperor, Friedrich was granted the right to crown himself Friedrich I, "King in Prussia," in the Prussian city of Königsberg (now Russian Kaliningrad) in 1701. (Not "King *of* Prussia" be-

15
Royal palace and Palace Bridge, 1913. Courtesy of Landesbildstelle.

cause part of Prussia belonged to the Polish crown.) Thus did Berlin become a royal capital, of a kingdom named for a territory far to the east.

Friedrich recognized that art and learning could also contribute to the glory of a grand court. But his queen, Sophie Charlotte, deserves credit for the establishment of the royal academies of arts and sciences (the latter first headed by the philosopher Leibniz). Friedrich also left a substantial physical legacy in Berlin. Most important was his expansion of the royal palace. His sixteenth-century predecessors had turned the medieval fortress into a Renaissance palace on the Cölln side of the Spree, but it was Friedrich who sponsored an enormous extension of the pal-

ace to the west, across the entire breadth of old Cölln. He found a gifted sculptor and architect, Andreas Schlüter, to design the new building, beginning in 1698. Schlüter added a courtyard enclosed by new and renovated wings on the west side of the old palace. The courtyard and the exterior portals were richly decorated with sculpture. His design has been praised as a masterwork—even *the* masterwork—of northern baroque architecture, effusively sculptural but more restrained than the better-known baroque of southern Europe (fig. 15). Its long and ornate facades, four stories and 100 feet high, established the final scale of the palace and—it has been argued—of all Berlin architecture. A second, larger courtyard and extension was subsequently designed in the same style by other architects, chiefly Johann Friedrich Eosander von Göthe. Eosander and others also built a palace several miles west of town for Queen Sophie Charlotte. After her death it would be named Charlottenburg.

By Friedrich's death in 1713, the royal palace had largely taken on the form it would have for more than two centuries. Each succeeding king, however, had his architects renovate and adapt the palace to contemporary tastes and needs. The largest later addition was a massive dome (1845–53) designed by August Stüler, rising to a height of 232 feet over Eosander's western portal. It sat atop the royal chapel and has been interpreted as the pious King Friedrich Wilhelm IV's reactionary response to the threatening tendencies of the modern world (in particular to the revolution of 1848). Others have seen it more benignly as an attempt to maintain the palace's profile in a rapidly growing city.

In the early 1700s, however, the twelve-hundred-room palace dominated a fairly small city. (After falling by half during the Thirty Years' War, the population tripled under the Great Elector and tripled again during Friedrich I's reign, but at 60,000 it was still about a tenth the size of London or Paris.) While rulers came and went—and often lived elsewhere—the palace's physical presence defined the city center, linking old Berlin across the Spree with the new, planned extensions to the west. The architects of all new buildings had to take account of it. Dominated by its new sections, the palace's orientation was now to the west. Its new facade marked the eastern terminus of Unter den Linden, which during the eighteenth century became the grand axis of royal Berlin. The intersection of boulevard and palace, at an oblique angle, became the pivotal point of Berlin's urban space. The same spot looms large in the planning of the reunified German capital in the 1990s.

Among Friedrich I's successors, three may be singled out for their notable contributions to the palace's immediate vicinity. Friedrich II (ruled 1740–86), grandson of his namesake and better (if perhaps not more accurately) known as Frederick the Great, was no great lover of the palace and resided there infrequently. His major contribution to Berlin urbanism is located a few steps down Unter den Linden. The "Forum Fridericianum" is a complex of buildings centered on Unter den Linden and an adjoining square. It consists of four buildings from Frederick the Great's reign, not built according to a unified plan (as originally foreseen) but nonetheless an impressive ensemble. The state opera house designed by Georg Wenzeslaus von Knobelsdorff (1741–43) was the first opera house anywhere built as a freestanding building. Behind it, St. Hedwig's Cathedral (1747–73), with its low dome modeled on Rome's Pantheon, is a Roman Catholic church built by Frederick the Great as a gesture of reconciliation with the Catholic inhabitants of the province of Silesia, which his armies seized from Austria. Across Unter den Linden stands the palace of the king's brother, Prince Heinrich, which has housed Berlin's university since its founding in 1810. Across the square from the opera house is the curved facade of the former royal library (nicknamed, in typical Berlin fashion, the "Commode"), built according to an old design for Vienna's Hofburg palace by the baroque architect Joseph Emanuel Fischer von Erlach. A later addition in the middle of Unter den Linden is the nineteenth-century equestrian statue of Frederick the Great, which the East Germans banished to Potsdam in 1950 and returned in 1980. Although the opera house alone has been badly damaged and rebuilt three times, this ensemble is happily intact and certain to remain so. The only touchy subjects were two plaques put up by the GDR. One commemorated Lenin's visit to the library; it has vanished. The other commemorates what happened in the square on May 10, 1933, when a Nazi bonfire consumed "un-German" books. It will apparently remain, although reunified Germany has added its own gesture, a sunken memorial to the book-burning under glass in the center of the square.

The immediate surroundings of the palace took their final

form during the reign of Friedrich Wilhelm III (from 1797 to 1840), more particularly through the efforts of the royal architect, Karl Friedrich Schinkel (1781–1841). As a result of Schinkel's work, the Lustgarten, the royal garden north of the palace, became the symbolic focal point of the state. On the south side stood the palace, representing the crown. To the east, representing the church, was the Protestant cathedral, a modest eighteenth-century building completely redesigned by Schinkel. To the west, representing the army, was the baroque arsenal (1695–1706), a graceful building designed in part by Schlüter and later used as a historical museum by both postwar German states. Finally, the north side, representing culture, was Schinkel's most original contribution, the long colonnade of his museum (1823–30), known as the Old Museum after four more museum buildings were added behind it in the course of the next century. (The "museum island" thus created is actually just the northern tip of old Cölln.)

What is remembered and honored about central Berlin is largely Schinkel's work. His plans shaped the Lustgarten itself; his recently restored Palace Bridge linked the palace and Unter den Linden with a double row of graceful statues; and among Schinkel's other notable buildings were two more in the immediate vicinity. On Friedrichswerder Market, across from the southwest corner of the palace, he built a neo-Gothic church (which still stands) as well as the brick and terra-cotta cube of his acclaimed Bauakademie, often seen as his most "modern" building. Despite its stature among modern architects, the East German authorities demolished the bomb-damaged building in 1961 to make way for their foreign ministry. That building's demolition in 1995 may open the way for the Bauakademie's reconstruction.

The last Hohenzollern ruler also left his mark. Kaiser (Emperor) Wilhelm II cleared away the houses on the west front of the palace for the construction of a massive National Monument (1892–97) featuring a large statue of his grandfather, Wilhelm I, who presided over the unification of Germany in 1871. The monument is long gone and unlamented; its foundation still projects into the western arm of the Spree but is recognized by few. Wilhelm II also authorized the razing of the old cathedral and its replacement by a much larger one (1893–1903). It was intended to cover Hohenzollern graves, to display Wilhelm's importance as protector of Protestants, and to compete with the grandeur of St. Peter's in Rome and St. Paul's in London. But Julius Raschdorff's neo-Renaissance design, towering over the Lustgarten and heavily laden with ornament, came at the very end of the era of unabashed historicist architecture, and it has never had a good press. It, like everything around it, suffered substantial damage in the war. The East German authorities (consistent only in their bad taste, some would say) eventually decided to keep the massive old building. Its restoration, financed mainly by the West German Protestant Church, began only in the 1970s and was not completed until 1993.

One other late-nineteenth-century change in the Lustgarten was a sign of the times. The northern tip of the old part of the palace along the Spree was torn down in 1885 to clear the way for construction of an east-west thoroughfare, Kaiser-Wilhelm-Strasse (now Karl-Liebknecht-Strasse). Only in the nineteenth century had the need to funnel traffic *past* the palace become an issue. Some of those who see the palace as Berlin's irreplaceable focus argue that its site has long been the symbolic meeting place of eastern and western Europe: Unter den Linden began the highways to the west; from the palace's southeast corner one embarked for Warsaw or Moscow. The same symbolism can also support the opposite conclusion, however: that the palace was or would be an impediment to communication. That argument emerged after 1918, when the palace (and Germany) ceased to have a king. The architect Adolf Behne argued (perhaps half-seriously) in 1932 that the palace no longer served to hold East and West together, so part of it would have to be torn down to establish rational traffic flows through Berlin and thus between Paris and Moscow (this, of course, a few years before autobahns). Echoes of his argument have cropped up in recent discussions of the palace's symbolic and practical value.

"Why do democracies need palaces?" inquired a visitor in the comment book at the 1993 exhibition on the palace. Another wrote sarcastically, "No palace without an emperor!" Those who would rebuild the Berlin palace confront the question of what to do with a monarchless palace. The problem is not unique to Germany, or to the 1990s. Berlin faced it after November 1918, when the emperor abdicated his throne and fled to Holland. The Weimar Republic of 1919–33 did not act decisively to transform the palace's identity, whether out of weakness in the face of monarchist sentiment or out of a desire to distance the new government symbolically from the monarchy. That is, unlike many former monarchies, it did not give the palace a new, high-profile use as, for example, a presidential residence. It employed the vast building for various purposes, mainly as museum space. The Third Reich made few changes; it, too, declined to occupy the palace's symbolic space.

The next regime was forced to make more difficult decisions. By 1945, bombs had seriously damaged much of the palace and burned out most of it. It was not a complete ruin, however, as evinced by four public exhibitions held in intact rooms between 1946 and 1948, while the city was under four-power occupation. In 1948, however, the municipal government was reorganized as four-power control broke down. In the Soviet sector, German Communists took firm control. Plans to rebuild Berlin as a socialist city took form in July 1950 at the Third Party Congress of the Socialist Unity Party (the name of the governing Communists after they absorbed the Social Democratic Party in the Soviet zone). In his speech to the Congress, Walter Ulbricht, the party's general secretary and undisputed leader, declared: "The center of our capital, the Lustgarten and the area of the palace's ruins, must become a grand square for demonstrations, upon which our people's will for struggle and for progress can find expression."[5] On August 23, the government decreed the palace's demolition.

This decision unleashed a storm of indignation in East as well as West Berlin. Protests came from prominent art historians in East Germany, notably Richard Hamann, an authority on baroque art who had come to East Berlin's Humboldt University after his retirement in West Germany. Hamann, keen to preserve a great architectural monument, argued that revolution and socialism were no enemies of old buildings: "The Louvre in Paris has survived all revolutions, and the Kremlin in Moscow, likewise the former seat of forces opposed by the government, is still today the seat of government."[6] Public replies from responsible officials did not challenge such claims. They defended their decision solely on the grounds that the palace was too badly damaged to be rebuilt. Mayor Friedrich Ebert (son of the Weimar Republic's first president) assured Hamann, "If the palace were still undestroyed, no one would have seriously considered tearing it down. Since, however, the English and American bombing attacks have left the palace eighty percent destroyed, as expert opinion has determined," there were only three choices. To leave the ruins standing would not be possible, "since the new Berlin must not become a city of ruins like Rome." To repair them would cost far too much in light of the city's other pressing obligations. Hence the decision to clear away the ruins.[7]

Ebert's allocation of blame typified the early Cold War: Hitler bore some responsibility, but the main source of troubles was the current capitalist enemy. East Berlin newspaper articles published during these days echoed the party line. According to the *Tägliche Rundschau,* "The destruction of this monument by American bombers was an act of cultural infamy that Berlin will long remember." The *National-Zeitung* wrote of "the barbaric vandalism of their flight crews, for whom unrestrained destruction was a mere matter of sport and of business, and from which they returned home with briefcases stuffed with dollars."[8] (One wonders how the crews could have managed such feats. Here we seem to have an overzealous Communist editor furiously mixing party-line metaphors.) But the question of blame was clearly beside the point. For whatever reasons, preservation of the palace was not a high priority. In fact, it appears that the palace's crucial location in the city—so important to its defenders—sealed its fate. Elsewhere ruins might be left for future disposition, but not at the vital center of the capital. The dynamiting began on September 6, 1950. Despite official assurances to the contrary, salvageable parts of the palace were not reerected elsewhere, with a single exception.

The removal of the ruins took months, but once they were gone the way was clear for construction of a reviewing stand from which Ulbricht and his colleagues could survey their grand demonstrations of proletarian power. While plans for new, monumental buildings came and went (see chapter 5), little changed for years on the site. As the proletarian will became less demonstrative (or as the GDR became more bourgeois), the palace's site came to be used for parking the proletariat's diminutive Trabant automobiles. The cathedral, museum, and arsenal, the other main buildings on the Lustgarten (now, in its expanded form, renamed Marx-Engels-Platz), remained. Across the Spree's western arm, Schinkel's Bauakademie sat in limbo until 1961, then was razed to make way for the long white slab of the new foreign ministry. To the south, a new Council of State building

16
Marx-Engels-Platz
and Palace of the
Republic, 1995

was also built during the 1960s. Into its facade was incorporated one of Eosander's baroque portals—the only piece of the palace that was indeed reerected, not for its architectural significance, but because Karl Liebknecht had stood on it to proclaim the socialist republic of Germany on November 9, 1918. Liebknecht was one of the pantheon of GDR heroes; in the following weeks he had helped to found the German Communist Party and been murdered by nationalist soldiers.

Thus we come to the clamor for rebuilding the palace—almost. The matter was enormously complicated by one more encumbrance on the site. In the 1970s, after having failed to act on all the grand schemes proposed over the years, the GDR finally constructed its new building atop the palace's site. By virtue of its location, if not its size or appearance, this "Palace of the Republic" became the old city center's most prominent structure. Designed by an architectural collective under the leadership of Heinz Graffunder, the building did not loom especially large in the enormous square. It took up only one side of Marx-Engels-Platz, covering approximately the site of the Renaissance palace, thus leaving a vast space—a parking lot most of the time—bordered by it, the Council of State building, and the foreign ministry. In most respects the exterior of the Palace of the Republic would not stand out in a suburban office park. It was not a cheap building, but its grandeur took the form of high-gloss international modernism (fig. 16). It was a rectangular box clad in white marble and bronze reflective glass; the best view of the cathedral was its reflection in this glass.

The Palace of the Republic accommodated an array of spaces and uses. One auditorium served as the meeting place of the East German parliament, a body that met infrequently and had as little public visibility as it had power. A five-thousand-seat assembly hall hosted more conspicuous but less frequent meetings such as party congresses and conventions of the national youth organization. The same hall was equally prominent, however, for the popular concerts held there, notably the infrequent (and hence legendary) appearances by Western rock musicians. The building also included other spaces for meetings, concerts, and theater performances, as well as restaurants, cafés, and a bowling alley. Perhaps nowhere else in the world did a parliament share quarters with a bowling alley.

In 1990, the building briefly became a center of attention. After the fall of the Communist regime, the new, freely elected parliament became the state's real government; here, on August 23, 1990, exactly forty years after the decision to raze the old palace, it voted to join the Federal Republic. Then came a twist of fate, the symbolism of which seems more farcical than tragic. Just two weeks before the parliament—and the state—would cease to exist, an official inspection declared the building hopelessly contaminated with asbestos and ordered it closed and sealed. And so it continued to stand for years, in many eyes the symbolic legacy of a poisonous state.

In March of 1993 came a decision to tear it down, but—as with the old palace in 1950, and innumerable recent cases—that only heated up the public debate. By no means all opponents of rebuilding the royal palace wanted to preserve the Palace of the Republic, but the empty GDR showpiece and the ghost of its baroque predecessor were competing for the same site. We can see rival nostalgias at work in the efforts of their respective advocates. Those who longed for a return of the royal palace wished to restore not the monarchy (though one could probably find a few monarchists among them), but rather a cityscape and with it a civic wholeness that had been lacking since 1950, or 1933, or 1918. Those who wished to keep the building that was there, the Palace of the Republic, may have had certain practical considerations on their side, but their deeper wishes were no less fixed on the past. They did not want to restore the Communists to power (though in this case there probably were a few more exceptions), but they sought to hold onto certain memories and experiences of life in the Communist state. A third group that wanted to wipe the square clean and start anew might present itself as free from these longings, but others have imputed to it yet another nostalgia: for the heroic architecture of the 1920s that claimed the ability to create a new urban world. The motivations on all sides deserve more careful attention, which will help us better understand what is at stake in their polemics.

The palace mockup that stood during 1993 and 1994 probably marked the high point of the debate. The scaffolding extended westward from the empty Palace of the Republic; a team of Parisian art students painted Schlüter's and Eosander's facades on strips of canvas which were then mounted on the outside. Since the Palace of the Republic (like the Renaissance portion of the old palace) extended farther to the north than the baroque wing, an additional scaffold covered the exposed part of its western facade and a mirror was mounted on it to give the illusion of a continuous baroque facade longer than had in fact ever existed. Inside the enclosed space was room for summer concerts and for a large exhibition on the history and future of the palace. All of this was privately financed—a most unusual initiative in Germany—by an organization especially created for the purpose. Though the exhibition's organizers strove to present different ideas about future plans for the site, the driving force clearly lay with proponents of rebuilding the palace, led by a Hamburg businessman, Wilhelm von Boddien. They were rewarded with large crowds of visitors willing to pay nine marks to view the exhibition. And they were further rewarded: the exhibition and the sight of the mockup generated a wave of popular enthusiasm for the idea of reconstruction. Even many who opposed reconstruction on one principle or another admitted being moved at the sight of the resplendent baroque facade on a sunny day.[9]

Especially in 1993, an enormous amount of ink and breath was expended in arguments about the two palaces. A look at the arguments reveals several issues at stake, but these issues—architectural aesthetics, urban form, civic and national identity, historical preservation, historical justice—were hopelessly intertwined with one another. The confusion was unavoidable: these arguments about buildings and squares are inevitably arguments about history and identity.

Some of the arguments were in fact explicitly about politics and symbolism. Those who were outraged over the Communists' act of destruction saw reconstruction as an act of justice. "The foul Communist crime must be reversed!" commented a Viennese visitor to the exhibition, adding that "German society needs to regain a healthy self-confidence." As another visitor wrote in the comment book, anything short of reconstruction "would be a German anti-historical vindication of the Red explosives expert Walter Ulbricht." This thirst for justice (or vengeance) had a particular historical context: a rebuilt palace would represent a declaration of victory in the Cold War. One of the palace's leading proponents, the journalist Joachim Fest, put particular weight on the Communists' justification for destroying the palace in 1950: they had wanted to create a Red Square to demonstrate their control of the masses. "In the worldwide conflict that lies behind us, not the least of our goals was to prevent the advance of that kind of control. If the destruction of the palace was supposed to be the symbol of its victory, reconstruction would be the symbol of its failure."[10]

Would it not be possible to erase the Red Square–cum–parking lot, actually and symbolically, without rebuilding the old palace? Fest is certainly right about the significance of the site in Ulbricht's mind. However, as we have seen, the Communist leaders did not admit to any enmity toward the palace itself. Fest's argument sprang in part from his conviction that the Communists intended the destruction of the palace as a symbolic death blow to Prussian militarism. Certainly some German Communists hated the building for its historical symbolism. One can speculate that self-hatred was at work: that Ulbricht and his fellow Communists took out on the palace their rage at the failure of revolutionaries to change the course of German history. But the architect Heinrich Moldenschardt, who made this argument, also turned it against conservative proponents of rebuilding the royal palace. He saw self-hatred arising from their sense of responsibility for the Third Reich and suggested that the return of the royal palace would soothe "the repressed recognition of having brought at least the destruction of the palace upon oneself."[11]

A rebuilt palace would celebrate victory in the Cold War by

wiping out all traces of East Germany on the site. Where did that leave the East Germans? Presumably they were invited to see themselves as victors too, victors over their own oppressive government. Many were happy to see themselves that way, but others' confusion was understandable. Until 1989, after all, the GDR's presentation of itself as an "antifascist" state had left some East German schoolchildren thinking that their People's Army had fought alongside the Red Army against Hitler. Many former citizens of the GDR saw the initiative to rebuild the royal palace, dominated by Westerners, as a denial of their experiences, or as an attempt to erase an unwanted chapter of recent German history.

Here East German history was embodied by the Palace of the Republic, itself a complex historical document. Earlier plans for the site had envisioned a monumental building that would serve as an unmistakable locus of centralized state power. But for one reason or another these plans were not realized. The Palace of the Republic was not very monumental, and in no way distinctly Eastern or Communist or totalitarian (as were, arguably, the bombastic Stalinist monuments of the 1950s). More important, for East Germans, was the fact that it served only secondarily as a government building. Unlike the government offices nearby, it was a public place—and a decentralized, unhierarchical one. It became one of the best spots in town to rendezvous with a friend or to take a visitor. Its thirteen bars and restaurants all catered to ordinary citizens—that is, they charged reasonable prices and (unlike those in first-class hotels) did not demand payment in Western currency—and they were among the most likely places to find an empty table in a city (and country) where that was notoriously difficult.

The 1993 decision to demolish the building raised a storm of protest. Former GDR citizens demonstrated, signed petitions, and formed an organization dedicated to saving it. They resented the Wessis who sought to control their lives, and they recalled with nostalgia the good times drinking, dancing, bowling, and attending concerts in the Palace of the Republic. Many remembered it as it had been officially designated: as a "house of the people," a place on which to pin positive memories of a previous, vanished life. It was a rare relic of an otherwise constricted public sphere in the GDR. For the West German preservationist Peter Findeisen this "gigantic attempt to pacify the people" was a worthy monument to the final years of the GDR.[12] Berlin's senator for cultural affairs, Ulrich Roloff-Momin, endorsed the warmer memories of many Easterners in calling it "an artifact of GDR identity in a positive sense."[13]

As the East German writer Friedrich Dieckmann argued, a wide gulf separated East Berliners' specific memories of a place of conviviality from Westerners' abstract condemnation of a Communist monument. The latter, Dieckmann explained, was the perspective of the victor, wishing to ratify a triumph, just as the Communist victors of 1945 had triumphantly cleared away the royal palace.[14] What many Easterners saw as Westerners' obvious failure to understand—in this case and many others—fueled their passionate attachment to a building that came to serve as an emblem for the fight to vindicate their former lives.

An enormous obstacle for the friends of the Palace of the Republic was the asbestos contamination that deprived the standing building of any salvageable value. This, at least, was an incontrovertible fact—or was it? For many of the building's supporters, it became an article of faith that the declaration of contamination had been a political decision, really directed at a different kind of contamination, a kind that could not be measured by any engineer. The application of asbestos during the building's construction had in fact been carried out according to procedures imported from the West, and experts put forward by the building's supporters argued that the contamination was no worse than in West Berlin's convention center, another 1970s building whose architecture was not widely admired—but a building that remained in use.

Other proponents of rebuilding the royal palace employed the language of urban planning and architecture to present their interpretation of Berlin's history and identity. For them, the Palace of the Republic had to go because its mediocre architecture was unworthy of its prominent site. This crucial point in the German capital, where Unter den Linden and the grid of Friedrichstadt are melded into old Berlin-Cölln and points east, held the key to the city's very identity. A city's identity is something that develops through history, and the importance of this site was stamped by the city's rulers and reinforced by its greatest architects and planners. The eastern terminus of Unter den Linden, the point that linked Berlin's elegant west to its proletarian east long before a wall intervened, was a focal point in the visual dynamics of Berlin precisely because other parts of the city were developed with an orientation to the palace and, later, to Marx-Engels-Platz. Indeed, the historical importance of the site is surely beyond dispute. But its future role in a nonroyal, noncommunist capital remains to be determined. Those who seek to maintain the importance of the site hope to link the twenty-first-century capital to its pre-twentieth-century forebears. In light of Berlin's history in the twentieth century, that is an understandable but nonetheless controversial desire.

Some who argued for the importance of the site went on to assert that only the baroque palace could fill the void there. This conclusion made no sense to the architectural historian Tilmann Buddensieg: "If you see this only as urban repair, then please leave out the Prussian and the historical elements of the building." Buddensieg opted for starting anew: if the need is for a building worthy of the site, "then we can have it built by a modern architect."[15] But here we come up against the sour reputation of modern architecture. For many, the old palace was the best solution precisely because they could not imagine a modern building that would not prove an embarrassment. The 1993 exhibition convinced many visitors—or confirmed them in their view—that reconstructing the old was preferable to creating the new. The comment books were filled with sweeping condemnations of modern architecture.

The publisher Wolf Jobst Siedler was the most articulate exponent of this point of view. Siedler, though a West Berliner, was clearly no single-minded opponent of Communist architecture: for decades he had passionately attacked Western urban development for the destruction it wrought on Berlin and other cities. He could praise the great modernist architects of the early twentieth century for the marvelous buildings they created, "but nowhere did this generation succeed in giving form to the center of a city."[16] Siedler and many others believe this is a task modernism has never mastered; hence, we must look to earlier eras for guidance. Moreover, Siedler added, the entire vicinity of the palace consisted of buildings designed with an awareness of and an orientation to the palace's dominant presence. According to Siedler, for example, Schinkel intended the classical simplicity of his museum to offer a dialogue with Schlüter's intricate baroque forms. Thus, only the palace would restore what was left of central Berlin to any kind of visual coherence.

For others, particularly architects, this conclusion amounted to an admission of defeat by contemporary architecture and perhaps a declaration of despair in the face of the modern world. Siedler did not entirely disagree: whereas his opponents continued to "believe in the genius of the new,"[17] his side was skeptical. It was with "melancholy" and "resignation" that he declared his support for rebuilding the palace.

Perhaps a gesture of resignation, even of despair, would not be the most inappropriate symbol of the new German capital, but it would not be a popular one, and such a sentiment surely did not explain the enthusiasm for rebuilding the royal palace. Nostalgia, rather, was at work. Nostalgia for what? As part of his plea for rebuilding the palace, Joachim Fest wrote a beguiling description of the palace's former role in Berlin life. Unlike most palaces, he observed, it was both a public place and part of the neighborhood, only steps away from ordinary houses and workshops, psychologically approachable because of Schlüter's inviting facades and physically approachable because most of the time anyone could pass through the inner courtyard.[18] Fest makes his readers feel the pain of the building's loss, and he also makes the point that the palace was not only—perhaps not even primarily—the king's house. The palace made the pieces of old Berlin fit together.

In the absence of a king, this fortunate combination of uses cannot be recovered, so what, exactly, *would* be rebuilt? The practical answer was that only the facade—and probably not all of that—would be reconstructed. The palace's friends agreed that rebuilding the interior—the magnificent throne rooms and ballrooms—would be pointless as well as impossible, since there would be no use for them. But they did believe that the city center needed the palace facade to help heal wounds and to restore a coherent urban identity. Opponents countered that a palace facade would repress half a century of historical memory and create the illusion of a continuity and wholeness that had never existed: "Neither in a monumental nor in a political sense could a palace function today as the city's crowning glory. For it would be—in the sense of its original purpose—empty. It would be an utterly misguided symbol for this state: an architectural lurch to the right and an enormous encouragement for restorative tendencies in society. It can be assumed that this is one of the palace lobby's intentions."[19]

This outburst came from a journalist writing for a respectable middle-of-the-road newspaper. Its imputation that the palace debate was really about right-wing politics should not surprise anyone who knows that deep philosophical and political divisions lurk just beneath the surface of German debates about form and identity, including debates about architectural form and urban identity. Many on the German left are deeply suspicious of anything reeking of nostalgia for the old Germany: how can anyone be nostalgic about German history? (Foreigners are likely to nod their heads in agreement at this point.) Nostalgia, according to this thinking, implies a denial of inconvenient facts, in particular, an exclusion from German history of the Third Reich and the GDR. And behind this selectivity lurks a conservative strategy to cleanse and unleash the left's bête noire, German nationalism.

What does this have to do with the royal palace? Its defenders would protest that the palace is not a symbol of Prussian militarism or German chauvinism—and they would be largely correct. The palace was essentially completed prior to the death of Friedrich I, before one can discern anything resembling Prussian militarism or German nationalism. Several later kings lived there seldom or never—including Wilhelm I, who presided over German unification and was the first Hohenzollern to be called emperor. Also—an important if rarely voiced argument for the palace's friends—it can be seen as uncontaminated by the stain of Nazism. It played essentially no role in the Third Reich. Hitler, wary of any sentiment to restore the monarchy, shunned the building.

Nevertheless, the attempt to salvage German traditions has been a project associated with the political right, despite some similar efforts by the GDR in the Honecker years. And the same political divisions carried over, by and large, to the debate over the royal palace. Berlin's Christian Democrats endorsed its reconstruction. The Social Democrats did not, leaning toward the support for the Palace of the Republic represented most vehemently by Eastern-based leftist opposition groups.

The lines in the debate over the two palaces were in large part determined by West German polemics about the Third Reich and German history in the 1980s, the so-called historians' debate. One aspect of that debate involved the left accusing the right of trying either to justify the Third Reich or to expunge its crimes from German history. The kind of history mistrusted by the left was exemplified by the Christian Democrats' parliamentary leader, Alfred Dregger, who boasted that he, like his American allies, had fought in the 1940s to save Western civilization from the tide of Bolshevism. (Dregger was a Wehrmacht officer on the eastern front.)

Similarly, after 1989 the left accused the right of trying to remove the GDR from the history of postwar Germany. Conservatives, suspected of sympathy for aspects of the Third Reich, in turn saw an affinity for Soviet-style socialism behind opposition to the royal palace. As one visitor wrote in the comment book at the 1993 palace exhibition: "Whoever is fundamentally against a reconstruction of the palace today puts himself at the same level as the narrow-minded philistines Ulbricht, the Socialist Unity Party, and company." But was the proper answer to Ulbricht's crime to undo it, or to avoid doing it again? Many pages away in the comment book someone else wrote that those who want to raze the Palace of the Republic "are at the aesthetic and moral level of Ulbricht and his apparachiks." In any case, Ulbricht was the standard of vituperation. Disagreement arose over how best to inscribe the differentiation from the GDR in the urban fabric.

Proponents of reconstruction cited many examples of projects they saw as comparable. Their favorite was postwar Warsaw, a city much more thoroughly destroyed than Berlin. Although (or because) there was virtually nothing left standing in the center of their capital, the Polish leadership decided soon after the war to undertake a careful restoration of the royal palace and the adjoining Old Town, returning it as closely as possible to its prewar appearance. The reconstructed buildings represented an obvious statement of national pride and defiance in the face of near obliteration. Statements of what might appear to be German national pride, however, make many people nervous—not least many Germans. Moreover, it is a different matter to envisage the reconstruction of a building gone for nearly half a century, one remembered firsthand by relatively few Berliners. The fact that this would be contemplated is itself evidence of a remarkably strong historical sense at work in the city. The obvious historical precedent for such an undertaking was in sight just across the river: the Nikolai Quarter. But the palace's proponents never mentioned it. Praise for any GDR project would presumably have been seen as tainting the palace proposal.

The lapse of two generations—evinced by the presence of the Palace of the Republic—separated the royal palace from any conventional understanding of historical preservation. Preservation has become professionalized and bureaucratized, giving preservationists a distinct identity and point of view. The professionals did not respond favorably to the idea of re-creating the palace. Current practices and theories of preservation have their roots in the nineteenth century's growing awareness of historical change and decay, manifested in the Romantic fascination with ruins as well as the conscious re-use of many historical styles of architecture. Schinkel himself played an important role in early efforts to protect historical monuments in Germany. But it was Schinkel's idea (fortunately never realized) to rebuild the Acropolis in Athens as a royal palace. A few years later, the Englishman John Ruskin taught that past works of art are unique and irreproducible, and that they should therefore be preserved, not restored. This practice slowly caught on and was encoded in theories of preservation around the turn of the century—in the German-speaking lands, for example, by Alois Riegl and Georg Dehio.

The fundamentals of modern preservationist practice still derive from these notions of historical authenticity. The only important change over the past century has been a gradual expansion of the class of structures or relics deemed worthy of preservation: from individual works of genius, to ensembles of buildings, to any artifacts of an era, and from a desire to preserve the very old to an interest in any style or epoch no longer current. Belief in the authenticity of the original artifact has remained constant among preservationists, but the enormous destruction of World War II forced a rethinking of their practices in Germany and other European countries. So much had been lost so quickly; ruins were the spectacle of daily life, not the exceptional reminders of a distant past. Compromises with principle, backed up by overwhelming public sentiment, permitted the restoration or, in a few notable cases, the complete reconstruction of destroyed buildings.

In Berlin, for example, those who wanted to save the royal palace in 1950 did not propose to leave it as a ruin. In West Berlin, the same was true of the Charlottenburg palace: the debate was between proponents of restoration and those who declared it irretrievably lost. The demolition of the royal palace in East Berlin may have been decisive in the victory of the former group shortly afterward. With a few notable exceptions left deliberately as ruins, West Berlin by the 1960s had chosen either obliteration or repair for all its major buildings. Things moved more slowly in the East, but the result was not radically different in the long run, although some Western observers thought the GDR too flexible with its heritage—for example, in reerecting old buildings on different sites. Many ruins still stood after 1970, but most of them had been slated for reconstruction. Even on the overgrown remnants of August Stüler's New Museum (the slightly newer neighbor of Schinkel's Old Museum) work had begun—just barely—by 1989.

Berlin's preservationists saw the proposed reconstruction of the royal palace as a clear case of the falsification of history. For them, and for other opponents, the project amounted to a declaration that the entire existence of East Germany had been some kind of aberration, not worthy of mention and best wiped from the urban tableau. Meeting at the old State Library just down Unter den Linden while the canvas facade was going up, many of them scorned the effort to erase authentic traces of one history in order to re-create a different one. For the preservationists, the proper course of action was to keep the Palace of the Republic, an authentic, existing monument. The coalition of that building's friends thus comprised professional preservationists in East and West, nostalgic former East Germans, and left-leaning Westerners opposed to whitewashing German history. The result was a fairly clear division along party lines. In January 1992, word got out that the city's preservation bureau was contemplating the designation of the Palace of the Republic as a historical landmark. It was, after all, the site of the GDR's historic decision to join the Federal Republic in 1990. One of the leading Christian Democrats in the Berlin legislature immediately denounced any protection for this "architectural monstrosity" as an expression of "historical ignorance."[20] (Ignorance of which history? Note that both sides make this charge.) His party and the Free Democrats declared their firm opposition to the move (and threatened to fire the city preservationist), while the Social Democrats announced that preservation was "acceptable" and a representative of the leftist Green Party accused the Christian Democrats and Free Democrats of politicizing preservation just as the GDR had.[21]

Among the general public, enthusiastic supporters of a rebuilt palace presumably cared little about the preservationists' notions of authenticity. The more thoughtful proponents of reconstruction had a reply, however. Siedler, Fest, and Boddien all conceded that a rebuilt palace would lack authenticity, but they denied that the concept had any relevance. Siedler noted that Unter den Linden today is a row of counterfeit buildings, some (like the Opera House) damaged and rebuilt more than once. "The architectural history of Berlin, like that of Europe, is a history of counterfeits"—whether Goethe's house in Frankfurt, the campanile in Venice, or the so-called crown prince's palace on Unter den Linden, which was totally destroyed during the war and then rebuilt from scratch twenty years later by the East Germans. Boddien added that the same inauthenticity would also apply to the Palace of the Republic if it were stripped to its frame to remove the asbestos and then restored to its earlier appearance.[22]

Few voices defended the Palace of the Republic on aesthetic grounds; many condemned it as an eyesore. Most preservationists believe aesthetic arguments should not be decisive in determining a building's historical value. In any case, they had good reason to be suspicious of assertions that Honecker's palace was just plain ugly. As the preservationists pointed out, similar-looking buildings in the West were never torn down just because they were unattractive (much as one might wish it!). On the other side, advocates of reconstructing the royal palace recognized that the sheer beauty of the old building—at best only partly reproducible—was not a sufficient reason for rebuilding it.

No party and no principle could claim a clear victory here. In the absence of any consensus, government budget cuts became decisive, forcing cancellation of plans to construct new buildings and to demolish old ones. In 1995, the decision to tear down the Palace of the Republic was reversed, leaving undecided how the asbestos would be removed, what the building would be used for, and what its long-term prospects were. The new lease on life for the Communists' vacant palace also left Marx-Engels-Platz empty, except for its ghosts.

The Brandenburg Gate

In a paradox typical of contemporary Berlin, supporters of the royal palace drew sustenance from the disdain for the building expressed by some of its owners. This strengthened their argument that the palace represented first and foremost the city center, not the king's house. After the death of its main patron, Friedrich I, in 1713, the palace was in fact shunned by many of the rulers that local patriots would most like to forget, from Friedrich Wilhelm I to Adolf Hitler.

Among the words that do not come to mind to describe Friedrich I's son and successor are charming, dashing, contemplative, and generous. Friedrich Wilhelm I hated his father—in this he was a true Hohenzollern—and scorned his parents' ambitions as patrons of the arts and the sciences. Facing large debts, the new king drastically cut royal expenditures, which meant canceling further plans to expand the palace. His thriftiness might perhaps be admired from afar, but his personality combined stinginess with cruelty: he liked to drive his point home by beating recalcitrant subjects with his own cane.

His one passion—and the one place he did not stint on money—was his army. If we want to find a tradition of Prussian militarism, here is its beginning. He removed the plants and statues from the Lustgarten and turned it into a military parade ground. Hitler, too, later had the Lustgarten paved for mass rallies, and Ulbricht, as we have seen, had the palace razed to accommodate his even bigger demonstrations. Though Friedrich Wilhelm greatly expanded his army, however, he avoided risking it in battle. His son and heir, a young man of very different temperament, longed to preside over a court filled with music and philosophy. But when the tyrannical father died in 1740 and Friedrich II inherited the large army as well as a full treasury, he decided instead to conquer Silesia. At one point his wars brought Prussia to the brink of destruction, but ultimate success brought him the appellation "Frederick the Great" and assured Prussia's reputation as a military power.

Berlin, it is worth remembering, came of age as a garrison town. Though Friedrich Wilhelm I was not interested in beautifying the city, he did seek to promote its growth. Needing more space to quarter soldiers and more artisans to supply their needs, he gave away hundreds of lots and compelled the recipients to build houses on them. He expanded the city limits and, in the 1730s, replaced the Great Elector's old fortifications with a new wall built around the expanded city (see fig. 14). This was not a fortification but a customs barrier to regulate commerce and

17
Brandenburg Gate and Pariser Platz, 1898. Courtesy of Landesbildstelle.

prevent soldiers from deserting. (For all the differences, in both these purposes we can see a resemblance to Ulbricht's later wall.) Among the wall's eighteen gates, the most prominent lay at the southern and western edges of the expanded Friedrichstadt, where large plazas were laid out inside the gates: a circular plaza inside the southern Halle Gate, an octagon at the Potsdam Gate, and a square at the western terminus of Unter den Linden. Friedrich Wilhelm envisioned all three spaces as military parade grounds.

The last of these gates concludes our look at the eighteenth-century city. It marks the outer end of the grand axis of Unter den Linden, scene of royal processions, military parades, and elegant promenades throughout the eighteenth and nineteenth centuries. Though it is not the original Brandenburg Gate, it is

all that remains of the eighteenth-century wall, apart from a fragment excavated in Stresemannstrasse. The original baroque gate that separated Unter den Linden from the Tiergarten was replaced at the order of King Friedrich Wilhelm II, Frederick the Great's successor. The commission given to the architect Carl Gotthard Langhans ushered in a new era in Berlin architecture. To the end of his long life (in 1786), Frederick the Great had insisted on building in ornate rococo forms that had long since fallen from favor in Europe's more fashionable capitals. Langhans's Brandenburg Gate, completed in 1791, brought the more severe lines of neoclassicism to Berlin (fig. 17).

Langhans's simple design, modeled on the Propylaea of Athens, comprises a double row of Doric columns that frame five openings. The gate's other famous feature is the copper quadriga that was mounted atop it in 1793. This work of the young sculptor Johann Gottfried Schadow portrays a goddess riding in a chariot drawn by four horses galloping into the city. The Brandenburg Gate, with its quadriga, has long been Berlin's most famous symbol, rivaled only by the more ephemeral Wall. Its image has adorned commemorative coins, playing cards, historicist and expressionist paintings, posters for all kinds of events, and East and West Berlin postcards and tourist brochures. It may be an admirable work of architecture and sculpture, but that does not explain its symbolic resonance. Nor does its intended function. Unlike many nineteenth-century structures, it was not erected as a national monument. Its size and form made it much more than a utilitarian structure, but it was nevertheless a functional gate in the city wall, flanked by guardhouses.

History has made the Brandenburg Gate a German monument. At first its official name was the "Gate of Peace"; it was not, after all, a Roman triumphal arch. But its identity changed in 1806, when Napoleon defeated Prussia and triumphantly entered its capital through the western gate. He showed his admiration for the quadriga by ordering that it be taken down and shipped to Paris to join his other confiscated art treasures. The emperor thus became known locally as the "horse thief of Berlin," and the denuded gate became the symbol of Prussian and German resistance. In 1813 Schadow himself proposed to fill the quadriga's place atop the gate with an enormous cast of the Iron Cross, the new military medal designed by Schinkel at the behest of King Friedrich Wilhelm III. Upon Napoleon's defeat in 1814, however, a triumphant procession returned the quadriga to Berlin, the neighboring square was renamed Paris Square (Pariser Platz), and the "Gate of Peace" became a "Gate of Victory." Schinkel designed new insignia for the goddess's staff: a Prussian eagle and, within a wreath, the Iron Cross.

Thereafter, the gate became ever more firmly established as a symbol of Prussia and its capital. It became the traditional backdrop for military parades (following Napoleon's example) and for the ceremonial reception of state guests. When the entire customs wall was torn down in the 1860s, the Brandenburg Gate remained; from then on, it was strictly a monument. After Germany was unified under Prussian leadership in 1871, the victorious troops returning from France were welcomed at the Brandenburg Gate. The Prussian monument had become firmly established as a German national symbol, the site of many more ceremonies before soldiers marched through it on their way back to France in 1914. The Nazis, too, embraced the old symbol of victory. The night Hitler was appointed chancellor, January 30, 1933, thousands of torch-bearing Nazi brownshirts marched through the gate.

When the bombers came, the Nazis generally did a better job of evacuating art treasures than saving people. But they apparently did not dare risk morale by removing the goddess and her horses. Instead, in 1942 they had plaster casts made of the quadriga. By 1945, when Soviet soldiers planted their red flag atop the gate, it was badly damaged and only fragments of the quadriga remained. The East German leaders who inherited these ruins decided to keep the gate and adopt it as their own. The shattered quadriga's fate was less certain. Artists and politicians entertained several proposals for a suitable new sculpture: a group of workers, children dancing around a globe, a mother with child, Picasso's dove of peace. A Western newspaper, hearing of the last proposal in 1949, declared that if the dove of peace were to nest placidly at the entrance to the Communist world, the West would be obliged to raise a banner in front of the gate with the words Dante had affixed to the gates of Hell in his *Inferno:* "Abandon all hope, ye who enter here."[23] Eventually, however, the East decided to restore the quadriga instead.

Unfortunately, the gate stood in the Soviet sector, the plaster casts were in the West, and during the 1950s the two regimes were busy denouncing each other as criminals and usurpers. After the failed uprising against the East German government on June 17, 1953, the West renamed the street that continued Unter den Linden west of the gate "the Street of 17 June." But the two Berlins had only one Brandenburg Gate, and it provided a rare opportunity for cooperation. West Berlin agreed to re-create the statues while the East restored the gate. This joint venture did not, of course, proceed without incident. In 1958 the reconstructed quadriga was brought to the sectoral boundary, a few steps from the gate, and simply left there for the East Germans to claim. Before putting it up, the Easterners sawed the Prussian eagle off the top of the goddess's staff and the Iron Cross out of the wreath. For the Western public, this was vandalism and deceit, but it should not really have been a surprise. In 1957 West Germany had legalized the display of the Iron Cross, which the GDR had banned as a militarist symbol. In 1958 the Eastern press was filled with editorials and letters demanding the removal of these "fascist" ornaments. The Brandenburg Gate was once again to be a gate of peace, declared the East Berlin government (fig. 18).[24]

With the goddess's staff crowned only by a wreath, the quadriga and gate would remain from 1958 until 1990; only their surroundings would change utterly. At first the gate still filtered traffic passing across the sector line between the Tiergarten and the shattered ruins along Unter den Linden. As the two halves of the city grew apart, the gate acquired a rich new symbolic resonance, captured, for example, in scenes of the 1961 American comedy film *One, Two, Three,* directed by Billy Wilder (whose ties to Berlin went back to the 1920s) and starring James Cagney as a representative of the Coca-Cola Company caught between the intrigues of Communists and ex-Nazis.

But the film was a commercial flop: by the time it was completed, the Wall had made crossing the Brandenburg Gate anything but a laughing matter. Because the western edge of the Mitte district coincided with the location of Friedrich Wilhelm I's wall, the sectoral boundary followed the same course after 1945, and after 1961, so did a long stretch of the new wall. The Brandenburg Gate was thus once again part of a wall. Here was a historical continuity that no one wanted to acknowledge. This time it was not a gate; the crossing points lay elsewhere. Erich Honecker, the Politburo member in charge of national security and hence the man directing construction of the Wall, apparently pressed for the gate's closure because he thought any activity around it would attract Western media attention, demonstrations, and provocations.[25] He was probably right, but he may also have been swayed by his own regime's frequent evocation of the Napoleon-like specter of West German troops marching triumphantly through the Brandenburg Gate on their way to destroy peace and socialism.

Both the gate and the quadriga had been designed to face into the city—that is, to the east. That is not what a visitor would expect, but the gate's intended audience was local residents, not outsiders. The folk memory of Berlin seems to offer evidence of confusion on this point. Visitors are often told that the quadriga originally faced the other direction and was turned around at some point—something that never happened. This is an old

18
Brandenburg Gate, 1959. Courtesy of German Information Center.

legend: an 1860 guidebook asserts that the goddess had faced away from town before Napoleon, but had been reerected looking inward in 1814.[26] Late-twentieth-century versions of the legend tend to be vaguer about the date of the reversal; Ulbricht as well as Napoleon comes under suspicion as a possible culprit.

In its uncertain stance toward inside and outside, residents and visitors, the Brandenburg Gate resembled nothing so much as its newer neighbor, the Berlin Wall. With the Wall's presence, the poignancy of the gate as symbol became stronger than ever. On its Eastern side, Pariser Platz starkly illustrated the desolation brought by the Wall. Once among Berlin's most elegant squares, a place of palaces, the French and U.S. embassies, the Academy of Arts, and the city's premier hotel, the Adlon, it was now bare except for the gate and the Wall. Tourists were restricted to its far end, but distinguished guests and officially invited delegations were brought to the gate and asked to admire the work of the border guards. From the Western side, the gate was now entirely

19
Brandenburg Gate, November 1989. Courtesy of German Information Center.

inaccessible, and could only be seen from a dead-end street in the middle of the Tiergarten. Nevertheless, tourist buses regularly came by, and state visitors were brought there too. In 1963, when John F. Kennedy came to see it, he found that the East had hung red banners between the columns to block any view beyond the gate—a Cold War gesture with more figurative meaning than the East had intended. In 1987, the gate served as the backdrop for Ronald Reagan's speech, with bulletproof glass erected behind the rostrum. (Bill Clinton, in 1994, was the first U.S. President privileged to speak on Pariser Platz, under the heads of the quadriga's horses instead of their posteriors.)

Both East and West Berliners claimed the gate as the symbol of their city and of their version of German unity. But it may have been the foreign media from the West that made the gate

the preeminent symbol of the less telegenic Berlin Wall. During the days after November 9, 1989, the TV networks made the Brandenburg Gate the backdrop for their cameras. It was a fortunate coincidence that the semicircular barrier blocking the gate was the only section of the Wall wide and flat enough to stand (and dance) on (fig. 19). Since the Brandenburg Gate was not a functioning gate, however, the hordes of East Germans actually passed through the Wall elsewhere for several weeks. Finally, on December 22, 1989, West German chancellor Helmut Kohl led a phalanx of politicians in a ceremony reopening the Brandenburg Gate. Evidence later surfaced that Kohl had in fact pressured the East Germans to delay the opening for five weeks so that he could be present.[27]

A few days later, New Year's revelers climbed up to the newly accessible quadriga and left it seriously damaged. Soon afterward, while the gate was being restored, the quadriga, too, was taken down for a careful restoration. Thereupon controversy erupted anew. The summer of 1991 saw a reprise of the 1958 debate about the quadriga, this time without the Cold War to define positions. A young Christian Democratic member of the Bundestag, Friedbert Pflüger, called for the Iron Cross and Prussian eagle to be left off the restored quadriga. (They had been preserved since 1958 in an East Berlin museum; the reunification of the quadriga coincided with that of Germany.) His campaign found supporters across the political spectrum, only some of whom could be dismissed as leftists antipathetic to any sign of German national pride. The Berlin press and public was nonetheless hard on Pflüger. He argued that symbols of Prussian patriotism had no place in the new Germany; but others suspected that his real motive was bitterness over the decision to move the government from Bonn. He was, more pointedly, accused of wanting to falsify history "à la Ulbricht." Little attention was paid to his claim that he wanted to restore the original "Gate of Peace" and the original quadriga as it had existed up to 1806. It was easy for Pflüger's supporters to conclude that Berlin was rejecting historical authenticity in favor of patriotic nostalgia.

In fact, no one was proposing the return of the goddess's original staff, gone since 1814, when Schinkel had not merely added the Iron Cross and Prussian eagle but had redesigned the entire staff. The quadriga Napoleon took, for example, had a Roman eagle where the Prussian one later perched. And that had actually been the goddess's *third* staff: Schadow's first two designs had proved so unpopular that he was obligated to replace each of them within months.[28] In other words, the debate in 1991 was between restoring the 1814 quadriga and the 1958 version. Since the latter's repudiation of Prussian militarism had been the work of Ulbricht's regime, it found few defenders. Amid good words for Prussian symbols—the Iron Cross, it was pointed out, came out of the wars of liberation against Napoleon, not World War I or II—Berlin's leaders ceremonially rededicated the restored quadriga, with the staff of 1814–1945 as well as an artificial patina, on August 6, 1991, the two hundredth anniversary of the gate.

The gate itself could thus claim its traditional place as the symbol of Berlin as well as its newer status as the preeminent symbol of unity. Yet it stood in the middle of the city's main east-west thoroughfare; the symbol of unity physically separated the two Berlins. The relationship between the gate and the all-important circulation of traffic sparked another debate. The attachment many Germans have to their cars has always stopped short of the American practice of tearing down cities to make way for cars, but the passion of German car lovers seems to arouse in Green-thinking Germans the same kind of suspicion that passionate patriotism does. Happily the question of driving through the Brandenburg Gate did not create clear battle lines. Some car haters wanted to reserve the gate for pedestrians and bicyclists, but others thought that the gate could serve to limit and slow auto traffic. Car lovers' favorite solutions were a tunnel under the gate or a scheme to circumvent it. The latter, in fact, had first been proposed at the turn of the century, and Nazi planners as well had sought to remove the buildings on each side of the gate to make way for traffic. In the 1990s, those buildings were long gone, but plans to direct traffic away from the gate were nevertheless opposed by some who thought it should serve as a gate, a symbol of German unity, not a traffic island, and by others who wanted to rebuild Pariser Platz as the enclosed space it once had been. An initial compromise permitted only buses and taxis through the gate, and they were restricted to the wider central passage, once reserved for the emperor's carriage.

When the monarchy ended in 1918, that central passage was not the only place that lost its identity. For all the turbulence of Berlin's history under the Hohenzollerns, they arguably presided over a degree of stability that has not been approached in the rest of the twentieth century. Many Berliners are understandably reluctant to frame their identity in terms of the troubled eras that followed: the weak Weimar Republic, the Third Reich, and the divided city. Hence the wish to reach back to the relatively placid era of monarchs. How can that nostalgia possibly be satisfied? Since hardly anyone actually wants a king, it is difficult to know just what to salvage from the royal past. The much-restored but never removed Brandenburg Gate, with its thrice-removed and twice-reconstructed quadriga, is as authentic a symbol as Berlin can offer. Other buildings, visible or remembered, embody too rich a variety of meanings to permit any consensus about the legacy of old Berlin, or about how to restore it.

Because Berlin is the site of the physical encounter of East and West, of two value systems and ways of life, it has the richest and most varied texture of any town in the world. The Reichstag is situated on the limit of that space and stands up in an open, strangely metaphysical area.[1]

—Christo, 1985

Ride back with bus number 5. Stand on the bus's platform, facing the Wertheim side of Leipziger Strasse. The picture of unbelievable movement of people, lights, and vehicles that now presents itself to the eye—that is Berlin![2]

—recommendation for visiting Potsdamer Platz in a 1912 travel guide

The cosmopolitan rabbits
Hop around on Potsdamer Platz
Looking at these pastures how should I
Believe what my grandfather told me
Here was the center of the world[3]

—Sarah Kirsch, "Naturschutzgebiet," 1982

A melting pot of everything that is evil—prostitution, drinking houses, cinemas, Marxism, Jews, strippers, negroes dancing, and all the vile offshoots of so-called "modern art."[4]

—Berlin as described by the Nazi Party newspaper, Völkischer Beobachter, 1928

Three

Metropolis

Berlin is a city of brick, stone, and concrete, but textiles have recently played a prominent role in its architecture. The years 1993 and 1994 saw the royal palace's facade re-created out of canvas; 1995, Christo's "wrapping" of the Reichstag. Their very transience enabled the two projects, different as they were, to make bold statements about Berlin's urban space as a repository of memory. The palace facade (see chapter 2) called attention to an invisible past; the wrapped Reichstag stirred buried memories about a visible, and visibly ravaged, building. If the vanished royal palace is the most notable absence among Berlin buildings, the Reichstag may be the single most resonant presence.

This pair of buildings, a mile apart at opposite ends of Unter den Linden, stand as symbolic centers of power from two eras and two kinds of government. The second era, the era of parliaments, saw a vastly larger and more diverse city, one less susceptible to domination by any central place or institution. After the middle of the nineteenth century, Berlin's expanse, appearance, social structure, and sources of livelihood changed rapidly and profoundly. And even things that didn't change *looked* different: thanks to modern technology—trains, then automobiles and airplanes—natives and visitors alike crossed the city via new routes and at new rates of speed. In this new world, no king could command the same allegiance as before, and no parliament could project the same kind of unity as a traditional king—especially when the palace still stood and (until 1918) still housed a royal resident. What came to Berlin in the late nineteenth and early twentieth centuries with startling speed was the bewildering set of changes that, for lack of a more precise formulation, we call modernity. It was a disorderly, disorienting, frightening era, but it was also exciting and liberating, and in light of what followed, it has come to be bathed in the light of nostalgia.

The Reichstag

Christo's "wrapping" was a peculiarly appropriate homage to the Reichstag, celebrating a conventional symbol of national dignity in an unconventional way. This forlorn building, the home of the German parliament, had become the symbol of German parliamentary democracy. That gave it a prominent place in Berlin's contested historical landscape, as Christo undoubtedly recognized. Parliaments and democracy have experienced many vicissitudes in modern German history—in Bismarck's Second Reich, the Weimar Republic, Hitler's Third Reich, divided Germany, and now the unified Federal Republic. The Reichstag's prominent role in each period makes it a monument to Germany's troubled national dignity.

The government of unified Germany after 1871 has often been described as pseudo-parliamentary. Perhaps semi-parliamentary would be more accurate: the powers of the Reichstag (or Imperial Parliament), for which all males over the age of twenty-five were eligible to vote, were circumscribed by those reserved for the emperor (the German title is Kaiser) and for the individual states (Prussia, Saxony, Bavaria, and twenty-two others), whose own parliaments were generally less democratic than the Reichstag. The empire's constitution created a peculiar balance of powers, reflecting the desire of its principal author, Otto von Bismarck, to combine traditional autocracy and modern representative government in a way that would leave the decisive power at the center. For Bismarck himself was the center: as imperial chancellor he was legally the servant of both Reichstag and emperor; but in fact, his ability to manipulate the political parties, on the one hand, and the old Emperor Wilhelm I, on the other, made him the effective master of both institutions.

In this compromise between representative government and monarchical rule, the Reichstag embodied both the hopes and frustrations of democrats. For autocrats, especially Bismarck, it served as an institution to keep democratic impulses under control. That control became more elusive as the Reichstag showed signs of growing independence. Particularly worrying, even for most of the liberal, conservative, and religious parties that sat in the Reichstag, was the growing strength of the avowedly Marxist Social Democrats, who in the 1912 elections became the Reichstag's largest single party.

Apart from the person of the emperor, however, the Reichstag was the most important institution of the new Reich, so the question of a worthy home for it was raised immediately in 1871. Bismarck saw no need for a monumental building, but parliamentary leaders begged to differ. It took twenty-three years to settle the issue. At first it proved difficult just to agree on a site for the new building. The location eventually chosen was the eastern side of Königsplatz (King's Square), some two hundred yards north of the Brandenburg Gate and just outside the area enclosed by the old customs wall (which had been torn down a few years before). Some parliamentary leaders found the location too remote—above all, too far from the traditional center of royal power at the other end of Unter den Linden. Before being renamed Königsplatz in 1864, the vast open space had been simply one of many army drill yards surrounding Berlin. Within a few years, however, a fashionable neighborhood grew up around it. The eastern side of the square was the side closest to town, but a building on that site would face away from the city—another complication. The location was never just a matter of convenience for Reichstag members: the symbolism of the building's site was inseparable from the unsettled question of the Reichstag's role in governing the new German state.

The same was true of the building's architecture. In 1872, the Reichstag held an international architectural competition for its building. A winner was chosen—Ludwig Bohnstedt of Gotha—but symptomatic of the Reichstag's weakness was its inability to acquire the proposed site on Königsplatz, meaning the entire competition had been for naught. A decade of uncertainty followed, punctuated by Bismarck's suggestion that the nation might be better served by a Reichstag meeting somewhere far away from Berlin, now a hectic city of a million, far too many of whom were, in Bismarck's view, untamed liberals and socialists. Finally, in 1882, the Reichstag announced a new architectural competition for the same site on Königsplatz, which it had by this time acquired. The existence of Bohnstedt's winning design of 1872 was passed over in embarrassed silence; it had been too much of a compromise choice between the mutually hostile advocates of Berlin neoclassicism and the neo-Gothic style.

This time the jury chose a design by the Frankfurt architect Paul Wallot. To meet the many demands put on the building, Wallot had to revise his design several times over the next two years. Finally his design was accepted, and the Reichstag was built over a ten-year period, 1884 to 1894. As the Reichstag's designer, the little-known Wallot suddenly became one of Germany's most prominent architects, but his only famous building has always been controversial. Wallot despaired of the difficulty of his task: he had to create a symbol of Germany and of German parliamentarism, when there was no model for either and little consensus about what they meant. (A century later, German architects and politicians understand his plight only too well.) He regretted "that we are building a national edifice without having a national style."[5] In hindsight, it is even easier to recognize how difficult the problem of architectural style was. Wallot's design came near the end of an age that had sought in vain to agree on a historical style appropriate to the modern world. A few years later, architectural modernism would challenge all historical styles and demand a completely different approach to design. So the first German parliament building would be one of the last examples of its kind of monumental architecture.

Wallot was more aware than most of his contemporaries of the changing spirit of architecture. Although the building was fundamentally an ornate Italian Renaissance design, with a richly decorated stone facade, abundant statuary, massive corner towers, and columned entrances, he worked to adapt the traditional style to the practical needs of a parliament and the symbolic needs of a new nation-state and an industrial age. Its most obviously modern element was a broad iron-and-glass cupola (fig. 20). The cupola in particular, and the building's design in general, have always enjoyed a somewhat better reputation than many contemporary structures—for example, the Berlin Cathedral—but Wallot could not singlehandedly create a national style in a divided and changing nation. In his history of the building, Michael S. Cullen has observed how the Reichstag reflected both the architecture and the politics of its time: it was "a building that presented a different appearance on nearly every facade and yet another different one in the cupola. It was a building that could not decide what it wanted. Or rather, it was supposed to be an expression of imperial unity and at the same time a monument of parliamentarism, but it became merely an example of the deep division in the German Empire and of a parliament's powerlessness to become master in its own house."[6]

It was in this unhappy sense that the Reichstag became a symbol of its age. Because of the building's combination of ornateness and size, it has often been labeled the epitome of bombastic "Wilhelmine" architecture, a usually pejorative term meant to suggest a style appropriate to the bluster and bombast of the autocratic Emperor Wilhelm II, who ruled from 1888 to 1918. Ironically, Wilhelm saw the building (which he set foot in only twice) as the "height of tastelessness," a judgment probably colored by his opinion of the Reichstag as an institution—the "imperial monkey house" *(Reichsaffenhaus)* as he once called it.[7]

The building has long been recognized by the inscription over its main entrance: DEM DEUTSCHEN VOLKE, "To the German People." Although the idea for the inscription dates to 1892, it has only been there since 1916—since the middle of World War I. It is not entirely clear who proposed the inscription, or who

20 Reichstag and Königsplatz, circa 1901. Courtesy of Landesbildstelle.

blocked it, but the notion of "the German people" did imply a democratic understanding of the empire's legitimacy, one by no means universally shared in a German Empire that was, legally speaking, a union of princes. The inability to agree on that or any other phrase meant that the stone surface remained blank until mobilization for total war gave a new and less controversial connotation to the role of "the German people."

From the beginning, as Cullen implies, the reputation of the building's architecture has been inseparable from its political function. Thus the pre–World War I Reichstag, as a building and as an institution, rarely satisfied either convinced democrats or autocrats. Although the role of the Reichstag changed at the end of World War I, its reputation remained poor and—more or less as a result—many people continued to consider its home an ugly building.

When the German war effort and, with it, the German monarchy collapsed late in 1918, the Reichstag came to embody the nation's hopes and fears for a future government. From its window on November 9, 1918, the moderate Social Democrat Philipp Scheidemann proclaimed the German republic, in an attempt to preempt the radical Karl Liebknecht's proclamation of a socialist republic from the royal palace on the same day. During the following days, the Reichstag building was occupied by members of the Workers' and Soldiers' Councils that sought radical changes in German government and society. Within a few months, however, they had given way to the Weimar Republic, a parliamentary regime in which the Reichstag was, for the first time, the real center of power. The unfortunate history of the republic—weak coalitions, economic chaos, and violent opposition—reinforced the association in many minds between the despised architecture (now, in the age of architectural modernism, more hated than ever) and the despised regime. Amid a discussion of plans to build a new, modern government quarter in the late 1920s, some architects proposed to demolish the ugly and impractical building, or to alter it beyond recognition.

By the early 1930s, the most disruptive force in the Reichstag was the National Socialist (Nazi) Party. Part of the Nazis' success lay in their ability to pose as the solution to the very disorder they sowed. The Nazis blamed the Reichstag and its many squabbling parties for Germany's troubles, and they came to power in 1933 promising to sweep away the chaos. The Reichstag building played a key role in the early days of Nazi Germany. On the night of February 27, 1933, it was seriously damaged by a fire that had been deliberately set. A Dutch anarchist, Marinus van der Lubbe, was arrested and charged with arson. The police—now under the control of the Nazis, specifically of Hermann Göring—announced the discovery of a Communist plot against the government. Two days later an emergency decree suspended civil rights, and the government shut down the opposition press and political parties. The Third Reich had begun, and the Reichstag building had become indelibly linked to its origins. Whether the Reichstag symbolized a Nazi or an anti-Nazi Germany was less clear.

The facts about the Reichstag fire have been in dispute ever since. Conventional wisdom first held that the Nazis set the fire themselves; later, that the mentally unstable van der Lubbe was guilty but acted alone. The story of a Communist plot is a transparent fabrication, rejected even by Germany's highest court. Though hardly anyone expected independent judgment from a German court in December 1933, it refused to convict the one German and three Bulgarian Communist leaders accused of planning the fire. One of the three, Georgi Dimitroff, acting as his own attorney, used his interrogation of Göring to denounce Nazi barbarism before the foreign press. His performance made him an international antifascist hero and he went on to become head of the Communist International and, after World War II, the premier of Bulgaria.

Whoever set the fire, the Nazis were clever enough to turn the occasion to their own purposes. Those who believe the Nazis set the fire point to the party's enmity toward the Reichstag as an institution. Paradoxically, however, Hitler himself always retained an affection for the building: its elaborate and oversized nineteenth-century grandeur matched his taste in architecture. Hitler vetoed all plans to demolish the damaged building, insisting that it remain as a historical monument in the new Nazi capital. During the Third Reich, the Reichstag also continued to exist as an institution. Meeting across Königsplatz in the Kroll Opera House, it served as a forum for Hitler's speeches and a rubber-stamp assembly of loyal Nazis.

For the Red Army, fighting its way into the city in April 1945, the Reichstag building was the paramount symbol of Hitler and Nazi Germany, and the ultimate prize in the Battle of Berlin.

21
Reichstag, after 1945. Courtesy of German Information Center.

By the time a Red Army soldier planted the Soviet flag atop the building, it had been badly damaged by shell fire and completely burned out (fig. 21). It is unlikely that the Soviets would have restored the building. However, it ended up just within the British sector of occupied Berlin; its fate thus passed into the hands of West Berlin and West Germany.

For years it sat in ruins and in limbo. The shattered building stood directly on the border with East Berlin and was not suitable for most practical uses, but the debate about its restoration was a debate about symbolic gestures. The very impracticality of the Reichstag made the Bonn government's commitment to restoring the building a measure of its commitment to reunifying Germany. But was it really appropriate for the federal parliament (Bundestag) of a functioning democracy to link itself to an imperial parliament (Reichstag) whose architecture as well as its name was a product of a discredited monarchy? One way of offering an affirmative answer was to purify the architecture and the history in a single blow. In the spirit of the postwar years, restoration entailed removal of much of the facade's architectural ornament, a change that was deemed an improvement of the building. And it was seen as an improvement of the building's pedigree as well. As Cullen has found, the history of the building was misremembered: newspaper accounts attributed the excessive ornament to the emperor's interference with Wallot's design.[8]

In 1961, the Berlin Wall was built a few steps from the Reichstag's rear entrance. The same year, however, its restoration began. Although its future use remained unclear, the interior was rebuilt with modern office space, meeting rooms, and an assembly chamber large enough for the Bundestag. Soviet objections blocked all proposals for the Bundestag or other West German government bodies to use the building. Beginning in 1971, it housed a permanent exhibition on German history. Tour guides informed foreign visitors, as they gazed out the window at the Wall, that this would be the meeting place of the German parliament when Germany was reunified. The promise seemed either quixotic or pathetic.

In 1971 Christo, an artist becoming known for his "wrapping" of all kinds of objects, received a picture postcard of the Reichstag from Michael Cullen, an American living in Berlin. Cullen asked Christo if he was interested in wrapping the building. Christo saw the pathos of the idea and decided to take on the project. Thus began a twenty-year struggle for official approval (during which Cullen wrote his history of the building).

The poignant political symbolism of Berlin and of the Reichstag helps explain both Christo's motivation and the varied reactions to his proposal. Europe's postwar division was a central motif in the work of Christo, who grew up in Dimitroff's Bulgaria and emigrated to Paris and then New York. His many walls and fences echoed the Cold War's most famous symbol, the Berlin Wall. An early work from 1962 is entitled *Iron Curtain—Wall of Oil Barrels.* "I understood it as a poetic gesture," he explained decades later, "an answer to the building of the Berlin Wall."[9] Christo came to see Berlin as more than a mere symbol, as "the living example of the division between East and West." The Reichstag itself, he noted, is "a political building," unlike any he had previously worked with. His proposal to wrap it sought deliberately to engage art with politics—and with politicians, who would have the final say. The project—not only wrapping the Reichstag, but also gaining approval to do so—interested him as a *process* that would bring history to light by stimulating "a discussion about the significance of the building and its place in Berlin, in Germany, and in history."[10]

He was certainly right: his plans became part of the postwar German debate about coming to terms with the past. The idea of digging through German history generally found more sympathy on the political left; so, therefore, did Christo. During the late 1970s the project attracted support from several leading German politicians, including the Social Democratic president of the Bundestag, Annemarie Renger. But her successor in 1977, the Christian Democrat Karl Carstens, decided that wrapping would "detract from the symbolic value of the Reichstag"; his opposition put the project on indefinite hold.[11] During the 1980s, Chancellor Helmut Kohl and other Bundestag leaders continued to block the project.

The demise of the Wall in 1989 changed everything. Suddenly the promises about the Reichstag's return to prominence were no longer empty ones. When the Bundestag decided, in 1991, to return the seat of government to Berlin, it was choosing the Reichstag as its future home. The venerable building would have to be renovated, but there was little agreement about how to adapt it to either the practical or the symbolic needs of the Federal Republic's parliament. The Bundestag's leaders fell back upon the favorite German solution of an architectural competition, passing the buck to a handful of talented architects. They displayed plenty of talent, but that was no substitute for decisions about what the Bundestag wanted. The competition jury divided its first prize among three spectacular but obviously impracticable designs by Santiago Calatrava, Pi de Bruijn, and Sir Norman Foster. In 1993, the Bundestag gave the commission to Foster with the understanding that the building's appearance would not be fundamentally altered. The final design long remained uncertain, particularly the form of a new cupola (the old one had been gone since its dilapidated ruins were removed in 1954).

Before the Bundestag moved in, and just before the renovation began, came the wrapping of the Reichstag in a million square feet of aluminum-coated fabric (fig. 22). Christo's growing ranks of supporters—including Berlin mayor Eberhard Diepgen and Bundestag president Rita Süssmuth, both Christian Democrats—saw the wrapping as an ideal rite of passage marking the Reichstag's initiation into a new era. They were taken with the idea that the layer of fabric, flapping in the breeze, would not only bring the building to life but would also draw new and thoughtful attention to it. Berliners, Germans, and foreigners would be forced to see it in a new way: a recognizable shape and at the same time a ghostly apparition. Chancellor Kohl agreed to bring the question of wrapping the Reichstag to a vote in the Bundestag in Bonn on February 25, 1994; after speeches from supporters and opponents on the floor, it was approved, 292 to 223.

It was surely unusual for a parliament to devote its time to debating an artist's work. But the debate was not really about art; it was about the German nation and its history. Was this, as proponents argued, an appropriate gesture to mark a historical transition? Wolfgang Schäuble, the Christian Democrats' parliamentary leader, thought not. (His was the main speech against the project; Kohl did not speak.) For him the building was too important, its symbolism too weighty, for it to be subject to an "experiment," and particularly to one that tried to underscore the irony of German history. No other land, Schäuble noted, has considered "making a building of comparable significance the object of such an act."[12] He specifically mentioned Westminster, Capitol Hill, and the Palais Bourbon—alluding to the democracies that many moderate and conservative Germans would like to

22
Wrapped
Reichstag, 1995

think of as their equals. This longing for "normality," particularly apparent among those (like Schäuble) close to Helmut Kohl, often appears as a plaintive wish that foreigners and fellow Germans would finally believe (or at least pretend) that Germans are no different from their Western neighbors. While it is true that other democracies have their historical blemishes too (though they generally do not care to be reminded of that by Germans), the Reichstag of 1871–1945 has a particularly dismal reputation. Many Germans, in turn, do not care to be reminded of that.

Schäuble also raised a more concrete objection: "State symbols, symbols in general, should unite people, bring people together. Wrapping the Reichstag would, however, not unite people, it would polarize them. Too many people would not be able to understand and accept it."[13] Schäuble might have found confirmation of his fears in a subsequent speech by the leftist Bundestag member Ulrich Briefs. Since opponents raised nationalist objections to the project, Briefs declared, he would endorse it as a gesture "against nationalism and narrowmindedness."[14]

Most supporters of Christo insisted that the project posed no threat to the nation's or the building's dignity. Quite the opposite, proclaimed the prominent Christian Democrat Heiner Geissler: "through Christo we get the chance to show the world Germany's tolerant and open-minded character."[15] This was art, after all, and educated Germans tend to take art, even whimsical art, very seriously, and to associate it with dignity. Christo's parliamentary supporters, as much as his opponents, wanted to treat the Reichstag as the proud symbol of a democratic tradition. But they were willing to cast a more critical eye on the history of the Reichstag and of German democracy. For all the achievements of the Federal Republic and its Bundestag, they decided that the Reichstag building's democratic credentials could use a boost, and that Christo would provide it. Already in 1977 former chancellor Willy Brandt had declared that the wrapping of the Reichstag "would show that the Germans have again achieved an unconstrained relationship to their history."[16] In the 1990s, according to the Social Democrat Peter Conradi, it would "mark a new beginning in the history of the building" and "a new chapter in the history of German parliamentary democracy."[17]

Christo had formulated his project when the Reichstag graced a divided city and continent. Ironically, its approval came after the Wall had vanished. This fact brought another objection from Schäuble: what exactly was the reason for wrapping the Reichstag in 1995? Was it another attempt to come to terms with the Nazi past? Or a dramatic gesture in the shadow of the Berlin Wall? Or the inauguration of a new unity of East and West? Or just art for art's sake? Indeed, the project was (or had been) about all of these things. No grand gesture in the center of Berlin could be unambiguous, just as none could be uncontroversial. Mayor Diepgen characteristically saw the positive side of the furor: just as controversy was an essential part of Christo's work, "living with productive antagonism" was a quintessential Berlin trait.[18] Christo earned praise all around as an artist who made debate and democracy a part of his work.

A more formal ceremony marking the Reichstag's new incarnation would certainly have stirred up controversy, if only in the form of demonstrators held at bay by swarms of police as politicians declaimed their interpretations of the national symbol. But as Christo and Jeanne-Claude, his wife and partner, supervised their team of climbers unrolling silver fabric from the roof of the Reichstag, polemics dissolved amid a mass celebration. During the two weeks of the *Wrapped Reichstag* in June and July of 1995, enormous, relaxed crowds came to stroll, gawk, relax, buy and sell snacks and souvenirs, and share the experience. In all, five million people saw the enormous work of temporary art. Rarely does anything emanating from the art world find such a large and happy public.

Part of what made the event so festive was the absence of any clear message. Christo and Jeanne-Claude declined to proclaim one, and neither their supporters nor their opponents had been able to agree on what it all meant. So it could be a celebration for some and a commemoration for others, one person's work of art and another's spectacle, a political event and a giant party. Berlin, once again basking in the world's attention, burned with "Christo fever": schoolchildren wrapped their classroom supplies, cartoonists offered every imaginable parody on the theme of wrapping, and cleverly "wrapped" people wandered among the crowds.

Christo transformed the battered building into a shimmering and abstract form, but its unkempt surroundings concealed no more of their secrets than usual. At the Reichstag's northeast corner, some visitors were bound to stumble upon the row of crosses remaining from the days of the Wall. On the opposite side stood a recently unveiled memorial to the many Reichstag members killed by the Nazis. To the northwest, where a fenced-off site marked the beginning of construction on offices for Bundestag members, special machines were removing underground obstructions left from excavations for the gigantic domed hall Hitler had planned here.

The Reichstag could easily accommodate the enormous crowds, however, because it stood nearly alone. Beyond the Platz der Republik (the former Königsplatz) lay open space in every direction, a legacy of Hitler, the war, and the Wall. The festival of 1995 marked the end of that era of division, of open space, and thus of West Berlin—a cause for celebration, but also for a tinge of nostalgia on the part of many West Berliners. They recognized that Christo had brought the last of the demonstrations, concerts, and summer afternoons that had drawn them to the Reichstag when it marked the edge of their island city. After the catharsis of wrapping it, the Reichstag would become a bustling place of politicians, a center of democracy rather than ruins. For a few days, however, this national symbol could include nearly everyone.

The Mietskaserne

The 1871 unification of Germany came at a time when German society was changing rapidly. Nowhere were the changes more dramatic than in Berlin. The city's population growth tells part of the story: a city of 170,000 in 1800, it grew to half a million by the early 1850s, one million in 1877, and two million at the turn of the century. By that time nearly all the growth was taking place outside the city limits; when its suburbs were annexed to Berlin in 1920, it became a city of four million, third largest in the world after London and New York (fig. 23). By the later nineteenth century, Berlin's status as capital was only secondarily and indirectly responsible for its growth. More than most national capitals, Berlin became a major industrial center. Men and women from the surrounding provinces and beyond poured into the city in search of work. At midcentury, the most striking growth was concentrated in its metalworking and machinery factories, such as Borsig, builder of railroad locomotives. A few decades later, the new electrical industry became dominated by such Berlin firms as AEG and Siemens.

The factories, at first concentrated by the city's northern gates, spread west down the Spree River to Moabit and ultimately in nearly every other direction as well. Around them clustered the city's teeming working-class districts such as Wedding in the north, Neukölln in the south, and the wide crescent of neighborhoods extending north and east from Alexanderplatz. Industrial wealth also helped create the booming middle-class suburbs to the west and southwest. Charlottenburg, Schöneberg, and Wilmersdorf became dominated by upscale apartments; beyond them lay exclusive villa suburbs such as Grunewald, Dahlem, and Zehlendorf, sprawling all the way to Potsdam.

Industrialization fundamentally reshaped the city's physical form. Apart from a few historic sites, on the one hand, and some new suburbs, on the other, the visible Berlin of today is fundamentally a product of the industrial age. The same is true,

23
Aerial view of central Berlin, 1939. The Spree is visible, flowing from east to west across the center, as is the Tiergarten, below the Spree at left, and Unter den Linden, extending eastward from the Tiergarten to the Cölln island and the royal palace. Courtesy of Landesbildstelle.

to a lesser and more elusive extent, of its people. West Berlin's industries only limped through the decades during which the half-city was a subsidized political symbol and an economic absurdity. But East Berlin remained a major industrial center until 1990. Only the demise of the East German economy shut down the old factories along the upper Spree and jerked it over to the Western European norm of empty factories and unemployed proletarians. Despite war and urban renewal, the valley of the Spree across much of Berlin remains a landscape of old industrial structures. Among them are the innovative and influential factory buildings built for AEG by Peter Behrens between 1909 and 1914 (years during which his assistants included Walter Gropius, Le Corbusier, and Ludwig Mies van der Rohe).

Very few of the city's older buildings predate 1850. Even the inner city was utterly transformed in the half-century before 1914, as old houses were replaced one by one with new and larger buildings. Years before the destruction wrought by World War II, only scattered buildings gave a sense of the city that existed in Schinkel's day. For those of us able to extract only limited information from old drawings and descriptions, the best way to get some sense of the preindustrial city is to take an excursion to nearby Potsdam, the garrison town and royal residence largely built up under Friedrich Wilhelm I and his son, Friedrich II.

There was an older part of Potsdam, but that old center was virtually wiped out in the one major Allied bombing raid that struck the city in 1945. The substantial eighteenth-century town extensions to the north and west were mostly spared, and they have survived the ravages of several regimes largely intact. That is, here one still finds streets lined almost entirely with two-story houses from the 1700s, most of them exhibiting little variation in style from their neighbors (fig. 24). After four decades of East German control, most looked terribly dilapidated, which at least suggests that they had been little altered during those years. (Their fate under the Federal Republic is another matter. Potsdam suddenly went from backwater to attractive Berlin suburb; amid skyrocketing real estate values, battles raged over badly needed redevelopment and badly needed historical preservation.)

These houses were put up under royal sponsorship and their designs conformed to standard models. Thus they help us to picture their vanished contemporaries in Berlin's Friedrichstadt,

24
Potsdam, Am Neuen Markt, eighteenth-century houses, 1993

the district south of Unter den Linden where the bulk of the city's eighteenth-century development took place. The king parceled out building lots, requiring each favored recipient to put up a house at his own expense, with its dimensions and facade often prescribed by royal decree. Most of these houses had two stories and simply decorated facades, although Friedrich II, seeking a more imposing urban appearance, required four-story buildings on a few streets. As in Potsdam, the goal was to develop the city and promote economic activity, but the most urgent need in both towns was to quarter soldiers, something each homeowner was required to do.

The early-nineteenth-century architectural innovations of Karl Friedrich Schinkel and his associates helped to change the design of the typical Berlin house, but it was only after 1850 or so that the pace of building activity fundamentally changed the face of the city. At this time, visitors as well as natives were most struck by the changes on the city's periphery. The typical transitional zone between the preindustrial town and its countryside—gardens, scattered houses, workshops, charitable and martial institutions—was giving way to large factories and imposing blocks of tenements. The economic boom around 1870 gave an enormous impetus to their construction. By the turn of the century, old Berlin was surrounded by a wide band of districts filled with five-story apartment houses. This kind of building had become the normal dwelling place for all Berliners except the very rich.

Yet they were not accepted as normal, and to this day they remain, as a type, the object of passion and polemics.

A name quickly emerged for these tenements, and it stuck: Mietskaserne, which means "rental barracks." The name came into common use as a pejorative label for Berlin apartment buildings. For our purposes, the term may apply to all of them built between 1860 and 1914. There is no point in offering a precise architectural definition: the notion of the Mietskaserne reflects a myth rather than an objective description. That is why it belongs in a book about Berlin's monuments. Like existing buildings (such as the Reichstag) and remembered ones (such as the royal palace), the image of the Mietskaserne embodies a set of beliefs about the history and identity of Berlin. The Mietskaserne is the preeminent symbol of Berlin as industrial metropolis. Attitudes toward that sometimes menacing city, in turn, were often projected onto the buildings identified as Mietskasernen. The history of the Mietskaserne, then, is a key part of our story of Berlin's identity.

The name "Mietskaserne" reflects the buildings' poor reputation, but also their provenance. Although the architecture of their facades reflected the influence of Schinkel's neoclassicism and, later, whatever styles were fashionable for villas, palaces, and banks, their true antecedent was indeed the army barracks. Before it became an industrial metropolis, Berlin was a garrison town, and the masses who had to be housed were soldiers. The architectural historian Goerd Peschken suggests that the enforced billeting of soldiers in private houses inspired the term "rental barracks."[19] In addition, though, there existed regular barracks built and maintained by the army itself. Transformations in the Prussian state and army in the early nineteenth century emptied many Berlin barracks of soldiers. In some cases, factory workers took their places. And—a fact often obscured in economic histories that trace the unfolding of a free market—the industrialization of Berlin was by no means unrelated to the military needs of the monarchy. The metalworking industry crucial to Berlin's early industrialization grew out of the state's own production of armaments. During the early nineteenth century, civilian workers also replaced soldiers in many military factories.

In the midcentury industrial boom it was left to an emerging private real estate market to respond to the enormous demand for housing. The Berlin tenement's typical form evolved out of private builders' attempts to profit from that demand. They developed new designs suited to traditional Berlin houses (including barracks), the emerging pattern of streets and blocks, and a minimal set of municipal regulations governing sanitation and fire protection. The city's planners have often been blamed for encouraging the spread of Mietskasernen, but in fact they neither foresaw nor knew how to control the real estate boom that created modern Berlin. As many thousands of poor people sought dwellings, high housing densities were probably unavoidable.

From the 1860s to 1914, the typical apartment building was five stories high, with a facade fifty to a hundred feet wide, decorated in whichever ornate historicist style was in fashion at the time of construction. Behind the massive front facade lay a narrow courtyard, enclosed—often on all four sides—by additional wings of the building. The largest buildings had wings on each side of the courtyard, which were connected in back by a transverse wing parallel to the street facade. On smaller lots, one side or the rear of the courtyard might face the walls of neighboring buildings, but each building's courtyards were accessible only through archways connected to its own street entrance (fig. 25). On particularly deep lots, there might be a second or even a third courtyard behind the first one. (The handful of buildings with five or six courtyards became famous, but were not typical.) Most apartments thus faced courtyards rather than the wide streets. Apart from the few streets of medieval provenance, Berlin was a city of wide streets and deep blocks. In contrast to a medieval city like Paris or a row-house city like London, the poor usually did not live on narrow lanes and alleys. Instead, they lived on courtyards.

This kind of building was a distinct Berlin type, although it influenced tenement designs in other cities. Because of the depth of Berlin blocks and the large size of building parcels, the tenements were enormous. A single building typically had a hundred or more residents. By 1910, the average number of residents per building in the entire city was seventy-six, the highest in the Western world. That statistic sounded ominous, but it actually said little about housing conditions. Indeed, compared to other housing for poor people—in foreign cities or in the German countryside—most of these tenements were of fairly good quality. They were solidly built and featured large rooms and high ceilings. In fact, the basic form of these buildings had not been developed as cheap housing for the poor. As Berlin became a vastly larger and more crowded city, its prosperous and expanding middle class became flat dwellers, and builders responded by creating designs intended to appeal to that lucrative market. A hallmark of the Mietskaserne remained its flexibility. Builders could reconfigure the long rows of similar rooms during or even after construction to satisfy a demand for larger or smaller apartments. It was common to place large apartments for the well-to-do on the street side and small ones for the poor behind them. Similarly, in buildings without elevators (something found only after the turn of the century and then only in a few luxury buildings), wealthier families lived on the lower floors.

Visible poverty has always accompanied rapid industrialization. The homes of Berlin's proletariat became the places where that

25 Middle-class apartment buildings from the turn of the century, Nürnberger Platz, Berlin-Wilmersdorf, circa 1935. Courtesy of Landesbildstelle.

poverty was most apparent to bourgeois visitors, who were typically struck by the gloom of the courtyards. Little sunlight penetrated their depths; colors of walls, floors, signs, and clothing were subdued; soot and dust could never be banished. In middle-class minds, the Mietskaserne came to embody all that was wrong with the industrial city. Muckrakers investigating the "social question" found squalid conditions in the tenements: large numbers of people, often not related to one another, sharing one-room and two-room apartments that faced dank courtyards. And this was in a city where, before the 1870s, running water was not available everywhere, and cesspools and open gutters offered the only drainage. Typhoid, tuberculosis, and (until the 1870s) cholera were often rampant, and in the minds of better-off outsiders those proletarian diseases were associated with other pathogens harder to trace: sexual misbehavior and socialist agitation.

A wide consensus condemned the Mietskaserne as an unhealthful place to live. For conservatives unhappy with the growth of cities and industry, it was the most visible symbol of the forces destroying traditional social bonds. For the urban middle classes, proud of the achievements of industry and commerce, the tenement homes of the restive working class represented the dark side of urban growth, threatening the march of progress. And for socialists, the Mietskaserne was the ugliest product of the bourgeois system of private property that ruthlessly exploited the working class.

It was the overcrowding in the apartments and the poverty of their residents that gave the Mietskaserne its dismal reputation. Most apartment seekers were poor, and hence most buildings ended up divided into small apartments. Even two-room apartments were too expensive for many families, so they took in boarders, typically single men for whom an apartment of their own was not even a remote possibility. Few apartments had bathrooms before the turn of the century, and the idea that a toilet in each apartment was not a luxury became accepted only slowly. Well into the twentieth century, the actual conditions in these overcrowded dwellings were clearly unhealthful, although improved water and sewer systems had already made an enormous difference even before 1900. After World War II, in a time of reduced population and greater prosperity, housing densities declined and the same buildings gradually acquired a new reputation.

Long before that happened, new ideas about architecture at the beginning of the twentieth century envisioned radically new forms of housing that would sweep away the Mietskaserne. These ideas took hold during the decade 1914–24, when war, political turmoil, and inflation brought construction to a virtual halt. The modernists of the 1920s proposed to abolish blocks, courtyards, and decorated facades in favor of generously spaced rows of sleek buildings that would afford their residents better access to light, air, and open space. Their particular architectural forms were matters of heated controversy, most famously between the purists who favored flat roofs and the more conservative adherents of pitched roofs. Nevertheless, architects and reformers agreed on many of the goals of new housing: decentralization, reduced densities, and abolition of the Mietskaserne. A new municipal building code in 1925 enshrined these goals in law. With the support of the Berlin government, nonprofit building societies constructed several large housing estates in outer districts of the city during the 1920s and early 1930s. The celebrated modern designs by Martin Wagner, Bruno Taut, Walter Gropius, Hans Scharoun, and Hugo Häring in the Britz Horseshoe Estate, Siemensstadt, and other projects did not reshape the existing city, but they became the model for alternatives to the Mietskaserne at least until the 1970s (fig. 26).

26
Britz Horseshoe Estate in 1931. Courtesy of Landesbildstelle.

The condemnation of the Mietskaserne was more widely shared than any particular alternative to it. In the Third Reich, for example, the leading modernists could get no work, and their most innovative designs were deemed unacceptable, but the Nazis, too, pledged to move Germans out of their tenement slums. After the war, housing and planning programs in both East and West Germany revived the modernist legacy, albeit inconsistently and in very different ways. Damaged pre–1914 apartment houses were rarely given the benefit of the doubt when deciding between repair and removal. Where buildings were intact, both East and West Berlin encouraged removal of the stucco facade ornamentation as an aesthetic measure; thousands of old buildings now have the same flat plaster exteriors as their postwar neighbors. Another postwar reform in some districts of East and West Berlin was the removal of all back buildings to eliminate the courtyards and create a large open space in the interior of the block. On a larger scale, West Berlin city plans from the 1950s to 1970s aimed to abolish the traditional city block and to separate residential, commercial, and industrial activities into dispersed zones connected by high-speed roads and rail lines. East Berlin's high-rise satellite cities of the 1970s and 1980s were in many ways a similar undertaking.

The 1970s marked a change in thinking. The Mietskaserne was rediscovered—that is, intellectuals and opinion makers embraced it. As West Berlin's alternative scene grew, students, artists, and nonconformists of many stripes discovered the unrenovated tenements. For them, a toilet down the hall and the absence of a bath merely meant a degree of inconvenience in return for an otherwise unaffordable large apartment, which could be renovated step by step. For rebels against the nuclear family and the traditional home, the large, high-ceilinged rooms continued to offer the flexibility of arrangement their builders had intended. The Mietskaserne presented an alternative to the modern apartment, designed for efficient use of space with small rooms carefully tailored for cooking, eating, or sleeping. As the old buildings attracted residents and small businesses, relatively intact tenement neighborhoods became Berlin's liveliest areas. Planners and urban critics began to praise the old buildings as incubators of neighborhood identity and attractive urbanity. They became charming rather than dilapidated.

World War II had already made the districts of Mietskasernen more bearable by thinning them out, as wings or entire buildings were reduced to rubble. Henceforth sunlight would quite literally dispel the permanent gloom in many narrow courtyards. The juxtaposition of enormous walls and vacant lots became a defining image of postwar Berlin, just as it had been when the Mietskasernen were going up at the turn of the century. Because the individual buildings had nearly always been planned and constructed one at a time, they faced inward, onto courtyards, and blank fire walls usually abutted each other on the property lines. When one building was demolished, its neighbors were suddenly exposed. A characteristic Berlin sight is a blank wall of rough bricks, seventy feet high and a hundred or more feet wide. Sometimes a single window has been punched through it, and a face peers out, supported by arms leaning on a cushion. Other walls display the faded remnants of enormous advertisements painted decades ago. These walls reveal Berlin to be an uncompleted city, and as a result they have often been deemed eyesores. By the 1980s they had become part of the charm of divided Berlin; in the 1990s many disappeared behind new construction.

Accompanying the rediscovery of the Mietskaserne was a rewriting of its history. Instead of the censorious point of view of the bourgeois reformers, the new historians, influenced by academic social history as well as community activism, proposed to enter the world of the working-class residents. Although their work sometimes sentimentalizes the lives it studies, it provides a fresh perspective on the connections between buildings and their residents—that is, on neighborhoods.

For the Mietskasernen were the homes of the true Berliners, the bluff proletarians known for their irreverence and quick wit, the men, women, and children lovingly caricatured in the famous sketches of Heinrich Zille. Although most of them presumably did not care for the dark, damp, and crowded conditions, the courtyards were nevertheless the settings of their family lives, where joyous as well as gloomy events took place. The turn-of-the-century Berliner's neighborhood often comprised little more than a few apartment houses, courtyards, and streets. When workers escaped their cramped apartments, they gathered in the courtyards or in the shops and pubs lodged in the street fronts of the buildings. Most residents of the same buildings in the late twentieth century had far more leisure and far more choices, but they sought to recapture the mystique of the old neighborhoods.

The most famous locus of change was Kreuzberg, the West Berlin district south of the old center. Eastern Kreuzberg contained the city's largest collection of buildings from the 1860s and 1870s, many with a mix of apartments and industrial lofts on the courtyards. Official policy classified these as slums; their proximity to the Wall made them even less desirable. Many Turkish workers moved in during the 1960s and 1970s, as did German students, artists, anarchists, and punks. The new residents recognized what official policy long denied: that the buildings were solid, adaptable, and represented the irreplaceable handiwork of craftsmen. By the 1980s, they were more sought-after than the postwar high-rises nearby.

Rents in these buildings were kept particularly low by rent controls enacted during the severe housing shortage after the war. West Berlin leftists suspected that the government was colluding with developers who wished to let the old buildings fall into disrepair until they could be demolished and replaced with more profitable structures. In 1980 squatters began to move into abandoned buildings, which then became centers of protest against everything from housing policies to exploitation of the Third World. Attempts by the police to evict the squatters grew into violent confrontations during the early 1980s.

The squatters' efforts to restore buildings and neighborhoods attracted public sympathy, as did similar work by less confrontational groups, and eventually the municipal government sponsored negotiations that legalized some of their efforts. Meanwhile, by the 1980s the government itself began to promote restoration of Mietskasernen. Its architectural showcase of that decade, the International Building Exhibition (Internationale Bauausstellung, or IBA), both rehabilitated old buildings and designed new ones to complement the attractions of the old tenement blocks.

In East Berlin, too, the old tenements became refuges for society's dropouts. Prenzlauer Berg, the most intact tenement district in the East, became the center of the German Democratic Republic's small and harassed alternative scene. The men and women who decided not to play by the rules—a much costlier decision in the East—found their niches of freedom and individuality in Prenzlauer Berg's tenements, where apartments were relatively easy to get because many had been abandoned after the decades of utter neglect the buildings had suffered.

By the 1980s even the East German government had jumped

on the bandwagon, if only in a small way. Imitating well-established efforts in the West, it began to renovate rows of old buildings in a few selected streets and to restore their facades, rather than stripping them of their ornament. Its grandest project was the renovation of both sides of a one-block stretch of Husemannstrasse in the middle of Prenzlauer Berg. It renovated the ornate facades, decorated the street with old-fashioned street lamps and water pumps, and opened cafés with period decor as well as museums catering to tourists, including the popular Museum of Hairdressing. For Berlin's 750th anniversary in 1987, the East Berlin government unveiled this block as the reconstruction of a typical Berlin workers' quarter from the turn of the century. For residents of Prenzlauer Berg, and for visitors who passed through streets lined with crumbling buildings to get there, it was a peculiar if not a galling sight. And the East Berlin planners obviously shared the common misconception that the Mietskaserne had been a working-class ghetto. Unlike many parts of Prenzlauer Berg, the grand facades of the Husemannstrasse had been built for bourgeois apartments. This "typical workers' street" only became a workers' street when the East German workers' state decreed its kitschy (and shoddy) renovation. (In the 1990s, however, it became the center of Prenzlauer Berg's hopping night life.)

After reunification, it was no surprise that city planners dedicated themselves to reinvigorating the old tenement neighborhoods. This was the Berlin version of an international trend: after decades of destroying the urban fabric, cities now sought to revive their endangered traditions of shared urbanity. And as the main focus of attention turned to the old city center, the hard-won lessons from districts like Kreuzberg and Prenzlauer Berg were applied there as well. The official goal in the 1990s became the "critical reconstruction" of the inner city. This program began in Friedrichstadt, the old commercial center, whose eighteenth-century grid of wide streets and rectangular blocks established the pattern later extended to the nineteenth-century districts. Much of that grid has been obliterated by megaprojects on both sides of the Wall (the southern Friedrichstadt belonged to West Berlin). Berlin's planners in the 1990s have partly restored the grid as a first step toward restoration of Berlin's traditional urban form. The scale they have in mind, though they rarely admit it and sometimes seem not to know it, is that of the late nineteenth century.

Friedrichstadt was originally built up in the eighteenth century with two-story houses, all of which have vanished (except an atypical pair of parsonages on Glinkastrasse). But neither their scale nor their style serve as the model for the new Friedrichstadt. During the second half of the nineteenth century, Friedrichstadt gradually changed from middle-class residential neighborhood to bustling commercial quarter. Entrepreneurs tore down the modest old houses and replaced them with ornate, five-story buildings. These new structures had the same dimensions as the new apartment buildings elsewhere in the city, but here they housed mainly offices and shops. The northern Friedrichstadt became the banking center of Germany; the southern part was the newspaper district; fashionable stores settled in between, along Leipziger Strasse. Like the new apartment houses, these buildings were usually built as tall as was permitted. The maximum height depended on the street width but could never exceed seventy-two feet.

This is the height limit applied to the cornices of new buildings in the "critically reconstructed" Friedrichstadt. In the old buildings, that permitted five stories; in new ones, seven or so (plus as many as four levels underground). Ironically, nineteenth-century reformers decried this height limit as too liberal, choking the light and air out of the city. Now it has become an honored tradition, like the once hated Mietskaserne. What had been the troubling specter of modernity and upheaval is now a comforting link to an idealized past. Critical reconstruction reaches back beyond world wars, dictatorships, and modern urban experiments and finds a Berlin identity in the decades before 1914.

This search for an urban identity ignores and even repudiates the famous Berlin housing estates of the 1920s. They represent the architectural high point of the first great move away from the city of Mietskasernen. The embrace of the nineteenth-century city excludes the work of the modernists from the prevailing conception of Berlin's architectural identity. Berlin's planners, and the critics and theorists whose lead they follow, have nothing but kind words for the beauty of the estates designed by Wagner, Taut, and their colleagues. But conventional wisdom sees 1920s modernism as the model for the inferior buildings that followed, especially the postwar plague of concrete high-rises in East and West. Even more important for planners is the belief that the 1920s established the practice of ignoring or destroying the extant fabric of streets and parcels, a process accelerated by the Third Reich and both postwar regimes. The result, in many people's minds, is a destroyed city; the solution is to restore links to the city of a century ago.

Revolution, Modernity, and Jewish Berlin

Among the things least changed by World War I and the advent of the republic was Baedecker's guide to Berlin, which continued to offer travelers an abundance of dry and useful information. Concluding its introductory section, however, the 1923 edition ventured a sweeping judgment: "The loss of the Great War has effected vast changes in the social composition of Berlin. The brilliance of the imperial court has disappeared. New classes of society with new aspirations have risen to commercial power, while the former calm based on assured prosperity has given way to a restless self-indulgence."[20]

Baedecker's elegiac tone captures one perspective on the Weimar Republic, the time of "the outsider as insider," in Peter Gay's phrase.[21] Better remembered today is the exhilarating cultural ferment, the liberating forces of modernity unleashed by the war and its aftermath. Much of what is famous about Berlin modernity began before World War I, but the demise of the monarchy stamped the new cultural forces with an indelible mark of revolution. In 1918, Berlin saw both the "revolution" of Dada and the revolution of soldiers, sailors, and socialists that toppled the monarchy, each in its own way both farcical and deeply earnest. In the years that followed, few traditions, institutions, or allegiances could be taken for granted; experimentation and contentiousness became the norm.

Images of the 1920s shape Berlin's reputation in much of the world: Berlin as the city of new architecture (Walter Gropius, Ludwig Mies van der Rohe, Erich Mendelsohn), new theater (Max Reinhardt, Erwin Piscator, Bertolt Brecht), new painting (Max Beckmann, George Grosz, Otto Dix), new music (Arnold Schoenberg, Paul Hindemith, Kurt Weill), the new cinema (Fritz Lang, F. W. Murnau, Marlene Dietrich), and the new physics (Max Planck, Albert Einstein, Leo Szilard). Fixed in the popular memory above all, however, is Berlin's night life and popular entertainment—not just legitimate theater, but the more experimental cabarets and especially the venues where sexual liberation and uncertain gender identities were on display: the nude stage shows; erotic dance, particularly as demonstrated by the visiting American Josephine Baker; the transvestite balls; and the open celebration of homosexuality. Liberation and experimentation went hand in hand with a sense of disquiet, disorder, and disgust that informs much of the artistic creation of the period, notably the painting of the famous (male) artists.

Berlin's golden twenties offered a concentrated brew of cultural and political turmoil. Foreigners' romantic images of it often leave out the politics. Christopher Isherwood, whose Berlin stories capture some of the tense political atmosphere of the city, returned in 1952 and wondered, "Hadn't there been something youthfully heartless in my enjoyment of the spectacle of Berlin in the early thirties, with its poverty, its political hatred and its despair?"[22] The Weimar Republic's turbulent birth had launched an era of uncertainty that culminated in the hyperinflation of 1923. The next several years appeared calm only by comparison with what came before and with what followed. By the early 1930s, in the depths of the depression, political violence was a daily event in Berlin. Street fights typically pitted Nazis against Communists, each claiming a mandate to destroy the established order.

Memories of Weimar Berlin are so vivid in part because its star rose and fell so quickly. After the Nazi reign of terror began in 1933, the rich crop of Berlin exiles spread the city's legacy of cultural experimentation and political dissent across the world. Many postwar West Berliners (and some East Berliners as well) also sought inspiration in the city's countercultural traditions. From the 1960s on, student protesters, squatters, anarchists, punks, and skinheads laid claim to Berlin's old tenement courtyards and stirred memories of the cultural ferment the Nazis had destroyed. But often they were indulging a nostalgia foreign to the 1920s.

The 1923 Baedecker offered one more observation about the visible change in postwar Berlin: "The large influx of foreigners, mainly from Eastern Europe, is readily noticed." Who were these foreigners? Baedecker does not elaborate, but in many minds the new age was inseparable from the Jews. Although most Berlin Jews were not foreigners, they could not entirely escape their status as outsiders. Baedecker's "foreigners" were not all Jewish, nor were the "outsiders" discussed by Peter Gay. But, as Gay notes, since the nineteenth century "the idea of a Berlin-Jewish symbiosis has become an article of faith, the only dogma that Jews, philo-Semites, and anti-Semites of all descriptions hold in common. Jews, it is said, making themselves at home in Berlin, transformed it, and imprinted upon it something of their rootlessness, their restlessness, their alienation from soil and tradition, their pervasive disrespect for authority, their mordant wit."[23] The mythical modern Berliner of the early 1900s "comes from the East and has no time," as a popular saying had it: a man or woman on the move, a restless outsider born (like so many Berliners) in Prussia's polyglot eastern provinces. This image clearly had a Jewish component: no one was unaware of the prominent roles in culture and business played by Berlin's Jews, many of whom could indeed trace their origins to Breslau, Posen, or other eastern towns. Many Jews played central roles in the creation of Berlin's modernity, and many non-Jews were quick to thank them or blame them.

The old image of the entrepreneurial Jew took form over centuries as Europe's Jews, excluded from most trades, developed skills in banking and retail trade. Jews have thus been broadly linked with the dynamic forces of capitalism (most famously by Karl Marx). More visibly, large numbers of them played prominent roles in Berlin journalism and publishing, in the garment business, and in the department stores. When department stores appeared in Berlin at the turn of the century, they became the greatest urban monuments to the brave new world of conspicuous consumption. Most of them, including the largest ones, were owned by Jews. The crown jewel of the main shopping street was Wertheim, at the corner of Leipziger Strasse and Leipziger Platz, begun in 1896 by the architect Alfred Messel and expanded several times in the following years. With its glass-roofed atrium, ten thousand light bulbs, and eighty-three elevators, it drew daily crowds of wealthy shoppers and less wealthy gawkers (fig. 27). (The GDR razed its bombed-out ruins, except for an underground vault that quickly became a trendy music club after reunification.) After 1907, the new Tiergarten commercial district in the west boasted a worthy competitor, the Hermann Tietz chain's Kaufhaus des Westens (KaDeWe, the "Department Store of the West") on Wittenbergplatz. Unlike

its eastern rival, KaDeWe was rebuilt after World War II. It carries on a tradition of tasteful indulgence that hardly anyone now associates with Jews.

27
Wertheim department store on Leipziger Platz, 1932. Courtesy of Landesbildstelle.

In general, Berlin's 170,000 Jews in the 1920s (4 percent of the city's population, but a third of all Jews in Germany) were thoroughly assimilated to German culture and had established themselves in the middle classes. From their ranks came Jewish shopkeepers, business magnates, doctors, and artists. Others, however—a quarter of Berlin's Jews by 1925—were "Ostjuden," Yiddish-speaking recent immigrants from Poland, Hungary, or Russia. They were certainly prominent among the foreigners noticed by Baedecker. While most of the assimilated Jews lived in western Berlin, the Ostjuden settled in the narrow streets behind Alexanderplatz, the area known as the Scheuenenviertel, "Shed Quarter," because animals had been housed there in the eighteenth century. By the turn of the century, as Ostjuden were first arriving in large numbers, the Scheunenviertel was already Berlin's most notorious slum, and its removal became the goal of Berlin's only major slum clearance project before World War II.

The Scheunenviertel is yet another Berlin ghost. The heart of it was leveled in 1906–8, but as the Ostjuden gathered in neighboring streets, the name of the quarter followed them. Additional clearance dragged on into the 1930s, when the Nazis openly linked the neighborhood's seedy reputation with its Jewish population. The Nazis despised the neighborhood doubly: the Communist Party, the leading vote-getter in the neighborhood, moved its headquarters here in 1926. That building, which the party named the Karl-Liebknecht-Haus, still stands, but of the old slum few traces remain.

Since 1989, however, the Scheunenviertel has been rediscovered. For Berliners, the name now evokes two lost worlds: the Jews and the underworld best known from Alfred Döblin's novel *Berlin Alexanderplatz.* Berliners attracted by these images from the past have worked to save, restore, or call attention to the old buildings that remain in the area. Since the Scheunenviertel, as originally known, is long gone, the resonant name is now broadly applied to the relatively intact nineteenth-century streets to the west. Here visitors can find the remnants of Berlin's first Jewish cemetery (in use from 1672 to 1827), names and symbols carved into stone facades that recall the Jewish boys' school on Grosse Hamburger Strasse and two rabbinical schools (liberal and Orthodox) on Tucholskystrasse, and, most notably, the New Synagogue on Oranienburger Strasse, completed in 1866 as a proud monument to Jews' civil equality and religious freedom in Germany. This grand building escaped from Kristallnacht in 1938 with only minor damage, but it was bombed out during the war and stood for decades as a ruin near the center of East Berlin. A plaque erected in 1966 explained that the facade would remain standing as a memorial; in 1988, the East German government authorized the restoration of the building's golden dome and front section (but not the three-thousand-seat sanctuary) for the use of its Jewish community, a task completed several years after reunification. Here and in a few other locales, the reunified city's small and inconspicuous Jewish community (most of whom are recent arrivals from Eastern Europe) is reviving its ties to the neighborhood.

Many Berliners today eagerly seek out the traces of Jewish Berlin, but most consider everything Jewish to belong to a remote and irretrievably lost era. Educated Germans sometimes observe that the disappearance of the Jews explains the loss of a certain cultural dynamism in Germany. When Nazi Germany drove out or murdered most Berlin Jews, it shattered the city's confident modernity. The unbearable memory of the Holocaust, and of Berlin's vanished Jews, casts its shadow across the golden 1920s too. The fate of the Jews reinforces an image of the 1920s as a time when Berliners threw off the shackles of tradition, with exhilarating but ultimately disastrous results. The century's later and greater disasters have thus reinforced the sense of loss expressed by the 1923 Baedecker. Even much of the recent rediscovery of modernity reaches back to the era before World War I. The New Synagogue and the other visible traces of Jewish Berlin date to the monarchy, for example. Before 1914, the Jews were emancipated, the arts were thriving, architecture was bold and inventive, but restrictions and inhibitions maintained a certain comforting order, and the restrictions were all the more comforting for reflecting tradition rather than choice. That, in any case, is the view from the 1990s, when a search for traditions, including Jewish ones, betrays a longing for order, limits, and rules. Berlin remains unsure how much modernity it wants.

Potsdamer Platz

Berlin in the early 1900s is one of the great cities that shaped the twentieth century's image of modernity: crowds, lights, noise, machines, buildings, all on a scale that dwarfed the individual. The experience of the metropolis stimulated cultural responses that exalted in, condemned, or creatively absorbed the new forms of human interaction. These responses, in turn, have shaped all later perceptions of the modern city. For our purposes, the most prominent symbol of the age is Potsdamer Platz, one of those Berlin places notable for what is not there. Like Hitler's bunker, the royal palace, and now the Wall, Potsdamer Platz is a significant void. And like them, its significance can only be recovered through memory and history.

Potsdamer Platz was never a real square, only an intersection. From the 1730s to the 1860s, it was simply the outer side of the Potsdam Gate and the beginning of the highway to Potsdam. (Its counterpart inside the gate was the octagonal plaza that has been named Leipziger Platz since 1814.) The following decades of explosive growth transformed this marginal location into a central one, as residential and then commercial development engulfed its immediate vicinity and continued spreading outward. Because the Tiergarten blocked urban growth to the west and northwest, commerce and traffic converged on Potsdamer Platz and made it something of a bottleneck. By 1900, with a new commercial center flourishing at the southwest corner of the Tiergarten, what had once been the city's edge was now virtually its center.

Potsdamer Platz came to symbolize above all the bustle, speed, and motion of the modern metropolis. Technology and capitalism had created both the means and the demand for the many modes of transportation that remade the city. A decisive step in the industrialization of Berlin (like the rest of Europe) had been the coming of the railroads, beginning in the 1830s. The first of the train stations that soon ringed Berlin, the Potsdam station, stood directly on Potsdamer Platz, and the busy Anhalt station was only a few blocks away. Urban rapid transit came with the elevated rail lines constructed in the 1870s and 1880s (now known as the S-Bahn): a circumferential ring and then an east-west line across the city center. Electric streetcars soon followed; by 1908, thirty-five lines crossed Potsdamer Platz. At the turn of the century came the first subway lines (U-Bahn), as well as a growing number of buses, trucks, and cars on the streets. All of these modes of transportation came to Potsdamer Platz and competed for space with pedestrians and horses (although the S-Bahn only arrived there in the 1930s with the construction of a new, underground line). They clattered, flashed their lights, shook the ground, and moved incessantly.

The central location of Potsdamer Platz attracted major hotels, followed by cavernous restaurants such as the Pschorr-Haus, outpost of the famous Munich brewery, and Kempinski Haus Vaterland, a constellation of fantasy worlds transporting guests to exotic Turkey, Spain, Hungary, and the Wild West. Commerce begat commerce, and the square became known above all for its traffic—and traffic jams, and traffic lights, and traffic policemen (fig. 28). The noise, lights, and motion of Potsdamer Platz attracted painters, poets, photographers, and cultural critics, and they made it famous. Their favored vantage point was the Café Josty, where even the idle came to watch the throbbing heart of the city. Otherwise the only repose could be found in an old church cemetery that lay, incongruously, next to the entrance to the Potsdam rail station. When the lease on its last plot expired in 1910, it too was swept away.

Potsdamer Platz *was* Berlin because Berlin was the city of bustle and speed. "There is no city in the world so restless as Berlin," wrote the British diplomat Harold Nicolson in 1932.[24] For Germans, the incessant movement of Berlin was the real and visible embodiment of the hypermodern urbanity they associated with the United States—thus it was an "American city," or a "German Chicago." The cosmopolitan restlessness also seemed somehow Jewish. A favorite word of the time was "Tempo"; when the Jewish-owned Ullstein press syndicate launched a racy tabloid newspaper of that name in 1928, it immediately acquired the nickname "die jüdische Hast"—"Jewish haste," a colloquial German phrase that recalls the linkage of Jews, commerce, and perpetual motion.[25]

28
Potsdamer Platz, circa 1930, looking southeast into Stresemannstrasse. The Potsdam rail station is set back from the street in right background. On the horizon is the roof of the Anhalt station. Traffic signal tower is in left foreground. Courtesy of Landesbildstelle.

What was striking about Potsdamer Platz by the 1960s, then, was the contrast between the memories (or, if you needed them, the pictures) of bustle and the utter desolation that had replaced it. By the 1960s, East and West Berlin, each in its own way, must have been among the least lively cities of their size in the world; the demoralized population on both sides of the Wall missed the activity and the personalities that typified early-twentieth-century Berlin. Potsdamer Platz thus embodied a Berlin state of mind in the 1960s, as it had half a century before.

Potsdamer Platz had largely taken its familiar form by 1914. Perhaps the most significant postwar addition was the traffic signal tower erected in 1925 at the center of the intersection, Europe's first traffic light. The technological modernity that the square embodied seemed to stand above the political turmoil that followed World War I. One evening in January 1919, during the Communists' abortive revolution, Count Harry Kessler, the perceptive diarist of Weimar Berlin, went to a cabaret near Potsdamer Platz. During a dance number a shot was heard:

> No one paid any attention. Slight impression of the revolution on big-city life. This life is so primordial that even a revolution of world-historical significance like the present one does not disturb it much. The Babylonian, immeasurable depth, chaos, and might of Berlin has only become clear to me during the revolution, as it became apparent that this colossal movement only caused slight disturbances in the much more colossal ebb and flow of Berlin. It is as if an elephant is stabbed with a penknife. It shakes itself and strides on as if nothing had happened.[26]

The following decade seemed to confirm Kessler's observation: the urban life that had survived world war and revolution also went on through the Kapp Putsch of 1920, when a general strike chased nationalist generals out of town; the hyperinflation of 1923, when the modern money economy temporarily broke down; and the rising tide of political street violence at the end of the 1920s. The proudest fomenter of the last was Joseph Goebbels, sent by Hitler in 1926 to become Gauleiter (Nazi Party leader) in the leftist stronghold of Berlin. The work of his brownshirted storm troopers ensured a steady diet of violence for readers of Goebbels's newspaper, *Der Angriff* (the Attack). Goebbels's public-relations machine also exploited Berlin street violence to create the most famous Nazi martyr, Horst Wessel, a storm trooper killed by a Communist in 1930.

After 1933, with the state's apparatus in their hands, the Nazis set out to prove Kessler wrong: their revolution would not leave the elephant unmoved. They chased Kessler and his freethinking friends into exile, prison, or hiding. The appearance and the bustle of Potsdamer Platz changed little during the next several years, as photographs show, but the appearance deceived. A building a few steps up Bellevuestrasse, for example, became the home of the Volksgerichtshof, Judge Roland Freisler's notorious special court established in 1934 to mete out summary death sentences to those judged traitors to the Third Reich. Meanwhile, the physical destruction of Potsdamer Platz began even before the war, as several nearby blocks were cleared in the first phase of Hitler's plans for rebuilding Berlin. World War II then left most of the remaining buildings in ruins.

After 1945, Potsdamer Platz marked the border between the Soviet and British sectors, where capitalism confronted Communism. Just after the war, a black market thrived here—itself a form of capitalist subversion, in Communist eyes—and during the 1950s the two sides waged a duel of signs. On the Western side, an electrical message sign beamed a running stream of news and information (the Communists called it propaganda) toward the East. The East responded with a sign advising wise Berliners to shop at its state-run "HO" stores. Potsdamer Platz was also the scene of a tense confrontation at the border during the East German uprising on June 17, 1953. As West Berliners watched angrily and the Western allies uneasily, Soviet tanks subdued Eastern protesters. When the Wall went up eight years later, the East Berlin side of the square became the death strip; all remaining buildings there were leveled.

On the Western side, most of the damaged buildings had already been demolished during the 1950s. Then, after the Wall went up, West Berlin turned its back on Potsdamer Platz. Beginning in the 1960s, the vacant area to its west was rebuilt with a widely dispersed array of buildings known as the Kulturforum, featuring the New National Gallery (designed by Mies van der Rohe) and two sprawling gold-roofed buildings by Hans Scharoun, Philharmonic Hall and the State Library. In building the

Kulturforum, the West even rearranged the old streets to shift the focal point away from the dead end at Potsdamer Platz.

Little remained at the square itself other than the souvenir stands that catered to busloads of tourists. Visitors came to gawk at the Wall and to buy postcards (or, for a time, see a billboard) showing contrasting pictures of Potsdamer Platz "then" and "now." Tour books and tour guides told them that this had been the busiest intersection in Germany, or Europe, or the world, dubious claims repeated enough to acquire the ring of authority. Visitors marveled at the power of the Wall to turn a central place into a marginal one. Along the hundred miles of the Berlin Wall, nowhere was it more clearly revealed as a physical and symbolic barrier stemming the motion of modernity (fig. 29). Wim Wenders's 1987 Berlin film *Wings of Desire* evokes this discontinuity. In one scene, an old man wanders across an expanse of weeds—recognizable as Potsdamer Platz in the 1980s—and laments that he can't find Potsdamer Platz. The old man is Curt Bois (1901–91), a star of stage and screen in 1920s Berlin, and a Jew who was forced to emigrate in 1933. *His* Potsdamer Platz is indeed nowhere to be found.

But perhaps it is not irretrievably lost—so hope the planners of the new Berlin. The Kulturforum and other steps to erase the historical urban fabric had their critics before 1989, but it was after the opening of the Wall that the spirit of "critical reconstruction" came to Potsdamer Platz. The idea of reconstructing Potsdamer Platz aroused widespread enthusiasm. It offered a symbolic as well as a practical reconciliation of East and West. And it built on the myth of bustling Potsdamer Platz—an image much in favor among the promoters of the new German capital. Leaders of government and business advertised Potsdamer Platz as a prestigious address that bespoke centrality and visibility as well as tradition.

The tradition that gave Potsdamer Platz its corporate cachet was a selective one: it was a glossy modernity without the subversive sexuality of the 1920s or the political terror of the 1930s. That is, it was fundamentally a pre-1918 tradition. Could a 1990s city be built on a 1910 model? Indeed, did the idea of a retrospective modernity make any sense at all? Skeptics thought not. For one thing, auto traffic was already threatening to choke the square in the 1920s, when few Germans could afford a car. In addition, the scale of real estate development had changed. On the old Potsdamer Platz, many buildings and businesses had developed in close proximity and had jostled for attention. No one has figured out how to plan that kind of unplanned liveliness, and many critics thought the Berlin government was not even trying. It moved quickly to sell large wedges of land bordering Potsdamer Platz to four major companies. The first, receiving the largest parcel, was Stuttgart-based Daimler-Benz, Germany's largest corporation (best known for its Mercedes automobiles, but also an electronics and aerospace conglomerate). The city government jumped at the chance to secure a high-profile Daimler-Benz presence in central Berlin, selling it fifteen acres of land cheaply. Next came Sony, proposing to build its European headquarters just across the street. The other parcels went to

29
Potsdamer Platz, 1972, looking east into Leipziger Strasse. East Berlin television tower is in background. Courtesy of Landesbildstelle.

the Hertie department store chain (the successor to Hermann Tietz, with its "Aryanized" name from the 1930s) and the multinational engineering company Asea Brown Boveri (ABB).

So much for diversity and street life, thought some critics, envisioning the area as a desolate zone of self-enclosed office towers. So much for planning, thought others: the decisions had been made before either planners or the public contributed their thoughts. What ensued was a messy set of negotiations between the city, trying to salvage something of Potsdamer Platz's urban diversity, and the corporate landowners, now functioning as real estate developers. The inevitable result was a compromise between the ideal of the corporate tower and that of critical reconstruction, and between the corporations' demand for eleven thousand parking spaces and the city's goal of a lively street scene. Daimler-Benz chose the Italian architect Renzo Piano to create an overall design for its complex of buildings, which were parceled out to several architects building for various clients. Sony chose a design by the German-American Helmut Jahn; ABB, that of another Italian, Giorgio Grassi. As the city demanded, each plan proposed a mixture of uses for the land and buildings, including shopping and a few apartments as well as offices. The result, for many years, was an enormous construction site; how the new Potsdamer Platz functions will not be clear until well into the twenty-first century.

Daimler-Benz and the others were attracted to the location because it offered the rare combination of a central and prestigious address and a nearly unencumbered tract of land, thanks to the events of the previous decades. Only two buildings stood nearby. Daimler-Benz agreed to keep the intact turn-of-the-century building of a former restaurant, the Weinhaus Huth, a decision it briefly regretted in 1995 when the building's residential tenants refused to move out and filed official complaints against the noise of the construction all around them. More controversial were Jahn's plans for the Esplanade, which had been among Berlin's leading hotels after it opened in 1908. The part of the building that still stood had been designated for preservation, but many critics were unhappy with Jahn's plan to remove its historic interior rooms and reconstruct them elsewhere within the Sony complex.

More important than the visible relics, however, were the memories and traditions that complicated the planning process.

30
Potsdamer Platz and Columbus Haus, circa 1933. Courtesy of Landesbildstelle.

Two ghosts hovered over the new Potsdamer Platz: radical 1920s modernism and its 1930s successor, Nazism. The first, architectural modernism, had begun to make inroads into Potsdamer Platz in the late 1920s, notably with the new Telschow Haus on the corner of Potsdamer Strasse. The more celebrated new building, completed in 1932 on the north side of the square, was Erich Mendelsohn's Columbus Haus. The smooth horizontal bands of its curved facade accentuated the tempo of the square, and suggested the possibility of an entirely new and different Potsdamer Platz, one that embraced the square's dynamism while discarding all its static forms (fig. 30). Mendelsohn's rejection of traditional styles was typical of architectural modernists, including those who built Berlin's famous housing estates at the same time, and it also expressed an oft-remarked tendency of modern Berlin. That tendency is captured in the concluding phrase of Karl Scheffler's 1910 book on Berlin, a phrase still quoted to characterize the city: "the tragedy of a fate that . . . condemns Berlin forever to become and never to be."[27]

What Scheffler called a tragic fate has often been celebrated. Certainly it suited Mendelsohn, a visionary architect who sought to create forms that expressed the dynamic movement of space and time. He felt a creative bond with Einstein and the theory of relativity; indeed, perhaps his most famous building is the Einstein Tower built in Potsdam for astrophysical research. (In 1929 the writer Wilhelm Hausenstein mused, "I could imagine the theory of relativity developed and proclaimed almost nowhere else" than in Berlin.)[28] In addition to Einstein, Mendelsohn professed an affinity for Nietzsche. His declaration in 1927, "Only he who cannot forget has no free mind," recalling Nietzsche's attack on historical consciousness half a century before, takes on a chilling ring in post-Holocaust Germany.[29] Germans who believe they can and should "never forget" the Third Reich's crimes know that their minds are indeed not free. Elements of Mendelsohn's radical modernism will be visible in the facades of the new Potsdamer Platz, but his celebration of change now strikes many planners as a plunge into the abyss.

This brings us to the second ghost of Potsdamer Platz, that of Hitler, who came to power a few months after Columbus Haus was completed. Nazis and modernists were enemies, and Hitler's new Berlin looked very unlike Mendelsohn's, but it is too easy to see Nazism and modernism as polar opposites. The Third Reich, after all, was the dark side of speed, motion, and industrial modernity: air travel and air forces, autobahns built for tanks and armies, boxcars full of Jewish prisoners, industrialized death on the battlefield and in concentration camps. Nazi Germany moved to the rhythm of a collective purpose, with no place for idling flaneurs or visionary Jewish architects.

In 1920, Scheffler was one of several critics asked by a newspaper to respond to the question, "How will Potsdamer Platz look in twenty-five years?"—that is, in 1945. Scheffler submitted an imaginary debate that included this vision:

> The buildings on the square will be ravaged, robbed of their usable materials; they will be ruins. The broken pavement will be overgrown with grass and bushes. No streetcars will run, a car will be seen but rarely, and only a few people will creep about timidly. The square will

> swarm with rats and mice from the neglected Tiergarten. Once a day a train will arrive in the station, and a handful of travelers clutching thin valises will scurry into the city, followed by the threatening eyes of the rabble living in the ruins. At night no lights will shine.[30]

Scheffler, the prophet of flux, was playing with ideas. Modernism did not cause the destruction of Potsdamer Platz, but the early modernists could contemplate transfiguration and destruction with an equanimity not possible after 1945. Mendelsohn's desire to transform Potsdamer Platz now reminds too many people of the disasters that followed, to which Columbus Haus also fell victim. Damaged in the war and again in the 1953 uprising, it was demolished by the East Germans in 1957. If it still stood, it would certainly be restored—but as a link to the past, not as a harbinger of the future.

Rebuilding Potsdamer Platz is supposed to enable Berlin to move out of the shadows of Hitler and the Wall. Perhaps that will not be so difficult amid the gleaming new buildings going up there, especially if the site of the Volksgerichtshof, now divided between Daimler-Benz, Sony, and the relocated Potsdamer Strasse, remains unmarked. But the remnants of Hitler's chancellery, Gestapo headquarters, and other centers of Nazi terror lie just a few steps away, and it is clear that not all of them will be forgotten. While Berlin is promoted as German capital, as business center, as city of modernity, it will also be commemorated as headquarters of the Third Reich. In rebuilding the Reichstag, Potsdamer Platz, and its old urban grid, Berlin has chosen to embrace an early phase of modernity that concluded in 1918, and to distance itself from more recent and disquieting assaults on tradition. Only this tentative embrace of modernity, it seems, might make it possible for Potsdamer Platz, symbol of dynamic change, to offer the new city a reassuring image of stability.

If Berlin were to meet the fate of Rome, then the coming generations could one day admire the department stores of some Jews, and the hotels of some corporations as the most imposing works of our time, the characteristic expression of the culture of our days.... Thus our cities of the present lack the outstanding symbol of national community, and hence it is no wonder that the community does not see any symbol of itself in its cities. This must lead to a spiritual dullness which manifests itself in practice in a wholesale indifference of the present-day city dweller towards the lot of his city.[1]

—Hitler, *Mein Kampf*

When peoples experience inwardly periods of greatness, they represent these periods through external forms. Their word thus expressed is more convincing than the spoken word: it is the word in stone.[2]

—Hitler, speech opening German Architecture and Applied Arts Exhibition, Munich, January 22, 1938

These buildings of ours should not be conceived for the year 1940, no, not for the year 2000, but like the cathedrals of our past they shall stretch into the millennia of the future.[3]

—Hitler, speech at Nuremberg Party Congress, 1937

What is ugly in Berlin, we shall remove, and Berlin shall now be given the very best that can be made. All who enter the Reich Chancellery must have the feeling that they are visiting the masters of the world. Even the route to it—through the Triumphal Arch, along the wide avenues, past the Soldiers' Hall, to the Square of the People—should take their breath away. Only thus shall we succeed in eclipsing our only rival, Rome. The Great Hall's size shall reduce St. Peter's and its square to insignificance.

For material, we'll use granite. Even the oldest boulders on the North German plain are barely weathered. In ten thousand years these buildings will still be standing, just as they are, unless meantime the sea has again covered the North German plain.[4]

—Hitler, table talk, night of October 21–22, 1941

Four

Nazi Berlin

A slim 1937 book offered its readers a guided tour to the memorable places of the Reich capital: here Hitler or Goebbels gave a stirring speech; here SA martyrs died at the hands of Communist thugs. Memorial plaques, the book noted, commemorated many of these events.[5] The book, in short, defined Berlin's historical landscape in accordance with the political authority and (perhaps) the popular taste of its time. Within a few years, those plaques and that authority had vanished. Berlin would no longer honor dead storm troopers; what would its historical attractions be? How would the years 1933–45 be commemorated? The Communists had some clear answers, while West Berlin, and now unified Berlin, have agonized over one site after another. The Nazis had broken radically with their predecessors in their treatment of the historical landscape and their sense of the relationship between past and present. They left their mark all over Berlin; their successors, determined to make their own break with the past, had to decide what to destroy, what to keep, and what to commemorate. These decisions, which are still being made (or avoided), reveal both explicit policies and deep-seated attitudes toward the place of the Third Reich in German history.

The Chancellery

During the years the Wall stood, visitors to Potsdamer Platz climbed stairs to a platform and gazed out over the desolate expanse of the death strip. Their tour guides usually pointed out a slight rise in the open space of no-man's-land and explained that under it had lain the bunker where Hitler committed suicide. This well-known fact was not entirely accurate: by the 1980s the mound one saw actually marked a different bunker. A second mound, visible in earlier years farther to the north and east, had indeed covered the so-called Führerbunker. In any case, the grassy mound offered a fitting monument. Hitler's legacy was devastation; the inexpressible horror of the Third Reich had ended at a place that was now grim, empty, and utterly inaccessible.

Unlike most of the historically burdened sites of Berlin, Hitler's chancellery and its bunkers probably attract less attention from Germans than from foreigners. The trivia of Hitler's final days hold little attraction for most Germans. They do not like to confront memories of the man once hailed as their national savior and later blamed for their national misfortune. Clearly, however, the site of the chancellery would have received more attention had it lain in West Berlin. East Germany's own treatment of its Nazi legacy did not encourage open debate and denied the significance of individual personalities. In accordance with reigning Marxist theories, Hitler's chancellery and nearby ministries deserved no more attention than the headquarters of the Deutsche Bank, still standing a few blocks away. The government enforced this belief with strict secrecy about the location and condition of the bunker. Only with reunification did the bunker's site become accessible and its disposition become a public issue.

The bunker had been built at the core of Berlin's main government quarter. This quarter was centered on Wilhelmstrasse, at the western edge of the eighteenth-century city. Under pressure from King Friedrich Wilhelm I, many noble families had built their town palaces there. In the late nineteenth century, a few bourgeois parvenus used their fortunes to build mansions on the same street. Notable among them were the railroad magnate Bethel Henry Strousberg, whose bankruptcy enabled the British to acquire his new mansion as their embassy, and the locomotive manufacturer Borsig, whose house was acquired for Hitler's use in 1933. During the nineteenth century, many of the palaces had come into the hands of the Prussian and Reich administrations, and Wilhelmstrasse became synonymous with government—especially with the foreign ministry, located here since 1819.

The west side of the street had attracted the grandest palaces, since it offered deep lots reaching back to Friedrich Wilhelm I's city wall. After these palaces passed to the government, this expanse became known as the "ministerial gardens." And this was space Hitler proposed to make use of. In addition to the chancellor's residence, a palace that had been taken over by Bismarck, Hitler in 1933 had at his disposal a new, compact chancellery, the Weimar Republic's main contribution to Wilhelmstrasse. Both in size and in style the building (described as "factory-like" in a Third Reich publication) was far too modest for the man who had promised to destroy the defeatist republic and make Germany great again. The Borsig palace next door soon provided some additional space, but there was no question of remaining in such makeshift quarters. Hitler therefore commissioned his architect, Albert Speer, to design a large addition to be built west of the existing structures. Its main facade would face Voss-Strasse, which marked the southern end of the ministerial gardens.

The new chancellery was by no means the Third Reich's first major building in Berlin, but it was the first (and, as it turned out, the only) completed part of Hitler's personal plans for rebuilding the city. The project confirmed Speer's reputation as a man who could get things done. Hitler wanted his building finished quickly. The hand-knotted rugs, which could not be made quickly, had to be ordered before Speer had determined the appearance of the rooms they would furnish; according to Speer, he then designed the rooms around the rugs. Construction began early in 1938 and was completed the following January. This speed, made possible by modern technology, represented a kind of modernity Hitler was proud to make his own. In a speech marking the ceremonial raising of the ridgepole, he declared, "This is no longer the American tempo; it has become the German tempo."[6]

Speer's design also pleased Hitler enormously. The entire building worked hard to impress—or intimidate. The overscaled and austere classicism of the main facade on Voss-Strasse was clearly intended by Speer and Hitler to express dignity and power (fig. 31). The more important part of the building, at least for Hitler, was the interior, most of which was devoted to purely ceremonial purposes. Specifically, it was intended to overawe foreign visitors coming to call on the Führer. They arrived by automobile in a court of honor, and from there walked through a succession of grand halls and anterooms for more than seven hundred feet before they reached the Führer's reception hall.

31
New Reich chancellery, facade on Voss-Strasse, 1939. Courtesy of Landesbildstelle.

Vast spaces and dark marble were the dominant features of these rooms. Hitler was particularly delighted with the central gallery, according to Speer, because it was twice as long as the Hall of Mirrors in Versailles.[7]

Much of the area of the former ministerial gardens was redesigned to complement the new chancellery. Several auxiliary structures were built there as guardhouses and maintenance facilities. And several bunkers were incorporated into the grounds of the chancellery. One of these was Hitler's personal command bunker, where he spent the final weeks of his life. It owes its fame to the many books that have described in minute detail the last days and hours of Hitler and his entourage. The earliest of these descriptions grew out of the Western powers' desire to assure themselves that Hitler was indeed dead. (Although many witnesses could confirm this basic fact, the penchant for secrecy in Stalin's Soviet Union helped to fuel decades of rumors to the contrary.) The attraction and repulsion of Hitler's personality has made this a story that continues to sell books.

Meanwhile, however, the actual site of these events fell into neglect. During the summer of 1945, many soldiers and other visitors from the West as well as the Soviet Union made their way into the Führerbunker. (Among them was Winston Churchill.) They found it little changed from the day of Hitler's death; many took away souvenirs. In 1948, however, the Soviet occupation authorities closed the bunkers and then leveled the

32
Removal of chancellery bunker, 1987

ruins of the chancellery and all the other buildings adjoining the ministerial gardens. They reused much of the stone in a nearby subway station and in the Soviet war memorials in the Tiergarten and in Treptow. After 1961, the Berlin Wall crossed the western edge of the site, and the new border fortifications covered much of the former chancellery grounds. The rest of the land west of Wilhelmstrasse simply sat untouched for years. (In 1964 the street was renamed Otto-Grotewohl-Strasse after the GDR's first prime minister.) Then, in the late 1980s, in the course of its redevelopment of central Berlin, the East German government built several large apartment buildings on the site. These quickly became known as the "Stasi" apartments, owing to the suspicion in East and West that only privileged citizens employed or vetted by the Ministry for State Security (the Stasi) would be given desirable new apartments next to the Wall. (The best-known tenant was perhaps the most famous East German, the skater Katarina Witt.) Two of these buildings were constructed directly atop the main chancellery bunker, which had to be laboriously demolished to make way for the new foundations (fig. 32).

When Berlin was reunified in 1990, Western leaders lamented the presence of these new buildings. In its final years, Honecker's regime had forestalled any other plans for disposal of the land, now once again in a prime location instead of a marginal one. The former death strip, however, was now available. How could the new German capital make use of a tract of vacant land, centrally located, where Bismarck had worked, and Hitler too? There was no rush to claim the real estate. Eventually it was allocated to twelve of the German federal states (some of whose predecessors had had quarters there until 1938) for their Berlin liaison offices.

But the past was not easily banished. On the former death strip between Potsdamer Platz and the Brandenburg Gate—that is, on the former ministerial gardens—the English rock band Pink Floyd planned a concert in the summer of 1990 to celebrate the Wall's destruction. Security officials, checking the land beforehand for mines and unexploded ammunition, stumbled across the roof of a bunker. It had belonged to Hitler's SS guard unit, and had lain untouched and forgotten since the closing days of World War II. When it was opened, visitors found furniture, weapons, silver, porcelain, and most notably, eight kitschy wall paintings depicting SS soldiers fighting to protect women and Germany.

The discovery was an embarrassment. The site's one saving grace had been the absence of any visible traces of Nazi contamination. Many people, especially conservatives, wished to destroy the bunker or cover it up and forget about it. Others just as predictably demanded its preservation. They were led by the head of the municipal archaeology office, Alfred Kernd'l, who had rushed to the scene of the newly discovered bunker. He was permitted only a brief peek inside it at the time, but returned two years later to reopen the bunker and inventory the site. His office's excavations, together with archival research and interviews with East German witnesses, finally settled long speculation about what was and was not extant here. The western part of the chancellery's capacious bunker—the part that had been under the Wall—remained. (The mound in no-man's-land had covered its entrance.) Nearby the archaeologists also discovered an intact courtyard, the only other part of Speer's building to survive. Easily the most interesting find, because it had not been looted, was the small SS bunker, which Kernd'l proposed to declare a historical landmark—a move that met with vehement opposition.

Kernd'l became Berlin's firmest and most consistent advocate of preserving traces of the Nazi past. Even after his retirement, he continued to argue his case in public and to show the site to foreign visitors. He acknowledged that one does not expect to find an archaeologist leading an investigation of twentieth-century history. But his office had jurisdiction over all underground landmarks, and, he explained, the thorough removal of above-ground traces of Hitler has made the search for the Third Reich largely an archaeological one. The little that remains should be kept, he argued. In his view, Germans' failure to confront their own past can be measured by the continuing destruction of its traces. This would be the last chance to preserve any remnant of Hitler's headquarters.

In the case of the SS bunker, he faced a broad coalition of opponents. Many Germans normally eager to confront the Nazi past—including Berlin's Jewish community—did not want to put Nazi art, however bad, on public display. They argued that the bunker might attract neo-Nazis. Kernd'l suggested that neo-Nazis were not really what his opponents feared. To destroy the murals, he argued, would in fact lead neo-Nazis to think Germany feared them. To the argument that the bunker was insignificant and the paintings banal, Kernd'l replied that they should be preserved for that very reason, as a warning about the "banality of evil." Their "typical mixture of adolescent arrogance and sentimental banality" illustrated the male fantasies and rigid stereotypes basic to Nazism, and they revealed that this mania reached far beyond the ranks of leading Nazis. According to Kernd'l, that was what made them worth preserving, but it was also what made them unwanted.

Kernd'l found some support for his proposal to make the bunker publicly accessible, but the city government decided against preserving it. It was willing to see the paintings removed to the German Historical Museum, but the museum's influential director, Christoph Stölzl, declared that he wanted nothing to do with them. The city hesitated to choose either preservation or destruction of the bunker. It was clear that any decision would be deferred until bulldozers were poised to begin new construction on the site.[8]

And what about Hitler's legendary bunker? Beginning in 1990, when visitors could stroll across the grassy mound, they wanted to learn more about the location and condition of the Führerbunker below. We now know that the Soviets only partially destroyed it after the war, but the East Germans largely completed the job in the 1980s. Apparently little more than its floor still remains, forty feet below an expanse of playground, parking lot,

33
Site of Hitler's bunker, 1995

and lawn adjoining the new apartment buildings. Typical German treatment of a historically burdened site, Kernd'l observed sardonically, is either to plant it with greenery or to use it for parking, and here we have both (fig. 33).

Germania

If Hitler had had his way, the site at Wilhelmstrasse and Voss-Strasse would not be so important. The suicide in the bunker there may have been a fitting end to the Third Reich, but it was not in Hitler's script. He had intended this chancellery, grand as it was, for temporary use. A new and larger "Führer's Palace" was slated to replace it by 1950. This building was to be just one small part of Hitler's grand plans for rebuilding Berlin, a city that held little attraction for him in its existing form.

Part of his animosity to the city was ideological and political. Hitler and many of his early supporters were motivated by an assortment of resentments and fears of modernity, as represented by capitalism and socialism, Jews and other "outsiders," and by big cities, especially Berlin. Berlin, for its part, was no Nazi stronghold. Although the party's local Gauleiter, Joseph Goebbels, managed to create a core of support and a great deal of violence in the city, the majority of its voters supported the Communists and the Social Democrats. So when the Nazis came to power in 1933, many of them felt they had seized the capital from their enemies.

Hitler wanted to make Berlin into a new city. When it had

been rebuilt according to his plans, in fact, it was to be renamed Germania. In the new city, Hitler wanted *new* buildings for himself and his regime. The idea that buildings represented traditions worth appropriating was foreign to him. He had no desire to emulate those leaders in Moscow or Prague who took over royal residences: "I am too proud to move into former palaces."[9] As we saw in chapter 2, he did in fact avoid the Prussian royal palace. Hitler also stayed away from the palace of the Reich president on Wilhelmstrasse, although he assumed the powers of the office after President Paul von Hindenburg died in 1934. "Why?" he explained in a speech dedicating the new chancellery. "That was once the house in which the Lord Chamberlain lived. And you know that the leader of the German nation does not live in the house once occupied by the Lord Chamberlain!"[10] It was "so unworthy" that the Weimar Republic had put its president in what for Hitler amounted to a servant's quarters. The republic's symbolic modesty will still appeal to many supporters of liberal democracy, but not even a royal palace was good enough for Hitler.

Beyond Unter den Linden, Hitler found little to like in Berlin. Architecture fascinated him, but only as an expression of monumentality. He found most of Berlin far too disorderly and mundane. His idea of good urban form was an amalgam of grand Parisian boulevards and prominently placed individual structures like those on Vienna's nineteenth-century Ringstrasse. His way of improving upon those models was to build something bigger.

We know that grand architectural schemes occupied Hitler's thoughts long before he had any prospect of carrying them out. As he solidified his hold on power, his thoughts increasingly turned to the great architectural monuments he wanted to leave behind. He chose several cities for grand projects: Nuremberg, Munich, Linz, and Hamburg, as well as the Reich capital. Plans for Berlin were already taking shape in 1937 when he appointed Albert Speer to head a special authority charged with replanning the city. Speer and his staff sought to turn Hitler's ideas into workable form. In fact, the two most prominent buildings in the final plan, the domed hall and the triumphal arch, were based on sketches Hitler had made during the 1920s. Hitler and Speer's cooperation on the plans for Berlin has become well known through Speer's memoirs. According to Speer, Hitler spent hours poring over plans and models for the new capital. He installed

Speer in the Academy of Arts on Pariser Platz, a building he could easily visit from his chancellery by walking across the ministerial gardens.

In accordance with Hitler's tastes, the Speer plan proposed a new monumental center standing largely apart from the existing core of Berlin. Its basic feature was an intersecting pair of grand boulevards, one north-south, one east-west (fig. 34). The east-west axis linked the plan to the existing city: it incorporated Unter den Linden and its western extension, the Charlottenburger Chaussee (now the Strasse des 17. Juni). It was to cross the proposed north-south axis just west of the Brandenburg Gate. Speer was given the power to create this north-south axis, the centerpiece of the capital, by removing all obstacles in its way: rail yards, a corner of the Tiergarten, and extensive built-up areas, including tens of thousands of apartments. It was to be lined with grand new buildings: government offices, corporate headquarters, theaters, and shops that would display the power and glory of Greater Germany. The only point at which it incorporated part of the existing city was its northern end at Königsplatz (which had been called Platz der Republik during the Weimar years). Here stood the one existing building that would remain on the grand boulevard: the Reichstag. Hitler liked the building's architecture even if he despised the institution, and he vetoed Speer's proposal to demolish it.

34
Model of "Germania." In the foreground are the south rail station, Tempelhof airport (at right), and triumphal arch (center). Beyond the arch runs the north-south axis leading to the Great Hall. Courtesy of Landesbildstelle.

35
Model of the Great Hall. Reichstag is at lower right. Courtesy of Landesbildstelle.

By late 1938, the plan had taken its final form. The redesigned Königsplatz would be a vast square intended to hold a million people. The Führer's Palace on its western side would face the Reichstag, augmented by a new addition. The northern end of the square would be dominated by an enormous hall capped by a dome 825 feet in diameter, rising to a height of 954 feet. This proposed building's volume was sixteen times that of St. Peter's cathedral in Rome. Its main purpose was to hold a crowd of more than 150,000 that would stand and hear Hitler speak. The scale model made for Speer gives us a sense of the hall's size when we see how it dwarfs the Reichstag—no doubt an intended effect (fig. 35).

The grand boulevard extending three miles south would be, as Hitler himself boasted, wider than the Champs Élysées. Its width would accommodate enormous martial processions. The Great Hall's counterpart at its southern end was the Great Arch, a Roman-style triumphal arch that differed from its model, Paris's Arc de Triomphe, mainly in being two and a half times as high, with a width and depth greater than its height and a volume forty-nine times that of the Parisian arch. On its walls would be carved the names of the 1.8 million Germans who died in World War I. Marking the ends of the great axis would be two enormous rail stations, north of the Great Hall and south of the arch, that would replace the existing stations scattered around the perimeter of the central city. All disembarking passengers would thus begin their visit with a view of Berlin's most awe-inspiring—or intimidating—sight.

By spoiling Speer's plans, the war saved Berlin from one destruction while subjecting it to another. The pressing needs of war slowed and eventually stopped all work, although the demolition of buildings continued as late as 1942. By then many blocks had been cleared to make way for the north-south axis, and British bombers were supplementing the work of Speer's crews. The journal of his office sardonically described the air raids as "valuable preparation for the goal of reorganization."[11] Visitors as well as Berliners usually blame wartime bombing for the utter desolation of the areas north of the Reichstag and west of Potsdamer Platz, but many buildings there were already gone when the bombers went to work.

Traces of the grand plan do remain, contrary to Speer's claim that only the deciduous trees in the Grunewald bear witness to his work. The Strasse des 17. Juni extending west from the Brandenburg Gate, though it predates the Third Reich, retains the enormous width given it during the 1930s as it passes through the Tiergarten, the campus of the Technical University, and on to the western edge of the city. Other fragments of its glorified status as the grand east-west axis can be encountered along the way. In the middle of the Tiergarten, it crosses a large circle known as the Great Star, which was widened from 296 to 658 feet in 1938 when the Victory Column and other monuments of Bismarck's age were moved here. Four small guardhouses built at the time in typical Third Reich style still mark the circle's periphery. At the western edge of the Tiergarten, a massive Third Reich building, not actually finished until the 1950s, still houses offices of the Association of German Cities, for which it was built. Just beyond it stands an ornamental neobaroque gate, built in 1908 to mark the eastern border of the then-independent city of Charlottenburg. Its two halves were pulled far apart to make way for the wide ranks of marching men. The entire stretch of road is lined with ornamental streetlamps designed by Speer specifically for this boulevard.

Other eerie reminders of Hitler's megalomania haunt the depths. The builders of the new Berlin in the 1990s have been forced to dig through the ground and through the archives to locate the numerous tunnels and foundations built and then forgotten. One such remnant has always been visible, although few recognize it. At the quiet corner of Loewenhardtdamm and General-Pape-Strasse, near where the districts of Tempelhof and Schöneberg meet, stands a massive cylinder of concrete, stained and cracked. This was to be the site of the Great Arch. The concrete was poured in 1941 to test the soil's ability to bear such an enormous weight. Too much trouble to remove, it has simply been left alone in an overgrown patch of weeds. It will probably long remain as an unintentional monument to a Berlin that very nearly was.

Although the Hitler-Speer plan showed scant regard for the existing city, it was not especially original. The north-south axis represented a new version of a street that had been proposed several times before: by Karl Friedrich Schinkel in 1840, by entries in a 1910 planning competition for Greater Berlin, and in a plan developed in 1917 by Martin Mächler, which Hitler had probably seen. After Hitler's fall, when the West Berlin government proposed an expressway following a similar course, opponents cast it as a return to Hitler's plan. Planners had also been urging a reorganization of the city's rail connections since the turn of the century. The division of the city after 1945 obviated the need to do so, but reunification has revived the issue. Plans for the new capital in the 1990s again foresee a centralization of rail lines along a north-south corridor. A north-south rail tunnel under the Tiergarten, first proposed by Speer, will finally be built.

In short, much of the planning for Nazi Berlin shared the technocratic rationality of all modern urban societies. The Third Reich differed from its predecessors—and perhaps its successors—in having the power to impose its plans on a large and complicated city. All urban planning contains an authoritarian element; planning and architecture are always linked closely to power. The opportunity for the ruthless exercise of power made the Third Reich a dream come true for an ambitious architect like Speer as well as a megalomaniac dreamer like Hitler. Few students of Speer's architecture have failed to reflect on the affinities between it and the new job Speer took on in 1942, when his organizational skill was put in charge of wartime industrial production.

There is something disturbing about the uncompleted Speer plan, something more than its scale and the name of its patron.

It proposed to subordinate the bustling city to a higher purpose. The rail stations, for example, represent an element of practical city planning, but they also contribute to the plan's essential theatricality. As the writer Elias Canetti has pointed out, Hitler's sense of power depended on the attraction and subjection of crowds.[12] Canetti sees the names of Hitler's fellow World War I soldiers, carved on the Great Arch, as his first crowd, but new crowds would perpetually have to be fed into his boulevard, his square, and his hall. The rail stations would produce them somehow, but not in the same way that rail stations and other transportation nodes produce the crowds in any city center. Hitler's Berlin would replace the chaotic bustle of shoppers and flaneurs with the regimented order of marching men and cheering hordes, something Speer partly recognized after serving a twenty-year sentence for war crimes. Upon his release from Spandau prison in 1966, he drove by the war-damaged ruins of the one building actually constructed for the north-south axis, the House of German Tourism near Potsdamer Platz. (It was demolished soon afterward to make way for Hans Scharoun's new State Library.) "I saw in a few seconds what I had been blind to for years: our plan completely lacked a sense of proportion."[13] In planning for vast, manipulated crowds, Hitler and Speer had (perhaps deliberately) lost all sense of the scale of individual human beings. Few would dissent from Speer's verdict on his own plans: "lifeless and regimented."

Hitler challenged Berlin—and still challenges it—because he envisioned a timeless, static city. In this sense, he was the polar opposite of the radical modernists of the 1920s: they embraced rapid change; he sought to control it and to stop it. The permanence he sought is apparent in his choice of a simplified classicism for his architecture and of granite for his facades, as well as in his contempt for the living urban traditions embodied in the streets and buildings he either ignored or demolished. Rarely has the intimate link between creation and destruction been so apparent. The unintended cooperation between Berlin's planners and the Royal Air Force underscores the connection between Hitler's plans for Berlin and his better-known ambitions. The creative work in which Hitler took such pride was built on the obliteration of cities, communities, and entire peoples—"races," in Nazi terminology.

Hitler's obsession with his architectural legacy is the obverse side of the apocalyptic bent that launched World War II and ended with his condemning Germany, and himself, to destruction. His desire to leave behind monuments that would rival the Egyptian pyramids betrayed a longing for immortality. This longing mingled with a sense of inevitable doom that drew him (like many others) to the music dramas of Richard Wagner. Speer's pretentious "theory of ruin value," which proposed that buildings be designed with an eye to their attractiveness as ruins in the distant future, revealed his own German Romantic longings.[14] The theory reinforced Hitler's aversion to concrete and steel as modern substitutes for building with granite, limestone, and marble. In endorsing Speer's theory, Hitler revealed the Romantic streak that would, ironically, carry him to his death in a reinforced concrete bunker.

The Nazi Presence

The Third Reich's architectural legacy in Berlin goes far beyond Hitler's personal plans. A great number of buildings were put up for one reason or another between 1933 and 1945, and many of them still stand. National Socialist architecture did not take a single form: industrial buildings continued to display glass, steel, and concrete in typically modernist fashion, and suburban and small-town houses were built in rustic, half-timbered styles. But in Berlin the Third Reich built mostly government offices, and buildings that displayed the power and authority of the Nazi state had to meet a different standard. Their style is distinctive; a moderately experienced eye can usually pick them out from among others built under earlier or later regimes. Stone facades, generous proportions, massive window and door frames, rigid symmetry, starkly simplified columns and other classical details—together these elements give a jolt of recognition to the unsuspecting passerby in many obscure Berlin streets and courtyards.

Does the style and date of construction taint these buildings as "Nazi"? In some eyes, yes. A more practical question is: Are these buildings disqualified for normal use? Or can they somehow be denazified? In the first postwar years these questions were rarely posed: an intact building was too precious to be subject to moral scruples, whereas it was easy to consign damaged Third Reich buildings to oblivion. (Except where extraterritorial rights intervened: the massive Spanish, Italian, and Japanese embassies south of the Tiergarten sat for decades in ruins and in limbo; the first two remain that way.)[15] After a generation had passed, doubts and questions were raised here and there: Should a particular building's history somehow be acknowledged, at least by a plaque if not by its entire function? Should a given ruin be saved to help keep alive memories of Nazi crimes? Usually the answer was no, but the questions lingered.

An uncontroversial example is Fehrbelliner Platz in the western district of Wilmersdorf, where a loosely coordinated ensemble of government and private offices was built during the Nazi years; the private companies displayed their loyalty by following the prevailing style. Public and private use of these intact buildings has continued without a break since the war. This square received little attention from the Nazi propaganda machine and housed offices that ranked relatively low in the Nazi hierarchy—facts that presumably help explain its smooth transition to democracy.

Doubts about buildings' continued use arose where there had been prominent tenants or notoriously unsavory activities. A typically complicated example is one of the Third Reich's largest projects, the grounds of the 1936 Olympic Games. Neither the 1936 games nor their grounds can be seen as exclusively Nazi. The International Olympic Committee awarded the games to Berlin before the Nazis came to power. By 1933 the architect Werner March had already developed a design for the Olympic Stadium, intended to replace one on the same site designed by his father, Otto March, for the 1916 Olympics (which had been canceled on account of war). The finished stadium, particularly the broad sweeping curve of its interior, has been much admired by Nazis and non-Nazis alike (fig. 36). But its genesis and its identity continue to be disputed. Hitler took a great interest in the Olympics and in the design of the grounds; scholars disagree on the extent of Nazi influence visible in the stadium's architecture. Did Hitler intervene to force March to change a modernist glass-and-steel design into a Nazi one, as Speer claims? Did March himself develop a design that expressed the spirit of the Third Reich? Or does March's stadium actually display a conservative style of modern architecture that predates the Third Reich? These questions matter to those who wish to save the reputation of the stadium, or of March, from the taint of Nazism.[16]

The stadium is the centerpiece of a large complex of buildings

36
Olympic Stadium and Olympic grounds, 1936. Courtesy of Landesbildstelle.

and athletic fields, an impressive and nearly intact ensemble of integrated architecture and landscape. Parts of it clearly reflect Nazi influence, for example, Langemarck Hall, dedicated to the memory of the fallen soldiers of World War I. The most unambiguously Nazi forms on the site are the specially commissioned sculptures of superhuman athletic heroes. But all judgments of the architecture are filtered through knowledge of the Nazis' symbolic use (or misuse) of the 1936 Olympics. While the Third Reich worked to convince the world of its commitment to peace, and met with considerable success, some perceptive observers recognized the extent to which the Nazis' rituals of sport thinly veiled their militarism and their cult of dead war heroes. The British diplomat Sir Robert Vansittart, for example, went away thinking that the Germans "are in strict training now, not for the Olympic Games, but for breaking some other and emphatically unsporting world records, and perhaps the world as well."[17]

The complex, with its capacity for enormous crowds, was never intended for athletic use alone; after the games it would—and did—serve "national" uses, which meant military or quasi-military activities. Thus, the events here during the closing months of World War II were arguably suited to its original purpose: hundreds of accused deserters were summarily shot in a ravine; and, as happened throughout Germany, very young and very old men gathered here for induction into the "Volkssturm," the defense of last resort. In April 1945, battles over the site left behind two thousand dead, mostly boys of thirteen and fourteen.

After the war, much of the grounds faded into obscurity, especially the part taken over by the British as their military headquarters from 1952 to 1994. However, the ruined Langemarck Hall with its bell tower, demolished by the British in 1947, was rebuilt according to its original plans in 1963. The Olympic Stadium itself remained in use as West Berlin's main soccer stadium, and was remodeled to host the 1974 World Cup.

These buildings returned to prominence in 1990 when, in one of its first acts, the reunified Berlin government applied to host the Olympic Games in the year 2000. Until a host city was chosen in 1993, the municipal government poured its resources into a lobbying campaign as well as a barrage of plans for Olympic facilities in the new Berlin. Berlin ultimately lost out to Sydney, but not before the city had thoroughly exploited a new opportunity to reopen old wounds. The city's application was certainly not helped by an active anti-Olympic organization that objected not only to the cost and effort diverted to a prestige project but also to the symbolism of an application so close on the heels of reunification. (There was even a committee of Berliners supporting Sydney's application.) For many Olympic opponents, a boost to national pride was the last thing Germany needed. Many of them feared that a second Berlin Olympics would represent a renewal of the dangerous traditions of 1936 and, at the same time, an attempt to wipe away the memory of them.

How would a second Berlin Olympics relate itself, explicitly or implicitly, to the games of 1936? Answers to this question naturally focused on the Olympic grounds and the stadium, still the only one in the city suitable for Olympic use. Easy answers abounded: the opponents' desire to keep the games away entirely; the preservationists' position, to leave the old facilities untouched and construct new ones elsewhere; and the local Olympic organizers' desire to use and remodel whatever facilities were available. Here and there some intellectuals acknowledged that the sports complex—like the entire Third Reich—formed an integral part of the city and of its history, a troubling legacy that could be wiped away by neither use nor disuse.[18]

Another massive structure from the Third Reich has been

even more thoroughly denazified. Tempelhof airport, originally established in 1923, was expanded during the mid-1930s in anticipation of an enormous increase in air traffic. Its terminal was replaced by a massive new building designed in 1936 by the architect Ernst Sagebiel. Sagebiel, Erich Mendelsohn's assistant until 1933, was a modernist who made the compromises necessary to get Third Reich commissions. Hitler's wishes influenced the final design, since he wanted to align the airport's entrance with the eastern approach to his triumphal arch. The terminal building faces the airfield in a long, sweeping curve; at the center of the curve it joins a large central hall connected to the airport's entrance, at its northwestern corner. The building's steel frame incorporated modern technology, and the curve of its layout and its roof betrayed the influence of Mendelsohn's modernism, but its stone facing, massive window frames, and monumental entrances bespoke a conservative opposition to radical modernism.

The airport was one of the largest Third Reich structures to survive the war, and the emphatic link between the Reich capital and air travel, as embodied in Tempelhof, was arguably a major Nazi contribution to city planning. But the growth of air transport was not unique to Nazis or dictators, so circumstances quickly weakened the link between Tempelhof and its creators. During the years of division, Tempelhof airport became associated with the U.S. military presence, since it served as the Americans' airfield—exclusively so from 1975 to 1990, when Tegel airport handled all civil air traffic. More notably, Tempelhof was the most prominent site of the Berlin Airlift of 1948–49: the "raisin bombers" landing there brought West Berliners much of their food and fuel for eleven months. Since 1951 the approach to the terminal, now named Airlift Square, has been marked by a soaring monument commemorating the airlift. One further event in the history of the building reveals how completely it has become associated with German-American friendship. In 1985 the Americans returned the head of an enormous stone eagle that Sagebiel had designed for the terminal's facade. The eagle's head, previously at home in a West Point museum, now stands on a pedestal in front of the building it had previously graced, accompanied by a plaque identifying the terminal's monumental entry court as "Eagle Square."[19] The Nazi eagle thus became a symbol of the German-American military alliance.

Sagebiel's other major building in Berlin, the former Reich

Ministry of Aviation, has also survived intact, and postwar events redefined it as well. But its redefinition took a different course because it stood in East Berlin. Like Tempelhof, this early Third Reich project was linked to the expansion of air travel, but here the emphasis was entirely martial. Although Hermann Göring's new ministry was responsible for both civil and military air travel, the impetus for the project—begun in 1935 and finished the next year—was clearly the establishment of a powerful air force.

The enormous building stretches south and west from the corner of Leipziger Strasse and Wilhelmstrasse, at the southern edge of the traditional government quarter. Several sprawling wings, ranging from four to seven stories high, contain two thousand rooms, among them grand halls in which Reich Marshal Göring received, entertained, and overawed visitors. Like Sagebiel's airport, its external appearance is modern in its stark and massive facades but traditional in its stone construction and monumental entrance courts (fig. 37). A Third Reich guidebook pronounced it a "document in stone displaying the reawakened military will and the reestablished military readiness of the new Germany."[20]

After the war its large size and intact state—in contrast to the rest of Wilhelmstrasse—made the building attractive to the new East German government. A dozen ministries were given office space there, and it was renamed the "House of Ministries," which it remained until 1990. In it was held the ceremony in 1949 officially establishing the German Democratic Republic. A mural along the building's north loggia commemorates this event. The building's importance as a center of government also made it a center of attention during the East German uprising in 1953: striking workers marched to the House of Ministries to present their demands for economic and political reforms. Not surprisingly, the GDR chose to leave no trace of that day. On the uprising's fortieth anniversary, therefore, the building's new masters dedicated a commemorative plaque. The plaque was mounted on a pillar directly in front of the GDR's mural. The building is thus marked by competing memorials of the GDR rather than any reference to its original use. Proposals for a plaque remembering the terror bombing planned here—of Guernica, Warsaw, Rotterdam, and Coventry—have come to nothing.

During the early 1990s, the building served as the headquar-

37
Aviation ministry, circa 1936, looking south down Wilhelmstrasse (at left) from corner of Leipziger Strasse. Courtesy of Landesbildstelle.

ters of the Treuhand, the special government agency charged with liquidating East Germany's state-owned economy. (In 1992 it was renamed Detlef-Rohwedder-Haus in honor of the head of the Treuhand who was assassinated by left-wing terrorists.) As the Treuhand's actions directly or indirectly eliminated hundreds of thousands of jobs, it became a hated institution in the eyes of many East Germans. Some of them chose to see the building as the fortresslike command center of an occupying power, the West German capitalists who had supplanted the Soviet Communists. Thus Göring's building, though denazified in the popular mind, remained a place of bureaucrats and autocrats issuing orders from behind their stone walls. For the private contractor hired to renovate the building for the Treuhand, in fact, its identity was uncomplicated. A temporary sign advertised "Berlin's largest office building."

Third Reich ministries and agencies left behind many other buildings. Their construction reflected both the growth of central government authority and the desire of leading Nazis to display their power in the most visible and permanent way. After the war, hard-pressed national and municipal authorities on both sides of the Wall understandably chose to see intact buildings as office space rather than as Nazi statements in stone. For example, the Third Reich's first major building in Berlin was the new Reichsbank, built just southwest of the royal palace, a project first proposed by the Weimar Republic but altered to suit Hitler's taste. In Marxist theory, the state bank symbolized the alliance of government and industry that brought Hitler to power. But here the East German authorities showed no fear of ghosts from the past. They removed the Nazi eagles and other sculptural decorations (as they did elsewhere) and used the huge building first for their finance ministry and then, from 1959 to 1989, as Communist Party headquarters.

A less prominent but more startling example of continuity can be found near Wilhelmstrasse. In 1933, Joseph Goebbels set up his new Ministry of Popular Enlightenment and Propaganda in an old palace opposite the chancellery. One of the Third Reich's most effective bureaucratic infighters, he found powerful new applications for radio, film, and the printed press in service to the regime. In the following years, the propaganda ministry expanded its quarters by building substantial additions behind the palace. The palace itself did not survive the war, but several of the new wings did. These structures, facing courtyards and side streets, were also pressed into use by the German Democratic Republic—as the Government Press Office and Ministry for Media Policy.

A few other characteristic monuments of the Third Reich survive not because they remained useful, not because they were deemed worthy of preservation, but because it was too much trouble to demolish them. Above-ground bunkers are tolerated presences here and there in the city. Other silent witnesses to the war, prominently visible in this very flat city, are the artificial hills built from the rubble of thousands of destroyed buildings. Two of them, in East Berlin's Friedrichshain and West Berlin's Humboldthain Parks, partially cover massive flak towers that were the scourge of British and American bomber crews. It is widely known that West Berlin's highest hill, "Devil's Mountain," is also made of rubble. Few know, however, that the American radar station there sat atop the never-completed building of the Berlin university's military science faculty. Speer had planned to relocate the entire university to the western end of the east-west axis; after the war this single remnant of the project was buried physically as well as symbolically.

Places of Resistance, Places of Terror

The landscape of Berlin was never dominated by the Third Reich's buildings and monuments, but the boots of marching

Nazis and the applause of onlookers echoed nearly everywhere. Apart from the edifices constructed during the Third Reich, how can particular streets and buildings be singled out to bear witness to that era? Every country chooses to mark some traces of its past as a way of anchoring its history and identity; a historical plaque, for example, links a person or event to a site. But not every country must look back at Hitler. Particularly where the Third Reich is concerned, many an innocuous-looking plaque or memorial in Berlin has provoked fierce controversy.

Both postwar German states, established under the aegis of conquering foreign powers, were forced to stake out unconventional relationships to their national past. Since it was out of the question to express any reverence for Hitler's regime, the new states were compelled either to ignore the twelve years from 1933 to 1945—as they did in many ways—or to seek to identify themselves as the heirs of non-Nazi Germans. Hence the great interest in resisters and victims of Nazism—two overlapping categories, since most resisters were persecuted. Neither group has proved to be an easy substitute for more traditional national heroes.

By most accounts, resistance to the Nazis within Germany was not especially widespread or effective; nevertheless, many different groups and kinds of resisters have been identified and honored. Among the best-organized resisters were Communists who fought the Nazis before and after 1933. The Communist resistance formed the cornerstone of the German Democratic Republic's identity as the antifascist German state. Many in the West accused the East of distorting history to exaggerate the Communist role in the resistance. (When the GDR ceased to exist, its monuments came under new scrutiny—a story we leave to the next chapter.)

The role of the resistance in the Federal Republic's identity has been more complicated. Here the central figures have been the leaders of the attempt to assassinate Hitler on July 20, 1944. Only gradually during the 1950s did the government's attempts to honor them overcome widespread opposition, since many Germans (including former Nazis still in high positions) considered them to have been what Goebbels's media had portrayed them as: traitors. At the former seat of the military high command, the so-called Bendlerblock, where the leading conspirators had been captured and killed, a statue dedicated to them was unveiled in 1953, but only in 1967 did it become a national memorial to the resistance. (The street in front, Bendlerstrasse, was renamed Stauffenbergstrasse in 1955 in honor of the man who planted the July 20 bomb, Count Claus Schenk von Stauffenberg.) This memorial, and all it stood for, came to play an important role in West German national psychology. The German visitor was invited to identify with the men and women of the resistance and thus to depart with a clear conscience. As a visitors' brochure from 1972 asserts, "The German resistance proves that the entire German people was not stricken with the disease of totalitarianism and that in Germany, too, the tradition of inalienable human rights could not be destroyed."[21]

What the Communist resistance was for the East, July 20 was the West. But while the Stasi enforced the former consensus, the latter was openly questioned. Was the Bendlerblock really an appropriate icon of German democracy, or just of the Cold War? The leading conspirators were conservative officers and aristocrats. Many of them supported the Third Reich until it began to lose the war—unlike Communists and other leftist resisters, whom the West did not honor. While Communist resisters were disqualified from recognition by their opposition to democracy, many of the conservative resisters had clearly preferred an authoritarian regime as well.

This critical spirit, informed by a growing body of research into all aspects of the German resistance, found its way into the memorial after Mayor Richard von Weizsäcker commissioned a revision of it in 1983. When the greatly expanded exhibit opened in 1989, if offered a carefully documented survey of resistance among upper and lower classes, Christians and Jews, conservatives, liberals, socialists, and communists. The new exhibit sought not to simplify history in order to find heroes, but rather to ask questions about the personal ideals and political circumstances that led a few Germans, and only a few, to resist Hitler.

But visitors encountered this thoughtful documentation in a historically resonant place: the room where, for example, the former army chief of staff General Ludwig Beck was given the chance to shoot himself rather than face the firing squad that awaited his fellow conspirators outside. These echoes of history had once served a clearer political purpose; not everyone found the new, more complicated story emotionally satisfying. Complaints came mainly from conservatives, who were more comfortable both with national pride and with the political views of the July 20 conspirators.

They objected to one specific part of the new exhibition. When Defense Minister Volker Rühe moved into his new Berlin office in the Bendlerblock in 1993, he decried the fact that Stauffenberg and his associates now shared their memorial space with Walter Ulbricht and Wilhelm Pieck, the founders of the GDR. The object of his ire was a small corner of the exhibition examining the National Committee for Free Germany, founded by German Communists in Soviet exile who hoped to stir up opposition to Hitler. In 1994, as the fiftieth anniversary of the assassination attempt approached, Stauffenberg's archconservative son drew headlines when he threatened to skip the ceremony in the Bendlerblock on July 20 if Ulbricht's and Pieck's photos were not removed. Rumors surfaced (and were then denied) that the federal government planned to separate the memorial from the exhibition, removing the latter from the Bendlerblock.

The organizers of the exhibition protested that Ulbricht and Pieck were not being honored; honor was not the point. But for the conservative *Frankfurter Allgemeine Zeitung,* it was. July 20 is among the "few events in the history of this century which a German can unreservedly endorse and even be proud of," it editorialized, and its meaning is lost when Stauffenberg and his allies are equated with "the founders of the second German dictatorship."[22] Jens Jessen, a writer for the same newspaper, offered a more ironic perspective a few days later. He agreed that "this distressing proximity" of the two groups was a scandal, "but it is the scandal of German history."[23] Germans in search of heroes, in other words, will have to recognize that Communists and high-minded aristocrats were among the few to resist Hitler. The exhibition's organizers think the resistance should not be honored unless it is understood; but the desire to understand it and the desire to honor it coexist uneasily at best.

It proved simpler, if less satisfying, for West Germans to identify with the broader category of the Nazis' victims. In 1952, the West Berlin government established a memorial to victims of the Hitler dictatorship at the Plötzensee prison in northwestern Berlin, which had served as the main place of execution for political prisoners. The most famous of the twenty-five hundred people killed there during the Nazi years were participants in the July 20 plot, but the memorial did not honor them specifically. It was dedicated to all the millions who had been persecuted or killed because of their "political convictions, religious beliefs, or racial heritage."[24]

Only slowly did Berlin mark the places where its Jews were persecuted. East Berlin led the way, but by the 1980s the West was discussing or building many kinds of new memorials. Recently erected plaques and memorial sculpture now mark many notorious sites: the places where Jews were assembled after being taken from their homes—including the synagogue in the Levetzowstrasse and the Jewish retirement home in the Grosse Hamburger Strasse, although neither building still stands—and the railroad freight ramps at Putlitzstrasse and Grunewald where they were herded into boxcars bound for the Polish ghettos and for Auschwitz.

The presence of a plaque raises but does not settle questions about how a place of death should function in a living city. The Grunewald rail station is an example. Here, between 1941 and 1945, the German national railway accepted thirty-six thousand Jewish passengers duly booked by the SS for their gruesome passage to the death camps. In 1973 a plaque, put up at private initiative, finally marked the entrance to the freight ramps. Amid renewed public debate about the site in the late 1980s, the plaque was stolen and replaced twice. The city then chose the Polish sculptor Karol Broniatowski to design a new memorial, a concrete wall with impressions of human forms, which was completed in 1991. But in 1993 the managers of the newly reunified national rail system, eager to modernize their lines, chose the rotting freight ramps as the site for a new facility to clean their high-speed trains. When the planned demolition of the freight ramps became known, the Jewish community, the Green Party, and many others raised a storm of protest against this "ignorance of and contempt for history." In the face of this controversy, the director of the rail system confessed his ignorance of the site's history but denied his contempt for it: he canceled the planned construction and agreed to leave the ramps as a memorial.

For all the difficulties of identifying with resisters and victims, it is of course much harder to acknowledge the perpetrators of crimes as one's forebears. By the 1970s and 1980s, resisters and victims were widely honored, but some younger West Germans were arguing that they had come to serve as the nation's alibi—

that Germany had to face up to its identity as the land of Nazis, not anti-Nazis. Why, they asked, do the places of the perpetrators remain unmarked and unacknowledged? Those who asked this question claimed to know the answer: because Germany denies its own past. Since victims rarely saw the offices of the "desk-bound criminals" *(Schreibtischtäter),* memorials to victims were placed elsewhere and sites like Hitler's chancellery and Göring's headquarters long remained unmarked. That began to change during the final years of West Berlin, indirectly at first, as the places of the perpetrators were dedicated to the honor of their victims.

At Tiergartenstrasse 4, for example, once stood the building in which bureaucrats planned and directed the mass killing of mental patients throughout Germany, meanwhile refining the practices later used on Jews and other death-camp inmates. The euthanasia operation was named "T4" after its address. This has long been a vacant spot next to Philharmonic Hall. In 1988 the city bought a Richard Serra sculpture, *Berlin Junction,* for the site; both the city and the artist subsequently agreed to install a plaque dedicating it as a memorial to the victims of T4.[25]

Even more than Tiergartenstrasse 4, the address Am Grossen Wannsee 56–58 is a place of worldwide notoriety, but until recently it was all but invisible to Berliners. The house here was the site of what became known as the Wannsee Conference on January 20, 1942. Here Reinhard Heydrich of the SS brought together a group of bureaucrats from various departments to discuss the mundane details of complicated plans for the "final solution to the Jewish question." Their chosen site was a quiet lakeside villa in the wealthy suburb of Wannsee, built by an industrialist on the eve of the First World War and acquired by the SS in 1940 for use as a guest house. We know of no other significant meetings that took place here. After the war the house returned to obscurity, passing through the hands of the Soviet and U.S. military and then, from 1952 to 1988, serving as a recreation center for schoolchildren. But Adolf Eichmann's minutes of the meeting turned up in the foreign ministry archives in 1947. While their cautious bureaucratic language makes no direct references to killing, extermination, or even concentration camps, the minutes outline a plan for removing eleven million Jews from all of Europe and leave no doubt about their ultimate fate. We have no comparable records of discussions or decisions among the top Nazi leadership, so students of the Holocaust have come to see the Wannsee Conference as the definitive beginning of that terrible set of events. As a result, over the course of decades scholars and Jewish organizations voiced a desire to dedicate the house to learning and remembrance. In the 1960s, the West Berlin government declined an offer by the World Jewish Congress to finance a documentation center in the house. It feared drawing the attention of neo-Nazis to the site, but it also feared the wrath of conservative voters. By 1986, however, German leaders no longer saw commemoration of the Holocaust as just a Jewish matter. The city agreed to turn the villa into a Holocaust Memorial Center, which opened on the fiftieth anniversary of the Wannsee Conference in 1992.

There is reason to cast doubt on the historical significance of the meeting, and hence of the site: as the minutes make clear, no major decisions were actually made here, since they had already been made by higher authorities. Most scholars also agree that the Holocaust did not begin here; it had already begun in 1941. And indeed the historical exhibition in the house dwells little on the particular event that took place here. Instead it presents a carefully factual and dispassionate history of the persecution and murder of European Jews, from Hitler's rise to power to the liberation of the death camps. Its organizers seek above all to fill a need for public education about the Holocaust, particularly among German schoolchildren. Thus it shares the usual emphasis on the Nazis' victims. The exhibition's existence is symbolically important, however, in its acknowledgment that the single terrible day in this house's history denied it the right to be a normal place in the city.

The Topography of Terror

The exhibition established during the 1980s on the site of the Gestapo and SS headquarters is perhaps the most self-conscious attempt to uncover the historical legacy of a particular place in Berlin. The exhibition's title, "The Topography of Terror," reveals its organizers' ambition: to link history (the Third Reich) and geography (Berlin and Europe). And there can be little doubt about the historical significance of the site in question. Unlike the Wannsee villa, its notoriety does not depend on a single day or event.

It lies at the southern edge of the former Wilhelmstrasse

government quarter (fig. 38). Until the 1930s, in fact, the block south of Prinz-Albrecht-Strasse and west of Wilhelmstrasse did not house any government offices. Goebbels's newspaper, *Der Angriff,* on the other hand, was headquartered here. The most important building on the block had long been the Prinz Albrecht palace. This was an eighteenth-century palace that Schinkel had completely renovated in 1830–32 for the Hohenzollern prince whose name it came to bear (the brother of Friedrich Wilhelm IV and Wilhelm I). The next major building constructed on the block was the Museum of Applied Art designed by Martin Gropius and Heino Schmieden (1877–81). Later joining it on the south side of Prinz-Albrecht-Strasse were the new buildings of the Ethnology Museum, the State School of Applied Art, and the Hotel Prinz Albrecht.

38
Prinz-Albrecht-Strasse (from upper left to upper right), looking north, circa 1935. North of the Prinz Albrecht palace's garden (right center) is Gestapo headquarters. Courtesy of Landesbildstelle.

In May 1933, the new Nazi government chose the applied art school's former building at Prinz-Albrecht-Strasse 8 as the headquarters of the newly established secret police agency, the Gestapo. (Despite its name—Gestapo is short for Geheime Staatspolizei, or Secret State Police—the location of its headquarters was always public knowledge.) The Gestapo was established under the authority of Hermann Göring, then prime minister of Prussia. But Heinrich Himmler, the "Reichsführer SS," soon sought control of all German police forces, and in April 1934 Göring named him head of the Gestapo. Shortly thereafter he moved SS headquarters from Munich to the Hotel Prinz Albrecht, next door to Gestapo headquarters. The same year, the Prinz Albrecht palace just behind was leased to the SS's Security Service (Sicherheitsdienst, or SD). The SD's job was to keep tabs on the Nazi Party's enemies. Its head, Reinhard Heydrich, was Himmler's closest aide, and under the latter's formal leadership he also ran the Gestapo from 1934 on. In 1939, in fact, the Gestapo, the criminal police, and the SD were formally united in the Reichssicherheitshauptamt (Reich Main Security Office), headed by Heydrich and officially headquartered at Prinz-Albrecht-Strasse 8.

The Reichssicherheitshauptamt was only one of twelve departments within the SS. The Nazi Party's Schutzstaffel began as an elite guard and, under Himmler's ambitious leadership, expanded its security functions into a vast bureaucracy of terror. It assumed responsibility for the regime's pseudoscientific program of racial purification. That meant above all the persecution of Jews, including the "final solution" carried out by SS execution squads and in SS-run death camps. The SS was also entrusted with the task of carving out "living space" for the racial elite in a newly ordered Europe. It therefore prepared plans for German colonization of conquered lands in the East. Out of its security functions and elite guard formations later developed the conventional military units of the Waffen-SS (Armed SS) as well. All of these far-flung activities were linked by a vague racial ideology and by Himmler's determination to create his own institutions that would rival and overshadow the traditional apparatus of ministries, police, and army. An awesome amount of power was exercised at SS headquarters in the former Hotel Prinz Albrecht. Along with Gestapo headquarters next door, it made Prinz-Albrecht-Strasse one of the most feared addresses in Europe.

From this location, then, Himmler and Heydrich laid plans for terror and mass murder that had their consequences elsewhere. (After Heydrich's assassination by Czech partisans in 1942, Ernst Kaltenbrunner assumed his duties.) By no means all the SS bureaucrats in Berlin worked here, not even all of those in the Reichssicherheitshauptamt; Adolf Eichmann's division of Jewish affairs, for example, was located in another part of town, at Kurfürstenstrasse 116. But the Gestapo's dealings with dissidents brought many people into direct contact with its headquarters. It converted sculptors' studios in the cellar of Prinz-Albrecht-Strasse 8 into jail cells. There prisoners were kept, usually for short periods, while they were being questioned. "Intensified interrogation" was the bureaucratic term for the torture that became routine practice here. Torture extracted information, brutalized victims, and—because the Gestapo's methods became well known—made most Germans careful to avoid any hint of impropriety. Some of the prisoners were released from here, many others sent on to concentration camps.

Like so much of Berlin, these buildings were badly damaged during the last two years of the war, and after the German surrender the SS and Gestapo ceased to operate. This once-feared address became one of many stretches of neglected ruins during the immediate postwar years. Certainly the new rulers, the U.S. Army, had trouble distinguishing one ruin from another. Its published guide to the city included a photograph of a building identified as Himmler's headquarters. But the building shown was actually the former Prussian House of Deputies, which stood across the street (and hence in the Soviet sector).[26]

The West Berlin government blew up the damaged remains of the Prinz Albrecht palace in 1949. Although this was one of Schinkel's few buildings in West Berlin, the preservation authorities were not informed and the public had no chance to speak up—in sharp contrast to the East Germans' demolition of the royal palace the following year. By the mid-1950s, the remains of all the SS buildings had been demolished. In the years that followed, the land was cleared of rubble and leveled, leaving no trace of the old buildings. Some of them could have been restored, but there was no will to do so. This site met the same fate as the rest of Wilhelmstrasse, across the border in East Berlin, where the chancellery and the old ministries had stood. Down Prinz-Albrecht-Strasse, the less seriously damaged Ethnology Museum remained standing—and in use—until it too was demolished in the early 1960s. Between it and the vanished Gestapo headquarters, the gutted and gashed shell of the former applied art museum continued to stand alone, its future uncertain.

Meanwhile, forward-looking plans for the new Berlin proposed practical new uses for the vacant site: in 1956, a helicopter landing pad; in 1957, a highway. But city planning once again yielded to world history—this time the Cold War. Prinz-Albrecht-Strasse marked the border between the Soviet and American sectors; hence the Berlin Wall ran the length of the street after 1961. By then the feared name had disappeared from the map: in 1951 the East Berlin government (to whom the street itself belonged) renamed it Niederkirchnerstrasse after Käte Niederkirchner, a Communist resistance fighter killed in the Ravensbrück concentration camp in 1944. But after 1961, only border guards walked or drove down Niederkirchnerstrasse.

The planned highway had arisen out of a Western initiative to draw up a master plan for all of Berlin. Officially the Wall merely delayed the plan's realization; the proposed road across the Prinz Albrecht site remained on the books until 1980. Meanwhile the land, made marginal by the Wall, was leased to two interim users in the 1970s. One used its land to store debris from construction work; piles of dirt it left behind still mark the site. The other tenant provided a place to drive cars without a license. Rutted paths left by the cars have gradually disappeared amid the weeds and trees that grew on the neglected land.

After the site faded into obscurity, a new generation of local scholars and activists began to accuse the city and its people of denying their roots in the Third Reich. At the end of the 1970s, their efforts brought the site's history back to public attention. At the time, West Berlin was beginning to redevelop inner-city areas near the Wall. It restored the former applied art museum and reopened it in 1981 as the Martin-Gropius-Bau, a museum for major exhibitions. While it was being restored, a local architectural historian, Dieter Hoffmann-Axthelm, led a tour of the adjoining Prinz Albrecht site and wrote an article on its invisible heritage. Architects and planners preparing Berlin's International Building Exhibition, who had been planning projects in the neighborhood, joined the discussion. Their efforts led to the cancellation of the long-planned road across the site, construction of which had been scheduled to begin in 1980.

An exhibition on the history of Prussia in the Martin-Gropius-Bau first brought crowds of people to the area in 1981. As they entered the museum, they passed a temporary sign that vaguely resembled the once-ubiquitous Berlin signs declaring that "you are leaving the American sector." This sign, too, was composed in German, Russian, English, and French, and it informed visitors about the history of their current location: "You are standing on the grounds of the former torture chambers of the Gestapo." Meanwhile, human rights groups and organizations of Nazi victims demanded that the site be marked with some kind of memorial. In 1982 the West Berlin city government agreed, and the next year Mayor Richard von Weizsäcker sponsored a design competition.

The 194 competition entries revealed a wide array of possible responses to the vacant site, including massive monuments, artificial ruins, and buildings or landscapes shaped into such symbols as swastikas or stars of David. The winning entry, by Jürgen Wenzel and Nikolaus Lang, proposed to "seal" the entire area with cast-iron plates set into the ground, punctuated only by rows of chestnut trees. On the plates would be marked the outline of the former buildings; other plates would reproduce documents of SS and Gestapo policy. The competition judges liked this entry because of its simplicity and uncompromising rigor. But that very rigor doomed the plan. The guidelines for the competition had specified that all designs provide both a suitable memorial and a recreational park to meet the needs of the densely built-up Kreuzberg district. Neighborhood representatives quickly attacked the Wenzel-Lang design because of its failure to fulfill the second goal. In hindsight everyone seems to agree that these two goals were irreconcilable; the demand to fulfill both at once betrayed an inability to agree on the proper use of the site. By the end of 1984, the Wenzel-Lang plan was officially dead.

Meanwhile, other proposals for use of the land emerged. In 1984, the federal government suggested using the Prinz Albrecht site for a new German Historical Museum. This favorite project of Chancellor Helmut Kohl aroused suspicions on the political left: Kohl's opponents accused him of wanting to foster national pride by whitewashing the dark spots of the German past. The question of how to reconcile Kohl's museum with the Gestapo was averted when the museum's site was shifted to the vicinity of the Reichstag (from which the unbuilt project was shifted again after German unification). In 1985, Weizsäcker's successor, Eberhard Diepgen, proposed to devote part of the land to rebuilding the Prinz Albrecht palace, which would then be used as a Jewish museum. Diepgen no doubt saw this as a suitable gesture of triumph over a dark past. But for advocates of confrontation with that past, reconstructing the palace for a new use meant repressing all memory of its time as Heydrich's headquarters.

The debate took a new turn during 1985 and 1986, when the physical facts of the site turned out to be different than previously assumed. The Wenzel-Lang plan, for example, had been predicated on the assumption that there was nothing to see here. But this proved not to be true, thanks to continued pressure for confrontation with the site's Nazi past. In 1983, advocates of that confrontation had formed the "Active Museum of Fascism and Resistance in Berlin," an organization dedicated to establishing an "active museum" to confront the Nazi past generally and this site in particular. On May 5, 1985—three days before the fortieth anniversary of the German surrender, and the same day Helmut Kohl and Ronald Reagan made their controversial visit to a cemetery in Bitburg where Waffen-SS soldiers were buried—the Active Museum held a symbolic dig on the Prinz Albrecht site. Their efforts to uncover traces of history bore fruit the following year, when the city government sponsored an archaeological excavation of the site. The extent of what was uncovered forced a rethinking of all plans that would have permanently covered or destroyed what was there. In addition to the foundation walls of the old buildings along both Niederkirchnerstrasse and Wilhelmstrasse, the excavation uncovered several cells of the Gestapo jail.

These ruins could not be ignored, particularly since the Martin-Gropius-Bau was slated to host the main historical exhibition marking Berlin's 750th anniversary in 1987. Amid many other commemorative events, the city government agreed to sponsor a provisional exhibition on the history of the Prinz Albrecht site. A simple, temporary building was put up to house the exhibition, next to the Gestapo cells and only a few steps from the Gropius-Bau's entrance. While digging its foundations, workers unexpectedly found more ruins—of what turned out to be a previously unknown outbuilding used as a kitchen by the Gestapo. The cellar walls of this building were incorporated into the exhibition, "Topography of Terror," which opened without fanfare in July 1987.

The exhibition invited visitors to explore the overgrown site (figs. 39 and 40). Here and there signs explained to them what had once stood on the spot and what had gone on there. The

39
"Topography of Terror" exhibition building and grounds, 1995

small exhibition building presented a carefully documented explication of the authority exercised from the desks upstairs as well as the fate of prisoners in the cells below. As the exhibition's name suggests, it attempted to situate the legacy of the SS and Gestapo in the geography of Berlin and of Europe. Thus it documented the many activities of espionage, repression, and terror planned and directed from here, and it explained how the tentacles of the SS bureaucracy reached across the city and the continent. Photographs of selected prisoners were accompanied by explanations of their fate. These victims included Germans and

40
"Topography of Terror" exhibition, 1991. At the bottom the excavated foundation of the Hotel Prinz Albrecht can be seen; above it, the Berlin Wall. In the background is the former Reich aviation ministry.

foreigners, Christians and Jews, conservatives, socialists, and military officers, but also dissident Nazis such as Gregor Strasser, murdered here in 1934, and Communists, notably Erich Honecker, interrogated here in 1935.

By nearly all accounts, the modest exhibition was a resounding success. The organizers' emphasis on documentation rather than interpretation or judgment successfully avoided the usual controversies about understanding the Third Reich's role in German history. Within the following year, the duration of the temporary exhibition was extended twice. The second extension was for an indefinite period, making the exhibition in effect a permanent one, although still in temporary quarters. It continued to draw three thousand visitors weekly and to be effusively praised—in the comment books at the exhibition, and in the local and international press.

Although both the exhibition's building and its administrative status remained provisional, by 1989 a broad consensus opposed any substantial alteration or development of the site. This consensus was enshrined in the report of a commission appointed by Berlin's government in February 1989. Most of the commission's members were well-known advocates of the site's preservation, and their report underscored the lessons that had emerged from years of heated debate. Above all, they had persistently argued that this place was fundamentally different from other Third Reich sites—from places of killing, like Plötzensee and the concentration camps, and from places of resistance like the Bendlerblock. Many victims had suffered here, and they could and should be honored. But this was a place of perpetrators more than of victims. The exhibition's central goal, therefore, should be to document the perpetrators' deeds and promote understanding of how these crimes came to be committed by the leaders of Germany.

No one openly contradicted this conclusion. Yet the distinction between honoring the victims and remembering the perpetrators has proved to be a major sticking point. As we have seen, Germans have long been willing to acknowledge the Nazis' opponents and victims in their midst. There has been much less interest in learning about those who persecuted these opponents and victims. After all, most Germans at the time were not arrested by the Gestapo and did not actively oppose the regime; indeed, most supported it. This is the uncomfortable fact that has to be confronted when looking at Himmler, Heydrich, and their thousands of employees. As Gerhard Schoenberner, chairman of the Active Museum organization, put it: "This is not about the 'evil Gestapo or SS,' who are often and conveniently seen as people from Mars who attacked and invaded a peaceful Germany."[27] The "Topography of Terror" approached the connections between Nazi repression and German society by examining the terror's geographical embeddedness in Berlin. The point of the exhibition was to confront the painful truths about the extent to which the Gestapo and SS controlled and corrupted the entire German government and most of the society.

But this approach has always met with subtle resistance. For example, the first official move to acknowledge the site came in 1982 when the opposition Social Democratic Party proposed a memorial for the victims as well as a center for exhibitions and documentation. When its resolution passed the city's parliament later that year, however, only the proposed memorial to victims remained. This step came, of course, after decades of complete neglect of the site, and it was followed by further years of uncertainty. Do the delays and opposition reflect many Germans' conscious desire to emphasize the good in their national past, or are unconscious forces at work, repressing feelings of guilt or shame? Both have been alleged; both have probably played a role. But neither repression nor an emphasis on the positive have succeeded in quelling the debate about Germany's Nazi past, the "past that will not pass away." It is now clear that destroying the buildings on Prinz-Albrecht-Strasse and covering their foundations neither obliterated the memory of them nor enabled Berliners to come to terms with their own history.

The commission in 1989, then, agreed that the ruins should be preserved, displayed, and explained. It recommended displays that encouraged active confrontation with the past. That meant keeping the existing "Topography of Terror" exhibit and adding facilities to provide access to more extensive documentation and to support public education, discussion, and research. The bulk of the site would remain untouched: no buildings, no landscaping, no beautification. This meant that the recently excavated walls would remain visible and unaltered. It also meant leaving the evidence of forty years of postwar neglect: nothing would be reconstructed; the shrubs and trees that had grown around the driving lanes would remain; and two large piles of earth left by the construction firm would also remain—incidentally offering a panoramic view of the entire area.[28]

While the commission was completing its work in late 1989, the context of the Prinz Albrecht site changed suddenly and profoundly. Already during the course of the previous decade, this part of West Berlin had ceased to be a forgotten wasteland, with the restoration of the Gropius-Bau and the redevelopment of many nearby blocks. But it had remained a marginal area as long as the Berlin Wall blocked Niederkirchnerstrasse, just a few steps from the newly excavated foundation walls. With the opening of the Wall in November 1989, this suddenly became a central location. The fact that it bordered on Wilhelmstrasse once again became significant: here was the southern edge of the old government quarter. Directly across the street was the largest building of that quarter, Göring's aviation ministry. Next to it, facing the Gropius-Bau, was the former Prussian House of Deputies, a century-old building that soon became the home of Berlin's municipal parliament. This, in short, was—or could be—prime real estate.

It is probably of great importance that the consensus in favor of preservation had emerged by 1989. It had been much easier to agree that history forbade any normal use of the land when the land was of little value anyway. The fall of the Wall delayed and complicated the planning for the site, but the basic decisions remained unchanged. After all—as several supporters of the "Topography of Terror" pointed out—the unification of Germany and the return of the capital to Berlin made it all the more certain that the world would be watching how the Germans come to terms with the darkest chapter of their history.

To act on the commission's recommendations, the Berlin government eventually turned to its favorite device—a design competition. In 1992, it invited twelve architectural firms to submit designs. They faced the difficult task of leaving the land largely untouched while providing an expanded, permanent exhibition space, plus a scholarly center to make available documents on Nazi terror, and facilities for international meetings on Nazi crimes and their present relevance. The winning entry, by the Swiss architect Peter Zumthor, proposed a narrow building of unadorned concrete and glass that drew the judges' praise for its unobtrusiveness: the site itself, not the building, remained the monument.

The small staff that had established and guided the Topography of Terror exhibit welcomed the new facilities, but they feared that Zumthor's building, four stories extending across the center of the site, might still be too much of an architectural gesture. Fundamental to their conception of the exhibit is its integration into the city. Unlike the Wannsee villa, it is centrally located, near or on the way to many other destinations. As the center of reunified Berlin is developed, the "open wound" of the Prinz Albrecht land stands out all the more, an intentional irritant and a lasting reminder of this bustling city's troubled past. Therefore, it was important that the ruins and the weeds, not the building, dominate the place. Otherwise the result might be too much like a traditional museum—a formidable place of serious culture and learning, to be approached with trepidation. It is supposed to attract visitors who have not planned to visit and passersby who are unaware of the exhibit's existence.

By 1995, when the Topography of Terror Foundation was put on a permanent footing, the "provisional" exhibition had drawn hundreds of thousands of visitors and had in some ways thrived on its temporary status. The long absence of any definitive design or organization forced Berlin's government and its cultural leaders to continue agonizing over the site for more than a decade. The combination of modest exhibition and lingering debate confronted the Nazi past more effectively than any "active museum" or any definitive plan for an "open wound."

If this confrontation has taught clear lessons about Berlin's Nazi past, however, the exhibition does not tell visitors what they are. It remains a "documentation" of the site and of the crimes committed here; its purpose is not to tell visitors what to think, but to inform them and encourage them to think for themselves. The result is bound to be a certain amount of confusion, since visitors probably assume that any ruins deliberately exposed in the center of a city carry great significance. Contrary to expectations, however, neither the foundation walls visible along the former Prinz-Albrecht-Strasse nor the cellar under the exhibition building housed prisoners. In fact, the Gestapo jail cells were covered up with sand in 1989 because they had rapidly deteriorated while exposed to the elements. They will remain invisible until plans are developed to protect them better.

Some sympathetic observers, including the former city archaeologist Alfred Kernd'l, complain that the effect is to divert attention from an authentic historical monument. But the exhibition's organizers do not want to present a selective history of the place. For example, they have insisted that the memory of forty years of unaesthetic neglect be preserved. For them, an important part of the site's history—and German history—is the generation that tried to ignore and forget what had happened here. To return the land to its appearance as of 1945 would thus be a falsification of history. As the writer Günter Grass put it in a public discussion of the site: "A part of the history of these crimes is naturally the period of forty years and more during which memories were suppressed, because the manner of suppression helps to explain the causes of the crimes."[29] But the exhibit's subtle effort to underscore this point is lost on most visitors. Even thoughtful visitors have gone home and written that the mounds of dirt are rubble left over from the war.

Since 1989, the thinking of planners as well as visitors has been further complicated by the presence of an additional set of ruins—those of the hacked-up Berlin Wall. The corner of Niederkirchnerstrasse and Wilhelmstrasse thus marks the intersection of two fierce debates about ruins in Berlin. During 1990, East and West Berlin's preservation authorities hastily agreed that the stretch of Wall between the aviation ministry and the Prinz Albrecht site would be one of those saved from immediate destruction, and they fenced it off to prevent further damage.

Since then visitors have been able to contemplate a striking sight here. Standing by the Gropius-Bau, they see two sets of ruins that arguably embody the essence of their respective states: on the right, the place where bureaucrats planned terror and genocide; on the left, the German Democratic Republic's most famous creation and most terrible obsession, without which, as it turned out, the Communist state could not survive. Here, one might proclaim, lies the end of two dictatorships.

But, warns Kernd'l, these were two very different dictatorships. Even while the Wall was intact, some visitors to the exhibit had gone away thinking that Hitler had built the Berlin Wall. Others had assumed that the entire exhibit was directed at the regime hiding behind that Wall. This conflation of the Third Reich and the GDR was a product of the Western theory of totalitarianism which, during the Cold War, equated Nazis and Communists. Many German conservatives saw nothing wrong with doing so. Most supporters of the Topography of Terror exhibit, however, whatever their opinions about the GDR, opposed any effort to equate it with the Third Reich and thus detract from the exhibition's attempt to measure the unique horrors of the Nazi regime. Kernd'l thought that the stretch of Wall should be removed in order not to "relativize and therefore dilute the crimes of the Nazis."[30] More rigorous preservationists, however, saw the Wall—and the division of Germany—as a part of the site's history that deserved protection along with the other traces of the past here. Again we see the dilemma of an exhibition that proposes to stimulate thinking but not to direct it: the exhibition's organizers actually do have some ideas about right and wrong interpretations of their material, but they want visitors to find the right answers on their own. Over the years, a recurring demand has been that the land "must be made to speak." But in the end someone must speak for it.

Hitler and the Holocaust Memorial

Theodor Adorno famously declared that after Auschwitz there must be no more poetry. What kind of a Berlin can there be after Hitler and the SS? Proposals to combine preservation with documentation—at the bunkers, the Bendlerblock, and the Topography of Terror—encouraged thoughtful and creative forms of interaction with the relics of the past, forms that would acknowledge the complicated tangle of memories and the multiplicity of meanings attached to a place. Advocates of these displays had no grand plan for a new Berlin, but they clearly understood what they did not want: a traditional commemorative monument. Not only would such a monument tend to focus on victims rather than perpetrators, it would also reduce the complex understanding of an urban site to a single aesthetic gesture. A work of art, in the form of sculpture, architecture, or landscape design, would leave the impression of a final statement that resolved the dilemmas and uncertainties of the site.

A traditional memorial, according to this thinking, presents itself as a closed book, inviting observers to dissociate themselves from the past that is being remembered. The authors of a 1983 study of the Prinz Albrecht site made this point with vehemence:

> The place of terror and of forgetting must become a place of awareness and confrontation. That certainly cannot be achieved with a "monument" in the nineteenth-

> century tradition. Characteristic of a monument is the reduction of a complex development to a single aspect that the monument's sponsors have identified as the most important. Such a monument is thus the result of a selection; it prevents the observer's own confrontation with the complex historical event. Insofar as the monument narrows one's perception and dictates the conclusions one draws from it, it is authoritarian.[31]

In other words, a monument can obscure an urban and historical context and replace a rational search for understanding with an emotionally gripping symbol. Most Berliners committed to a deeper examination of the Nazi past feared that symbolic gestures encouraged the very nationalism exploited by the Nazis, from which, they believed, Germans could only be liberated by the tools of reason.

The activists who had been grappling with the Prinz Albrecht site soon saw the specter of just such a "nineteenth-century" monument. In 1988, a new initiative led by the television talk-show hostess Lea Rosh proposed building an enormous memorial to Jewish victims of the Holocaust there. Supporters of the Topography of Terror won out against her, but the fall of the Wall opened up new possibilities in East Berlin, and Rosh chose the site of Hitler's chancellery for her memorial. She and her group, Perspektive Berlin, organized a vigorous publicity campaign, enlisting prominent names from business and politics, and in 1992 gained the approval of the federal and municipal governments.

If it is built, this truly monumental project, not the Topography of Terror, will be Berlin's grand urban response to the Third Reich. A design competition in 1995 attracted 527 entries, most of which sought to fulfill the spirit of the project by proposing gigantic symbols that would dominate the five-acre site. Among the entries were enormous ovens, towers, boxcars, and stars of David. Rosh's personal favorite emerged as the winner. It envisioned a slanted concrete slab larger than two football fields, covered with granite plates containing the engraved names of the 4.2 million identified Holocaust victims. The sheer size of it beggared the imagination, including, apparently, the imagination of Chancellor Kohl, who quickly vetoed the design as too monstrous and too controversial. He declared that no memorial should be approved without a broad consensus of support, a stipulation that could effectively sabotage a project he had long supported: a broad consensus on a German Holocaust memorial is scarcely imaginable.

In 1988, Rosh declared that it was time for Germany to follow the lead of other nations that had established central memorials to the Holocaust. She rejected the attempts to draw attention to the perpetrators, arguing that such an approach ignored the Nazis' victims. She also opposed all efforts to widen the definition of Nazi victims; this would be a memorial to the Jews. Rosh's ally, the distinguished historian Eberhard Jäckel, presented a sound historical argument for this exclusivity: "the murder of the European Jews was the essential goal of National Socialism."[32] Opponents questioned whether this justified a memorial to Jewish victims, as opposed to some kind of attention to their killers. But Rosh managed to override all objections, thanks in part to her unwavering self-confidence in an area—the relations between Germans and Jews—where everyone else is plagued by doubt and suspicion.

The decision to build a central memorial to victims led, perhaps inevitably, to an unseemly squabble among the victims. Representatives of the Roma (Gypsies) argued that the extermination of their people must not be separated from that of the Jews. After an ugly debate in which each side invoked Nazi racial categories to characterize the Third Reich's treatment of the two groups, the Roma were promised their own memorial, although city leaders disagreed about whether it should be nearby or at the suburban location of a former Gypsy prison camp. Roma leaders, in turn, declined to share their memorial with homosexuals or Communists, who, they argued, had not been persecuted for racial reasons. Soon skeptics began to raise the specter of a landscape of segregated victims' memorials.

Perspektive Berlin presented itself as the agent of memory; in making its case, it did not distinguish between opponents who feared too much remembrance and those who feared too little. It suggested the character of its detractors by including, in a publication, a statement from supporters of the Topography of Terror amid several anonymous and threatening letters it received from anti-Semites and fanatical nationalists.[33] In fact, the Active Museum led the opposition, arguing that a central memorial to victims was fine in Washington or Jerusalem, but that the land of the perpetrators had more pressing tasks of remembrance. Germany could honor its victims at dozens of concentration camps, including Sachsenhausen and Ravensbrück, both just outside Berlin and both sadly neglected. These were authentic places of victims, in other words, while the chancellery was an authentic place of perpetrators, where attention should be devoted to the causes of mass murder, not its effects. A memorial on a site closely associated with Hitler, the Active Museum argued, would seem to place responsibility for the Holocaust on him alone, and thus would serve to absolve other Germans.

The arbitrary location of the memorial was underscored by the fact that it is actually not the site of Hitler's chancellery or its bunkers, but rather lies a few steps away on the northern part of the old ministerial gardens, the former no-man's-land just south of the Brandenburg Gate. The available land above the bunkers had been allocated to the federal states for their Berlin offices; the nearby Holocaust memorial would commemorate the site's history, but only in a vague and approximate way. Alfred Kernd'l suggested that the ruins of the bunkers—slated for demolition—would attract more visitors than any artificial monument. He argued that it was scandalous to build a memorial in this historic place "as if nothing was there," while ignoring authentic ruins. His belief that the memorial served as an "alibi" rather than a place of real remembrance seemed to be confirmed by city officials' argument that the bunker had to go because it lay too near the proposed memorial.[34] And when the city building director, Hans Stimmann, wrote about the development of Potsdamer Platz, he assured his readers that all the gleaming new buildings did not mean that the city was trying to suppress memories of Nazi terror—as its approval of the Holocaust memorial showed.[35] The memories would not be suppressed, that is, but rather centralized at a convenient location.

How could an artist's design give form to Germany's need to remember the Holocaust? This was the skeptical question posed by those who saw Rosh's proposal as a "nineteenth-century" monument. Its massive dimensions, its detachment from any authentic site, and its lack of subtlety and paradoxical vagueness of purpose seemed to preclude any connection to the lives of Berliners and other Germans. Commenting on an earlier project, Dieter Hoffmann-Axthelm had feared that "reality disappears when art is put in its place." Whenever that most painful of legacies, the extermination of the Jews, is at issue, he added, "suddenly our society displays an unbelievable trust in art."[36]

Elsewhere in Berlin, smaller memorial projects sponsored by several districts in the 1990s have grappled directly with the question of how to integrate art and remembrance into urban life. These works, rooted in conceptual art, demand intellectual engagement and call attention to the complex conditions and processes through which Nazi Germany persecuted Jews and others. To commemorate the once-lively Jewish life around Bayerischer Platz, the district of Schöneberg chose a project by Renate Stih and Frieder Schnock. Throughout the neighborhood, they mounted eighty small signs that recall vanished street names, businesses, and cultural activities, and quote some of the petty and pernicious government regulations that systematically destroyed Jewish life between 1933 and 1945. In the district of Neukölln, an installation by Norbert Rademacher projects lighted explanatory texts onto a city sidewalk next to the long-forgotten site of a forced labor camp. In Steglitz, a slightly more traditional monument takes the form of a large reflective wall. The combination of its prominent location on a busy square and its detailed listing of the names and addresses of deported Jews obviously irritated residents: Christian Democrats and Free Democrats on the district council joined with the far-right Republican Party in 1994 to block the erection of the completed wall. An embarrassed city government had to overrule the district council in order to avoid a scandal that threatened to "damage Berlin's reputation far beyond the city."[37]

Advocates of these "countermonuments" feared that the effect, or even the purpose, of Rosh's central memorial would be to separate the events of the Third Reich from the collective memory of the city.[38] They saw it as a step backward, a large version of the all-too-harmless signs that have stood in two squares in Schöneberg since 1967. Each of these signs lists the names of ten (since 1995, twelve) concentration camps under the heading, "Places of terror that we must never forget." The signs, though they probably still shock some passersby, have long been mocked for the apparently arbitrary placement that makes them easy to ignore. If it is built, the new memorial will of course be far more impressive—at least in size—and will dominate its surroundings more effectively. But it will also be more permanent, a final statement rather than an invitation to discussion or interaction. Berliners quickly scorned the project as a "wreath-dumping place" *(Kranzabwurfstelle).* As a protest, Stih and Schnock entered the competition with a proposal to devote the land to a bus stop from which visitors could catch rides to the authentic sites of concentration camps.

In 1988, when Rosh's group first proposed its memorial on the Prinz Albrecht site, Berlin's opposition Social Democratic Party countered by suggesting that it be placed in front of the Reichstag to acknowledge the responsibility all Germans bore for the crimes committed. The idea received little attention and less support, but Rosh explicitly rejected it with reference to the inscription on the Reichstag's facade: "Did 'the German people' murder the Jews? Hardly."[39] Rosh presented her organization as a private initiative of non-Jewish Germans trying to make a statement on behalf of the German nation, a minority of which had carried out the Holocaust. Critics complained that Germany's victims were being used to make a nationalist statement, citing the group's declaration that "we Germans" not only "accept the burden of our history but we also intend to write a new chapter in our history." Rosh, a declared "antinationalist," was not a political ally of Helmut Kohl, but her opponents saw the same motive at work: the desire to end the postwar era, overcome the burden of the past, end the mourning, and make Germany a normal nation.[40]

This step is often and more abstrusely labeled the "historicization" of the Third Reich. Some see it as desirable, others as inevitable, still others as something to be resisted at all costs. The historians and artists who have so creatively engaged history in the city—in the Bendlerblock, the Topography of Terror, and elsewhere—generally see their work as contributing to a confrontation with the Nazi past that is far from complete. They use the power of place to make that past vivid, comprehensible, and inextricable from the lives of today's Berliners. In showing how thoroughly the Third Reich permeated the daily life of the city, their work implies that that era is far more than mere history.

Rosh's Holocaust memorial, standing apart from the visible remnants of Nazi Berlin, would offer a different message. Perhaps it should not be directly compared to these other, lesser memorials: it is larger, simpler, more palatable, and therefore likely to reach a far wider public. Most important, it eschews the relentlessly rational confrontation with the past in favor of a grand symbolic gesture. That does not guarantee that it will be built; it is, after all, remarkable enough that a nation contemplates building a memorial for its own crimes against others. If it is built, in whatever form, it will be condemned as an effort to repress the past, and praised as a gesture of coming to terms with the Third Reich, and will presumably represent some combination of the two.

It is clear that the traces of the past in Berlin's twenty-first-century cityscape will not tell a story of unblemished triumph. It is less certain how pride and admonishment will be balanced in presenting traces of the Third Reich. Through the attention given to unholy sites, those responsible for the new Berlin will be seeking to distinguish themselves from their unsavory predecessors. At the same time, however, they will be acknowledging as their own the legacy of twentieth-century Berlin.

The ruins of Berlin should be preserved as a modern Babylon or Carthage—as a memorial to Prussian militarism and the Nazi regime. The city is completely deserted. You can drive miles through smoking ruins and see nothing that is habitable. This city can never be rebuilt.[1]

—Air Chief Marshal
Sir Arthur Tedder, 1945

The Reichstag and the Chancellory are already sights for sightseers, as they might well be in another five hundred years. They are the scenes of a collapse so complete that it already has the remoteness of all final disasters which make a dramatic and ghostly impression whilst at the same time withdrawing their secrets and leaving everything to the imagination.[2]

—Stephen Spender, 1946

The symbols of the old Germany—the imperial palace in Berlin, the Hindenburg palace, Hitler's Reich chancellery, and the police headquarters—were destroyed in the Second World War. The men and women of the new Germany are clearing away the ruins of the old imperial Germany. From the ruins of the old Germany a new one arises.[3]

—Walter Ulbricht, 1951

Karl-Marx-Allee, Alexanderplatz, and the Lustgarten, once centers of urban life, today serve only as showcases for the government. They have been degraded to monuments of an authoritarian order whose models can be found in Moscow, Kiev, or Odessa.[4]

—Rolf Schwedler,
West Berlin Senator
for Construction and Housing, 1971

Five

Divided Berlin

Ruins

On September 15, 1994, workers excavating a construction site in eastern Berlin struck and detonated a World War II bomb buried in the ground. The explosion killed three people, injured seventeen, and blew an enormous hole in the wall of an apartment house next door. Berliners did not need such a cruel reminder that memories of the war lurk in the depths of their city. Fifteen thousand unexploded bombs (by one estimate) remain buried somewhere in Berlin, threatening at any moment to make a mockery of a writer's metaphors about an "explosive" past.[5] The legacy of the war makes itself felt in more subtle ways as well. Half a century after its end, and years after the division it spawned has been overcome, Hitler's war remains the event that has defined and shaped Berlin.

May 1945 was supposed to be "Stunde Null"—zero hour. It was easy to believe that all of Prussian and German history had been wiped away in the purgatory of the final war years. Trying to cope with night after night of bombing raids and fires, Berliners and other Germans had few thoughts to spare for ideologies, traditions, symbols, and abstract loyalties. And when it all stopped, Berliners emerged to face new uncertainties. How would they be treated by the foreign troops at whose mercy they were? Where would they get food and water? In the coming months, their strength would be devoted to getting ration cards, looking for black-market food, planting vegetable gardens on balconies, and cutting down trees in the parks to heat their rooms. Whatever national pride lingered from the efforts of Hitler and Goebbels soon yielded to resignation or resentment.

Hitler was dead, the German armed forces had surrendered, and the German state had ceased to exist. So too, many people thought, had Berlin. Eighteen months of relentless Anglo-American bombing followed by days of a street-by-street Red Army advance had left behind a landscape of rubble (fig. 41). Tens of thousands of buildings had been destroyed, more were badly damaged, and hundreds of thousands of people had lost their homes. We think of riots, floods, earthquakes, or tropical storms as devastating to a city, but total war is far more thorough.

Ruins became the symbol of "zero hour" in Berlin, along with the ubiquitous "rubble women" who patiently cleaned and

41 Ifflandstrasse, near Alexanderplatz, 1949. Courtesy of Landesbildstelle.

stacked millions of bricks from thousands of smashed walls. Sentimental attachment to the ruins only came years later, when there were far fewer of them. In the late 1950s, when the West Berlin authorities proposed to remove the ruins of the Kaiser Wilhelm Memorial Church at the head of Kurfürstendamm, they were simply continuing the work they had begun a decade before. What was new was the public outcry in favor of preserving what was left of the church. The authorities yielded, and the church's shattered tower became one of West Berlin's landmarks, a lasting reminder of how much of the city looked in 1945.

In fact, however, ruins were not all that remained of the old Berlin. Even the best efforts of the British, American, and Soviet armed forces had not sufficed to wipe Berlin off the map: *most* of its buildings still stood, reparable if not intact. The photographs and film footage we often see of postwar Berlin understandably focus on the scenes of most utter devastation—which were not hard to find. In a perverse way, those who proclaimed Berlin a total loss were guilty of wishful thinking. They included reformers who had long wished to sweep away the city of Mietskasernen—that is, to correct the errors of nineteenth-century urban development. That reformist impulse was powerfully reinforced by the widespread desire to suppress all possible links to the capital of the Third Reich, whether that desire was motivated by revulsion at the Nazis or by a sense of guilt. Although the ruins were real enough, "zero hour"—and thus a new beginning—was more of a hope than a fact.

The desire to break with the past is most evident in the first and most ambitious of the immediate postwar plans. In the municipal government set up in 1945 under Soviet auspices, which comprised a broad coalition of antifascists, the prominent architect Hans Scharoun took charge of building and planning. He gathered a group of architects and planners whose "collective plan" of 1946 applied principles of urban modernism to the design of Berlin. For these planners, the destruction of the war offered the opportunity to cast off the shackles of the past and to create a new city adapted to the natural landscape of the Spree River valley in place of the haphazard historical accumulation of streets and buildings. The planners sought a decentralization and functional division of the city. That is, they envisioned the creation of many individual "cells," with a few thousand residents each. Separate industrial and commercial areas would likewise be set aside, and the entire urban region would be connected by a new and efficient network of road and rail connections. The "collective plan's" visionary urban design was intended to be democratic rather than hierarchical and thus to break with the German past in politics as well as planning.

In the long run, many parts of this modernist agenda profoundly influenced Berlin, as old tenements gave way to expressways, high-rise buildings, and satellite cities. But in 1945, the time for utopia had not come. Just as important as the many salvageable buildings was the presence of the urban infrastructure, much of it invisible below ground. These sinews of the modern city—water, sewer, and gas lines, street paving and subway tunnels—were more than 90 percent intact. A fundamental reorganization of the city would have required rebuilding these systems at enormous cost. Quickly, then, Berlin after "zero hour" had to acknowledge its physical heritage. The "collective plan" remained on paper, while planners after Scharoun salvaged what they could from the ruins. And with the practical uses of old buildings and streets came historical continuities and symbolic baggage.

Cold War Planning: Stalinallee

Soon postwar planning became hostage to international politics as well as German history. The Soviet blockade and Western airlift of 1948–49 hastened the division of the city into two separate administrative entities: one under the control of the Western allies and increasingly associated with the new West German state; the other, the Soviet sector, a de facto part (and the capital) of the new East German state. By the late 1940s, then, planners worked for one side or the other, and plans for the entire city—which continued to emerge from West Berlin—took on an air of fantasy. It was clear, not for the first or the last time, that both the economic and physical development of the city depended on decisions about its political status.

Berlin, as a city, only gradually split into two. During the Cold War, each side sought to free itself from dependence on or contamination by the other side, and thus faced the task of turning a half city into a whole and autonomous one. During the blockade, two separate administrative apparatuses established themselves and claimed jurisdiction over public services in their respective sectors of the city. After the blockade, contacts between East and West resumed, but in many cases only temporarily. In 1952, when the East German government sealed the border between East and West Germany, it further isolated West Berlin: the electrical grids were separated and the telephone lines were cut. The culmination of the schism came only in 1961 with the building of the Berlin Wall, which completely divided the city at ground level and left the public transit systems entirely separated.

Even then the two Berlins were not totally isolated from one another, but the extent of remaining contacts was very limited: postal service, a teletype connection between the police forces, telephone connections between the transit systems and the fire departments, Western subway lines that traveled under Eastern territory without stopping, a train system in the West operated by the East, Eastern water serving a few corners of West Berlin, and sewage flowing freely under the Wall wherever gravity so dictated. The result was a need for a few discreet technical discussions and an occasional skirmish over fees or sovereignty. The thaw in East-West relations around 1970 led to a resumption of telephone service, a few more opportunities for people to cross the Wall, and negotiations to share supplies of electricity, gas, and garbage.

The process of reattachment has been slow and complicated, in its practical aspects, its politics, and its symbolism. It began, of course, in every sense, with the breaching of the Wall in 1989. Since then the West has poured enormous sums of money into projects to reattach all those sinews that were severed: utility grids, telephone lines, surface streets, subway tunnels. These were the prerequisites for the routine human contact out of which, in turn, some renewed sense of civic community might grow. But there was much to overcome: not only expensive physical obstacles, but also the cultural gap between two cities that had gone their own ways for decades.

Before the Wall, Berlin had been a unique battlefield in the Cold War, where the ideological combat was hand to hand. Crackdowns on dissent in East Berlin had sent fear throughout the city: Westerners who criticized the GDR occasionally disappeared from West Berlin streets and reappeared in Eastern prisons. Meanwhile, Communists who lived in the West had discovered that it was they, not former Nazis, who were denied jobs and mistrusted as subversives. As long as the inner-city border was open, however, East and West Berliners at least shared many of the same complications in their lives. Here, for a time, East was West and West was East. For example, West Berliners at first saw little of the economic growth transforming West Germany. Well into the 1950s, the standard of living was not greatly different on the two sides of town: most people were fairly poor, and they did what they could to profit, legally or otherwise, from the juxtaposition of two currencies and two economies. It is also important to remember that in the postwar years, even after the airlift, many Germans took seriously the GDR's aspirations to be the "antifascist" German state, a place open not only to Communists but to all who wished to build a new Germany unlike the Third Reich. After the city government split, in fact, Scharoun and some of his associates at first continued to work for East Berlin. Neither they nor anyone else could have predicted the ways the Cold War would give new meanings to architectural forms.

It soon became obvious to everyone, however, that East-West competition would shape the planning of postwar Berlin. Neither side ever fully acknowledged the division of the city; the official view in East and West was that Berlin was one city and the other side was responsible for its unfortunate partition. Planners maintained direct contact until 1956 and thereafter upheld a certain unspoken cooperation, trying to avoid projects that would negate their counterparts' work, should the Wall disappear. In other words, both sides continued to some extent to plan as if Berlin were a single city—but as if that city were theirs. Each side's desire to appropriate urban traditions belied its claim to be making a fresh start. Paradoxically, then, while each German regime granted the other the honor of being the Third Reich's true successor, each nevertheless claimed the legacy of Berlin for itself.[6]

The West upheld more insistently the fiction of unity. In 1957–58, it sponsored an international competition to gather comprehensive plans for the entire city, plans intended to guide the process of returning the seat of government from Bonn to a reunified Berlin. The political dimension of this gesture was obvious, its practical effects negligible. As an exercise in architectural fantasy, though, it provided a showcase for Western ideas of modern, decentralized urban form, and its results were no

42
Europa Center (at center) and ruined tower of Kaiser Wilhelm Memorial Church, 1995

more ephemeral than those of many other Berlin architectural competitions.

After the Wall was built and these grand plans put on indefinite hold, Western investors turned their attention to the area around the Kaiser Wilhelm Memorial Church and the Kurfürstendamm, which was becoming the closest thing to a city center that West Berlin could offer. Since the officially recognized center lay in the East, this area became a genuine capitalist showcase: no obvious governmental presence, no serene palace gardens, few old buildings; instead, crowds of tourists, expensive shops, and cafés by day, and movies, discotheques, and prostitutes by night. Since 1965, the tallest building in the area has been the twenty-two-story glass box of the Europa Center, best known for the three-pointed Mercedes-Benz star that rotates on its roof (fig. 42).

The German Democratic Republic, founded in 1949, claimed Berlin as its capital but did not waste effort on plans extending beyond the Soviet sector that it controlled. Early plans emphasized development along an east-west axis extending eastward from the Brandenburg Gate. Here the continuity with the Third Reich (as well as earlier regimes) is obvious. Apart from the demolition of the royal palace, however, the historic center itself was at first neglected in favor of Friedrichshain, the devastated district just to its east. The centerpiece of the Friedrichshain project was an east-west boulevard, Frankfurter Allee, renamed in honor of Josef Stalin on his seventieth birthday in 1949. The first buildings on Stalinallee, built in 1949–50, were designed by Ludmilla Herzenstein, one of Scharoun's associates. They are long, unadorned, five-story blocks entirely in the German modernist tradition of the 1920s.

But an abrupt shift in architecture and planning followed during the course of the year 1950, as modernist architecture and functionalist planning acquired a taint of Western capitalist decadence. Soviet influence was decisive: the USSR under Stalin, which had rejected modernist experiments in favor of ornate monumentality nearly two decades before, was during these years building its most bombastic skyscrapers and subway stations in Moscow. East German politicians and architects certainly were familiar with this style. Even those who had not lingered in exile in Moscow could see the three major Soviet war memorials in Berlin, all of which had been completed by 1949, as well as the new Soviet embassy under construction on Unter den Linden. The relevance of these models became crystal clear in the spring of 1950, when the East German government sent a delegation of planners and architects to Moscow to confer with their Soviet colleagues. The lessons they brought back seem to have sealed the fate—for a while—of the architectural style represented by the 1920s housing estates scattered across East and West Berlin. According to the new official line, a capital city's design had to display centralization, hierarchy, and monumentality. In addition, since the GDR during its early years sought to unite all of Germany, the appearance of its capital city was supposed to reflect national traditions.

Walter Ulbricht, the East German Communist leader, took a direct interest in matters of city planning. The new policy clearly suited his wishes, and he helped to usher it in. In a speech at the Third Party Congress in July 1950, he accused unnamed municipal architects of wanting to diminish the significance of Germany's capital by rebuilding it with low buildings. In their "cosmopolitan fantasies," he continued, they believed that "one could build houses in Berlin that would be just as appropriate to the South African landscape."[7] The following year, the editor of the Communist Party newspaper denounced the practice of housing people in "egg cartons." These mass-produced boxes "are the natural products of the greed for profit and contempt for humanity of the dying capitalist system."[8]

In the Stalinist vocabulary, "formalism" and "cosmopolitanism" characterized international modernism and were antithetical to the victorious working class as well as the German nation. "Formalism," the opposite of "realism," meant an emphasis on pure artistic form to the exclusion of social and economic concerns. The charge of "cosmopolitanism" was an even stronger echo of Nazi polemics. For the Nazis "cosmopolitan" meant Jewish, which in turn often implied either Communism or capitalism, depending on the context. For the East German Communists the term connoted above all the leveling tendencies of American capitalism. They thought they could rescue their national culture, including its architecture, from the Nazis' clutches. The party newspaper, discussing the legacy of the Bauhaus, tried to explain the difference: "We must not be confused by the fact that the Nazis misused the people's healthy aversion to this American cultural barbarism for the chauvinistic purpose of inflaming a vicious agitation against the Communists, whom they blamed for these manifestations of degeneracy."[9]

The GDR officially welcomed "progressive" German traditions, which not incidentally underscored its claim to be building the capital of all Germany. In architecture, this policy opened the way for a conscious return to national and local styles—meaning above all the Berlin neoclassicism of Karl Friedrich Schinkel. By 1951, construction had begun on buildings in the new style, an amalgam of Schinkel and Stalin. Work on these seven-to-ten-story buildings on Stalinallee was divided among a half dozen of the GDR's most prominent architects. In sharp contrast to Herzenstein's plain gallery apartments, the facades of the newer and larger apartment buildings are generously proportioned, articulated vertically and horizontally, and profusely ornamented with classical detail (figs. 43 and 44). The bases are clad in stone and many are pillared. The stories above are faced with ceramic tiles from Meissen. In deliberately echoing the era before World War I, the buildings embodied the promise of a new society in which ordinary workers would enjoy the comforts of the old bourgeoisie.

Not only the architecture but the planning as well turned away from modernism. The "Sixteen Principles of City Planning" issued by the government in 1950 emphasized the political and visual importance of the city center, arguing against the modernist ideal of the decentralized city.[10] Stalinallee clearly demonstrates this return to classical and baroque traditions. It is laid

43
Karl-Marx-Allee, the former Stalinallee, 1991. One of Herzenstein's modernist buildings from 1950 is visible in center.

44
Detail of building on former Stalinallee, 1987

out as an immensely wide, tree-lined boulevard in the tradition of Unter den Linden or the Champs Élysées. The individual buildings, ostentatious as they are, function as walls enclosing the street, which is the center of attention (fig. 45). With space for stores, restaurants, and cultural institutions, it was intended to be a street for shopping and strolling as well as residence. The street's commanding presence is marked above all by the pairs of towers designed by Hermann Henselmann that frame each end of the grand boulevard. Henselmann (1905–95), a political chameleon who until 1951 had been a proponent of the modernist style, became the GDR's most famous architect and is often falsely credited with designing the entire Stalinallee.

The history of Stalinallee's reputation is a case study in the political interpretation of architecture. As Berlin became the

45
Former Stalinallee, looking east from Strausberger Platz, 1968. Courtesy of Landesbildstelle.

front line in the Cold War, the East was the first to present a clear urbanistic profile. A contemporary East German publication is stridently assertive even in its title: *Stalinallee—The First Socialist Street of the German Capital, Berlin.* It continues: "On the seventh anniversary of one of the heaviest terror attacks on the German capital by Anglo-American air gangsters, on February 3, 1952, Prime Minister Otto Grotewohl laid the cornerstone on Block E-South of Stalinallee for the buildings of the National Reconstruction Program in Berlin."[11]

Much of the ritual praise of Stalinallee thus made no reference to its particular style. The boulevard was the first step in the "socialist" reconstruction of Berlin and above all in the provision of new housing. (It is ironic, then, that the 1953 uprising began as a strike by overtaxed construction workers on Stalinallee.) The spacious and attractive apartments remained among the most desirable in East Berlin throughout the GDR's history. Most were allocated to those who had distinguished themselves in arts and letters, in resistance to the Nazis, or in rebuilding the city. They were not cheap to build—and that fact helped to guarantee that Stalinallee would remain a unique development. In 1954, the year after Stalin's death, Nikita Khrushchev began to speak out against Stalinist architecture. He criticized it above all on grounds of efficiency: the best way to house the masses, he argued, was to develop prefabricated industrial forms for apartment buildings. This line was quickly picked up by the East Germans, although construction of ornate Stalinallee buildings continued for several more years. For the East Germans, Khrushchev's critique conveniently coincided with the recognition that German unification was not imminent, which led to a marked de-emphasis on German national traditions, including architectural ones. By the end of the 1950s, unadorned concrete-and-steel apartment blocks were the rule in East Berlin. For example, the western part of Stalinallee, linking it to Alexanderplatz and thus to the city center, was built up with apartment houses in the new style during the early 1960s. These buildings were lined up in parallel rows, did not face the street, and contained only residences. In short, the "international style" of modern architecture had returned to East Berlin, only a decade after it had been condemned as decadent and dehumanizing. The change in style accompanied Khrushchev's program of de-Stalinization. The final symbolic steps were taken in 1961: the street was renamed Karl-

Marx-Allee; and one night the Stalin monument on it was removed, pedestal and all, leaving no sign by morning that anything had ever stood there.

During the 1950s, and long after, Western critics relentlessly pilloried both the architecture and the planning of Stalinallee. For the architectural modernists who held sway in the West, these buildings were the worst kind of overwrought kitsch. But their ugliness was political as much as aesthetic: they embodied the epitome of Communist centralization, regimentation, and false pomp.[12] It was easy to list the resemblances to Speer's work: the classical ornamentation influenced by Schinkel, the axial design, and the monumental scale of buildings and street. Even the streetlamps bear a striking resemblance to those designed by Speer and still found on the other side of the Brandenburg Gate. The point was clear, and usually explicit: Stalinallee revealed the essential similarity between the totalitarian systems of Hitler and Stalin (or Ulbricht).

After its style fell from favor in the East, the former Stalinallee ceased to attract much attention. It no longer offered a current ideological target; it lay just far enough from the center of East Berlin to be seen by few visitors; and it crumbled along with the rest of the city, as the Meissen tiles discolored and fell off. But a curious thing has happened since reunification: Western architectural critics have come to admire Stalinallee. Speaking in Berlin in 1993, the American architect Philip Johnson announced that even in the 1950s he had found Stalinallee to be "true city planning in the grand style."[13] The venerable Johnson, himself the chameleon architect of high capitalism, clearly saw a kindred spirit in Henselmann, his equally venerable contemporary who had negotiated the changing winds of Communist fashion. For the Italian architect and theorist Aldo Rossi, Stalinallee is "Europe's last great street." These postmodern architects, disillusioned with the formal purity of modernism, saw Stalinallee as a rare twentieth-century example of the kind of revival of urban decoration they aspired to—despite its Communist origins and despite its resemblance to Speer's work. (A few postmodernists, it should be noted, have sought to rehabilitate Speer's reputation as well.)

The day before German unification in 1990, the East Berlin government declared the entire former Stalinallee a protected historical landmark. Preservation, however, has hindered its adaptation to the capitalist world, at least in the short run. With garish new storefronts prohibited, the grand but shabby street attracted few new shops. Years after unification, its appearance remained little changed, an empty and quiet boulevard (apart from the cars of commuters racing by) with its old businesses closed or struggling to survive. It was an unattractive commercial location in part because the street's residents tended to have low incomes; many were pensioners who had lived there for decades and had no desire to give up their apartments. Another problem for shop owners was the fact that the enormously wide street included no parking spaces anywhere—a situation inconceivable in the West but temporarily frozen into place by the entire street's landmark status. Nevertheless, the street's architectural cachet has given it a bright future. West Berlin's planners have abandoned their Cold War grudges against the former Stalinallee. If the necessary financing appears and the compromises can be worked out with the preservation rules, they envision Berlin's "first socialist street" becoming a grand showcase of capitalist ostentation.

During the 1950s, West Berlin's leaders, scrambling to present a worthy alternative to Stalinallee, certainly never considered imitating it. They intended to present "free" Berlin (as opposed to the "democratic"—that is, Soviet—sector) as a clear alternative to Communism. The first grand Western project was the International Building Exhibition of 1957, devoted to the reconstruction of the Hansa Quarter, a neighborhood in ruins since the war and centrally located on the northwestern corner of the Tiergarten. The city commissioned internationally prominent architects (Le Corbusier, Gropius, Scharoun, Aalto, Niemeyer, and many others) to design individual low-rise and high-rise buildings scattered across the neighborhood—all more or less in the modernist style, none remotely resembling the ornate facades of Stalinallee. As a conscious counterpoint to Stalinallee, the design of the Hansa Quarter reflected a deliberate renunciation of axial orientation, centralized order, or anything that smacked of regimentation or totalitarianism (fig. 46).

Western politicians and architectural critics long praised the Hansa Quarter as the embodiment of Western liberal principles of freedom, individuality, and the nonauthoritarian order of democracy and the marketplace.[14] Unlike its crosstown rival, it never faced controversy; instead, it has faded into a comfortable obscurity. Many of the characteristics that set its design apart from Stalinallee—a parklike setting, individual buildings not oriented to one another, the separation of housing, shopping, and streets—caused it to fall from favor when the Mietskaserne, the street, the courtyard, and other aspects of traditional Berlin urbanity became fashionable in the 1980s. The Hansa Quarter shared a more practical problem with Stalinallee: contrary to its purpose, its construction costs were too high to make it a model for the tens of thousands of subsidized apartments that had to be built in the following years.

One might have expected the construction of the Wall to encourage a further divergence in urban form between East and West. Thanks to Khrushchev's initiative, however, the opposite happened. Buildings from the 1960s and 1970s in East and West Berlin are by no means identical, but to the outside observer the general resemblance is striking. A good illustration is a pair of intersections that might be said to mark the outer limits of Berlin's sprawling inner city: Ernst-Reuter-Platz in the west and Alexanderplatz in the east. Both acquired their current form

46
Hansa Quarter, 1962. Courtesy of Landesbildstelle.

mainly during the 1960s. Both are dominated by undistinguished high-rise steel-and-glass buildings. Although Alexanderplatz has long been closed to cars, whereas Ernst-Reuter-Platz is dominated by their movement, both vast squares seem windswept and desolate in a way that makes pedestrians want to hunch over and hurry across to their destinations. Neither place pleased the planning experts of the 1980s and 1990s. Ernst-Reuter-Platz is unlikely to see any significant change anytime soon, whereas planners intend to transform Alexanderplatz into a landscape of *new* skyscrapers—which some critics think will merely trade Eastern bleakness for its more lucrative Western equivalent.

The landscape of scattered towers at Alexanderplatz illustrated the GDR's new policies toward urban form as well as architecture. Its leaders had, not surprisingly, seen the 1957 Western planning competition for all of Berlin as a challenge to their authority. They countered in 1958 with their own competition for central Berlin that ignored the existence of West Berlin just as pointedly as the West had ignored the fact of division. Entries sought to achieve the centralization and monumentality that had been GDR policy since 1950. Specifically, the party leadership favored the creation of an urban focal point in the form of a large government building on Marx-Engels-Platz, the former site of the royal palace. The most controversial design, by Hermann Henselmann, proposed that the dominant structure there be a television tower. The Politburo promptly denounced the idea that the city's visual focus would be a symbol of modern technology with no specifically German or socialist characteristics. A decade later, however, technological modernity had become the East's accepted architectural language and a television tower based on Henselmann's design was in fact built. It stands northeast of Marx-Engels-Platz, near Alexanderplatz, and at twelve hundred feet, it is by far the tallest structure in Berlin. It became one of the best-known symbols of East Berlin, which inevitably meant that after reunification there were demands to tear it down.

Erich Honecker, who succeeded Ulbricht as party leader in 1971, never showed the same interest in city planning and introduced no dramatic new policies. Although he was responsible for building the Palace of the Republic on Marx-Engels-Platz, his priority was clearly the construction of badly needed new housing. Beginning in the 1970s, and continuing until his regime

47
Marzahn, 1991

collapsed, the GDR built enormous satellite cities of mid-rise and high-rise apartment buildings constructed with prefabricated concrete panels. One encounters their characteristically bleak appearance on the edge of every major East German city. By 1989, nearly a third of East Berlin's residents lived in its three satellite cities, Marzahn, Hohenschönhausen, and Hellersdorf. Marzahn alone has fifty-six thousand apartments (fig. 47). West Berlin, too, built satellite cities in the 1960s and 1970s, notably the Märkisches Viertel and Gropius-Stadt, but they are far smaller, and during the 1980s the West spent millions to give them a less monolithic appearance and to better integrate their buildings and residents into the city.

The satellite cities represent one of the GDR's most substantial bequests to the new Berlin, in terms of both social and physical presence. Most Westerners find them ugly, and after reunification some demanded that they be demolished—a completely impractical idea in a city already suffering a housing shortage. Westerners made the false assumption that such complexes were slums inhabited by the dregs of society. In fact, their apartments had been eagerly sought and well liked by skilled workers and professionals. However, there is considerable reason to worry about the future of these districts in a "free," capitalist society. Their smooth functioning depended on several conditions that quickly disappeared after 1990: full employment, a broad range of state-provided social services (especially child care and youth activities), and a society in which cooperation among neighbors was taken for granted. If these satellite cities continue to deteriorate into ghettos of unemployed adults and disaffected youth, plagued by crime and vandalism, Westerners will be all the more inclined to curse the GDR authorities who built them, but Easterners will see the problem differently.

The GDR's Monuments

East Berlin contained hundreds of memorial plaques put up by the GDR, as well as dozens of stone and bronze monuments. Everyone in East Berlin encountered some of these either in daily life or in official ceremonies. The GDR worked hard to make its memorials a part of its people's consciousness and identity. The design and placement of monuments in the GDR was planned at the highest levels of government. The great majority of them clearly fit into a political program intended to stamp Berlin with the image of the socialist state. Most commemorated personages or events in the history of the workers' movement, "antifascist" resistance, or the GDR. When the GDR ceased to exist, the fate of its monuments became a measure of the new Germany's success in supplanting the old one.

In contrast to government buildings or the Wall, statues and memorials would seem to be simpler and purer symbols. They are what we normally think of as "monuments," as opposed to the practical structures whose symbolic meaning is intertwined with their mundane functions. But statues and memorials also stand in urban space, and their location, size, and form all color their message. It quickly became clear that a Lenin monument, for example, was in the minds of Berliners not just a political statement but also a neighborhood icon, a repository of memories, or a vital piece of urban architecture.

The revolutionary enthusiasm that swept Eastern Europe at the end of the 1980s was directed against many a monument that symbolized the Bolshevik regime. But celebratory fervor in the divided city of Berlin took a different form. East German activists, less interested in symbols, seized the sprawling headquarters of the Ministry of State Security (Stasi), with its tons of secret records; they have since turned its main building into a museum. It was mainly West Berliners who engaged in acts of ritual destruction, and their target was the Wall, the GDR monument best known to them. Other monuments mostly escaped unscathed, leaving their fate to be decided by official deliberation. The first steps were taken during the GDR's final months by the democratically elected councils of East Berlin's districts. At least three district councils ordered the prompt removal of plaques whose offense was that their inscriptions carried the words and the name of Erich Honecker. At the time, everyone could agree in blaming the discredited former dictator for his regime. There was no consensus about where else blame might lie—with socialism, for example, or with other East German citizens—so Honecker became the scapegoat. Many West Germans saw a disturbing parallel to their own past, one captured by someone who defaced a poster on East Berlin's Alexanderplatz in 1990. The poster advertised a long-running West Berlin play whose title caricatured German denial of the Nazi past: "It's not me, it was Adolf Hitler!" The graffitist had crossed out "Adolf Hitler" and written in "Erich Honecker."

Since Honecker was still alive, however, there had been no Honecker monuments as such. When the city was officially reunified in October 1990, East Berlin still had a full complement of statues and memorials, although some had been vandalized. It was above all Western conservative politicians who wanted to ratify their triumph by sweeping away the Communist past—either by demolishing the monuments or removing them all to a park dedicated to the failure of Communism (as had happened in Budapest and Moscow). Their demand was expressed in the headlines of Germany's largest-circulation newspaper, the conservative and nationalist tabloid *Bild.* In an East German edition, it assured its readers that "everyone agrees" the "Red" monuments must go. "Everyone" in the article specifically included two Bonn politicians, a man from East Berlin, and a woman from Halle who was quoted as saying, "After the fortunate reunification I don't want to be constantly reminded of the forty terrible years of socialism."[15] This sentiment, first directed against the Wall, now condemned the monuments as further vestiges of a past best forgotten.

Certainly the question had to come up: it made sense to argue that the political postures of the Communist regime, even those carved in stone, had no place in the unified German democracy. But it was equally certain that these claims, when made by Western Christian Democrats, would arouse suspicion—first among their leftist opponents, then among "Ossis" who felt manipulated by the "Wessis." The demand to remove every monument erected by the poisoned hand of the GDR soon gave way to discussions about specific sites, and to a sometimes enlightening, sometimes nasty public debate about the monuments' meaning. In 1990 a group of art history students from East and West Berlin (mostly the latter) formed an "Initiative Politische Denkmäler der DDR" (Initiative on political monuments of the GDR) to promote public discussion and study of the GDR's monuments. Joined by the Active Museum of Fascism and Resistance, the group previously organized to preserve the Gestapo site, they sponsored an exhibition that showed the diversity of East Berlin monuments and the range of ideological, aesthetic, and historical motives that could argue for or against preserving them.

As the Active Museum's involvement suggests, impetus for this initiative arose out of the West German debate about the Nazi past. Advocates of removing the GDR monuments offered an analogy to the situation in 1945: no one then, and surely no one now, wanted the swastikas and Nazi monuments to stay in place. Western leftists, long allergic to the Cold War posturing that equated the "Brown" and "Red" dictatorships, argued that the Third Reich's unique crimes disqualified it from any comparison to the GDR. At the same time, many used the example of the Third Reich to draw a different lesson: Gestapo headquarters and other sites revealed how postwar West Germany had unwisely buried and denied its Nazi past, a mistake that would be repeated if all signs of the GDR were wiped away.

The best way to begin understanding the GDR's monuments is to look at the Soviet war memorials in Berlin. Their fate would be a matter of heated debate, were it not for the 1990 treaty in which the Soviet Union acquiesced to German unification. In the treaty, Germany pledged to preserve the numerous Soviet memorials. There are several in Berlin, three of them enormous, each containing the graves of thousands of Soviet soldiers. The first, completed before the end of 1945, is the best known because it stands in the former West Berlin, just west of the Brandenburg Gate. Westerners and tourists knew it well, although the British authorities kept them at a distance for many years after the Wall was built (which did not prevent a neo-Nazi from shooting and wounding one of its Soviet guards in 1970). With this memorial, the Soviets staked their claim to the historical landscape: within sight of the Reichstag, astride the former site of the Hohenzollerns' statue-laden Victory Boulevard, and at the point where Speer's north-south and east-west axes were to meet. The lesser-known memorial cemetery in Schönholz is

48
Soviet war memorial, Berlin-Treptow

much larger, however, and it in turn pales before the main Soviet memorial in Treptow (fig. 48). Here the visitor passes across an expansive landscape of memorial sculpture, including quotations from Stalin carved in granite. Its culmination is a thirty-eight-foot-tall figure of a soldier, standing on a pedestal high above the surrounding field. The soldier holds a sword in one hand and cradles a child in the other while trampling on a swastika.

This is a grand expression of heroism and triumph—a style

49
Lenin monument

the GDR's leaders embraced in the name of the antifascist German state, born of the alliance with Soviet antifascism. In glorifying the Soviet Union and the Communist resistance, the GDR's own memorials contributed both to the creation of indigenous traditions and to Cold War propaganda. Perhaps the best-known example was the sixty-three-foot-tall Lenin statue fashioned from blocks of Ukrainian red granite by the Soviet sculptor Nikolai Tomsky. Walter Ulbricht dedicated it on Lenin's hundredth birthday in 1970 (fig. 49). The statue was the focal point of a twelve-hundred-unit apartment complex based on a design by Hermann Henselmann—until the Berlin government decided in 1991 to remove it.

In late 1990, the city had cleaned the statue after vandals splashed it with paint. Why had it suddenly become important to bring down Lenin? The government presented itself as the instrument of the people's wrath, completing the revolution of 1989. Mayor Eberhard Diepgen declared that it was simply unacceptable for Berlin to honor this "despot and murderer."[16] Both parties in the new centrist coalition government, Social Democrats and Christian Democrats, approved the statue's removal. Surely, it seemed to them, only unreformed Communist fossils could disagree. The fact that the statue was a protected landmark caused a brief furor, but in the end the government simply revoked its landmark status. A legal challenge to this decision failed, as did another by Tomsky's widow and daughter.

As a sculpture, Tomsky's work earned at best grudging respect. More convincing aesthetic arguments against its removal came from those who pointed out that the statue was an integral part of Leninplatz and that its removal would leave behind a desolate square. Too many observers, however, judged the square to be already desolate and not worth preservation. In any case, aesthetic arguments swayed hardly anyone.

Nevertheless, opposition to the removal was growing. Both sides claimed popular support, and in particular the support of the neighborhood around Leninplatz. A radio station drummed up support for Lenin's removal and raised forty thousand marks to help pay for the demolition. Opponents countered with protest meetings and demonstrations. No doubt some of their support came from unreconstructed Leninists, but Lenin and Communism quickly became almost irrelevant to the discussion, as the *Berliner Zeitung* observed: "For opponents as well as supporters of demolition his statue has instead become the symbol of GDR history." The government was shocked to discover that its eagerness to wipe that history from the cityscape had become deeply divisive. In the words of one neighborhood resident, "For me it's not about Lenin, but rather about demonstrating our power and not letting ourselves be pushed around."[17]

The furor over the Lenin statue revealed the extent to which former East Germans were choosing between assimilation into West German society and insistence on a separate identity. The East Berlin representatives of the established West German parties tended to support Lenin's removal, but the defense of the granite Lenin became a rallying point for other Ossis who resented what they saw as a forced adaptation to West German ways. This new sense of Ossi identity within united Germany took form in various organizations, the most successful of which was the reorganized Communist Party, now known as the Party of Democratic Socialism (PDS), which exploited Ossi resentment to revive its fortunes.

The Lenin statue and, soon after, the Palace of the Republic became touchstones of Ossi resentment because they appeared to be clear cases of Wessis trying to claim that only the Federal Republic had represented postwar Germany. Some Easterners were happy to identify themselves with the Federal Republic, but many found it to be foreign and sought refuge in an Ossi identity. Monika Maron, a writer who had emigrated from East Germany only a few years before, was baffled by the latter group:

> Before, under Erich, the Thälmann monument was built, as was the Lenin monument, and the Palace of the Republic, which disfigured Unter den Linden. For reasons I find impossible to fathom, enormous numbers of people who call themselves Berliners designate these abominations of socialist art and architecture as monuments to their own identity. I always thought that a particular way of baking cherry pies or cleaning one's nose had more to do with identity than the urbanistic bungling of crazed dictators under whom it is one's misfortune to live.[18]

Most Westerners likewise found this Ossi identity unfathomable. The former symbols of Communist authority were becoming monuments to an ominous crack in the facade of German unity.

The issue of the Lenin statue grew into an enormous confrontation during the fall of 1991. Amid the various protests, opponents of its removal hired a crane to drape Lenin with an enormous sash reading "No violence!"—a decidedly non-Leninist slogan that recalled the peaceful East German revolution of 1989. The government's resolve held, but its final decision was to dismantle the statue rather than destroy it—revealing, according to one's point of view, a characteristic lack of resolve or a refusal to practice Leninist ruthlessness.

What followed was acutely embarrassing. The government found a demolition firm that promised to do the job in a week at a cost of one hundred thousand marks. When the statue's concrete core proved unexpectedly intractable, the contractor gave up. The government scrambled to find another firm and finally, after three months and five hundred thousand marks were gone, the enormous statue had been removed and its pieces put to rest in a gravel pit. In an apparent attempt to replace Communist solidarity with a new internationalist piety, Leninplatz was then renamed Platz der Vereinten Nationen (United Nations Square), and in place of the statue came a modest fountain consisting of boulders from all corners of the earth.

The Initiative Politische Denkmäler had wanted to make the point that monuments in both East and West were a form of political propaganda, a fact that should guarantee neither their preservation nor their removal. At the height of the Lenin controversy, members of the PDS and Green Party clearly wanted to make a similar point when they introduced a resolution in the municipal parliament demanding the demolition of one of West Berlin's most recognized landmarks, the Victory Column. (The same year someone planted a bomb in it.) The architect Heinrich Strack had been commissioned to design this monument to commemorate Prussia's victory over Denmark in 1864. Before it was completed in 1873, however, there were two more, greater victories to celebrate: over Austria in 1866 and France in 1871, the combined result of which was the creation of the German Empire under Prussian leadership. The sandstone column, inlaid with the barrels of captured cannons, stands on a base decorated with commemorative reliefs and mosaics and is crowned with an enormous golden victory goddess. It stood at the center of Königsplatz, by the Reichstag, until 1938, when it was moved a mile west to the Great Star in the middle of the Tiergarten. There Hitler and his planners intended it as a memorial to the lesser, preliminary glories of Bismarck's Second Reich. The Nazis acknowledged it as one of the principal monuments to Prussian military prowess.

Today the 220-foot column's imposing physical presence retains little connection to its origins as a victory monument. The goddess figures prominently, for example, in Wim Wenders's film *Wings of Desire,* without any militaristic connotations. In other words, despite the cannon barrels, the Victory Column has shed its militarist symbolism and become one of Berlin's least controversial monuments. It is usually noticed from afar or from passing cars and buses (fig. 50). Most of those who stop to visit it do so

50
Victory Column,
1995

mainly for the privilege of climbing 285 steps to view Berlin from its observation platform. Yet the parliamentary resolution in 1991 denounced it as a "symbol of German national self-importance, claims to imperial power, and the glorification of militarism and war." (Other leftists dissented, one of them arguing that it must remain as a "phallic symbol" and "expression of masculinity on the city skyline.")[19]

The major parties dismissed the resolution without debate. But for those who cared to listen, the point had been made: anachronistic monuments with dubious messages are not unique to East Berlin or the GDR. The Initiative Politische Denkmäler argued that by 1990, after the Cold War, monuments in both East and West should be judged for their historical rather than political value. Similar thinking lies behind the numerous recent proposals to plant vegetation in the paved ceremonial spaces around many GDR monuments, or even to grow ivy on the statues. These proposals represent deliberate attempts to preserve statues, affirm tradition, and at the same time turn politically defined urban spaces into something different.

After the public relations fiasco over Lenin, the Berlin government was eager to find face-saving compromises. In March 1992, it established an independent commission to study East Berlin's monuments, something it had promised to do a year before. The commission's membership was weighted toward East Berliners and preservationists, and after a year's work it issued a moderate and thoughtful report. After explaining the significance of the various monuments in the context of the GDR's interpretation of history, the commission recommended the outright removal of only a few monuments. In other cases it proposed alterations, particularly in the text of plaques. For example, it judged many commemorations of the antifascist resistance to be misleading in their emphasis on the Communists' role, but it concluded that most of these monuments were worth preserving.[20]

Among the monuments recommended for removal were those dedicated to border guards. Even these found a few defenders, but several arguments converged against them. The monuments had already been damaged by vandals, who presumably shared the widespread belief that these men were criminals, not victims or heroes. In addition, the typical language carved into the monuments was probably untrue as well as inflammatory: "treacherously murdered by members of the West Berlin police"; "treacherously murdered by fascist bandits from West Berlin."

In its most controversial recommendation, the commission approved the removal of the single largest East Berlin monument, the Ernst Thälmann memorial. Thälmann is an interesting figure for anyone attempting to understand the place of Communism in German history. He was unquestionably an opponent and victim of the Nazis: after eleven years in prison, he was murdered at Buchenwald in 1944. However, as chairman of the German Communist Party from 1925 to 1933, he presided over its transformation into a loyal instrument of Stalin, and his steadfast

51
Ernst Thälmann monument, 1991. Graffiti on the pedestal reads: "Don't you have it in a larger size?"

opposition to the Weimar Republic may indirectly have helped Hitler come to power. Yet this Stalinist can also be seen as a victim of Stalinism: evidence suggests that the Soviet Union could have bought his freedom but declined to do so.

Plans to honor Thälmann had been in the works since the late 1940s. For many years, the government planned to build a monument on Wilhelmstrasse across from the Reich chancellery's site. In 1979, however, the Politburo decided to make the Thälmann monument the centerpiece of a new housing complex in the northern district of Prenzlauer Berg. The party leadership—apparently Erich Honecker himself—rejected all the designs presented by East German artists as insufficiently monumental; Honecker then commissioned the Soviet sculptor Lev Kerbel. Kerbel's monument, unveiled in 1986, is a massive, forty-three-foot-high bronze bust of Thälmann, in a heroic style closely related to Tomsky's Lenin, which looked slim and elegant by comparison. Apparently Thälmann was even equipped with a heated nose to prevent snow from accumulating there. Like most major GDR monuments, it stands in a large paved square that was frequently used for official ceremonies. The square in turn is framed by trees and grass, behind which rise the high-rise apartment buildings of Ernst Thälmann Park. Thus the enormous statue dominates a vast space (fig. 51).

This superhuman figure had little to do with the man Ernst

Thälmann and a great deal to do with the image cultivated by the GDR's leadership. They fashioned a Thälmann who would serve the function that Lenin served for Stalin and his successors: the hero whose prestige and authority they inherited. They suppressed all portrayals of Thälmann as a suffering concentration camp inmate in favor of Thälmann as antifascist hero. The combination of historical falsification, authoritarian gesture, and bombastic design understandably made the statue unpopular after 1989. Thälmann the antifascist still had his defenders, although it was easy to dismiss them as lingering victims of Communist miseducation. On the other hand, the arguments against honoring his life sometimes took a form one is tempted to label anticommunist miseducation: *if* he had lived, wrote at least two conservatives, he would have become an oppressor of Germans.[21]

Despite all the sound arguments against the monument, the defenders of GDR traditions were too active by 1993 for the commission's recommendation to meet with universal acceptance. Many leftists and Easterners who had lost the battle over Lenin used the Thälmann case to revive their challenge to the establishment. The passage of time worked in their favor: after several years of united Germany, the Thälmann monument was on its way to becoming a historical relic of a past regime, perhaps worth preserving as a document of GDR political ritual. But the strongest argument in favor of keeping the monument, at least provisionally, was its size: no one was willing to pay for its demolition. Meanwhile, the accumulating graffiti around the statue's base made it clear enough that the heroic Thälmann no longer met with official favor. By 1995, three neatly stenciled words higher on the pedestal commented on the fate of the man and his monument: "Imprisoned—murdered—besmeared."

A degree of diversity in GDR political monuments is apparent when we look at a work contemporary with the Thälmann memorial: Marx-Engels-Forum. It better illustrates East German sculptors' treatment of an urban space—a style the GDR leadership rejected when it chose Kerbel to design the Thälmann monument. Marx-Engels-Forum, too, is the product of many years of deliberations and changing plans, but in this case the result was different: a less bombastic sculpture in a far more prominent location.

After the royal palace was demolished in 1950, plans called for an enormous memorial to Marx and Engels on its site, which had been renamed Marx-Engels-Platz. Eventually, however, the royal palace's former location at the eastern terminus of Unter den Linden was given over to the more modest Palace of the Republic. Marx-Engels-Forum, only completed in 1986, is separated from Marx-Engels-Platz by the Spree and the Palace of the Republic. It marks the western end of a swath of open space that extends the entire width of medieval Berlin; at the opposite end is the television tower. This area was a densely built-up neighborhood from the Middle Ages until 1945, but only the forlorn medieval church of St. Mary remains as evidence of what once stood there. Because this open space lacks a historical identity, it is frequently and inaccurately identified as Alexanderplatz, which in fact lies behind the elevated train tracks just northeast of the television tower.

Marx-Engels-Forum comprises an ensemble of sculptures by several artists intended to illustrate the triumph of Marx and Engels's "scientific socialism." Across an expanse of two hundred feet, historical progress is arranged as a kind of pilgrimage route from west to east. At the western end, a white marble wall is carved with reliefs illustrating the suffering of the oppressed. The opposite end is marked by bronze reliefs of human figures intended to show the happiness of life under socialism. The central statue of Marx and Engels (by Ludwig Engelhardt) thus marks the passage from the former to the latter. The paths to the central statue are framed by steel pillars into which photographs illustrating the history of the workers' movement have been etched.

Although the bronze figures of Marx and Engels are twice life size, they are accessible at ground level, as is the entire complex, which one can enter on paths from several directions. The figures of Marx and Engels reinforce the impression of undemonstrative and unheroic design. Marx sits and Engels stands; both are gazing to the east, but neither makes any gesture of triumph or militancy (fig. 52). Their static postures and their unruffled clothing make them appear strikingly stiff and passive, which is probably why they acquired the unofficial and irreverent nickname "the Pensioners." According to another typical East Berlin folk explication of the statue, they are sitting on their suitcases and waiting for permission to emigrate. Unification in 1990 did not put an immediate stop to the humor: for months the pedestal bore the spray-painted declarations "We're not guilty" and "Next time everything will be better."

52
Marx-Engels-Forum. In the background is the Palace of the Republic.

In the 1990s, a steady stream of tourists wander across the site and stop to look at the various sculptures. Many probably recognize Marx and Engels; others might identify the history of the workers' movement as the general theme of the photographs; but hardly anyone without prior knowledge will apprehend the entire conception of the monument. What visitors do implicitly grasp, however, is the nonauthoritarian design that invites wandering and touching rather than a transfixed gaze. Marx's lap is a popular spot to have one's snapshot taken. It is precisely the lack of heroic monumentality that led the special commission to recommend keeping the sculptures in place, despite all objections to such prominent honors for the two socialists. The ensemble functions more as public sculpture than as political statement. As the commission observed, for example, the bronze and marble reliefs appear as dynamic human figures, not political allegories.

The fact that this site was not a park before 1945, however, puts its future in jeopardy. The many expropriated former owners have a legal right to claim their property. That includes those whose land was taken by the GDR; but some of them, in turn, acquired their property from Jews who were forced out in the 1930s, and *their* heirs can also stake claims. Here, as in many other places in the former GDR, it will be years before due compensation is paid and legal ownership of the land is clearly established. At that point Marx and Engels might have to move elsewhere, if the land is to be built on again. Meanwhile, they are likely to enjoy years of placid retirement.

The differences between the Thälmann monument and Marx-Engels-Forum reveal the plurality of GDR traditions. Although Marx-Engels-Forum claims to illustrate the triumph of socialism, its modesty may be cited in future histories as evidence of the decline of East German Communism. Thälmann and Lenin, by contrast, clearly stand in a tradition imported from the Soviet Union—one embraced by the GDR's leaders more than its artists. This heroic style was foreign to the West in the second half of the twentieth century. No one of any political persuasion would contemplate a monument to Helmut Kohl even remotely resembling that to Thälmann—or, for that matter, resembling the colossal Bismarck statue that towers over Hamburg harbor. In the West, we associate triumphal monuments with the nineteenth century. We might see the Soviet-style monuments either as anachronistic relics of that bygone era (like Marxism itself) or as evidence of a historical optimism the West has lost—or perhaps as both.

It would be too simple to dismiss this optimism as a Soviet import that disappeared when the Soviets' puppet state collapsed in 1990. The GDR's official identity as an antifascist state has bequeathed its former citizens a very different disposition toward the Nazi past. That fact is bound to create tensions as long as the treatment of the Third Reich remains as explosive an issue as it has long been in the Federal Republic, which did not pretend to make such a clean break with the Nazis. The West did link its identity to anti-Nazis such as the men of July 20, 1944. But its monuments commemorated them and others as suffering victims, not conquering heroes. Differences in the iconography of memorial sculpture in East and West reveal a divergence in attitude that goes beyond political programs. West Germany was a land of victims, East Germany a land of heroes.

Another genre of cultural production—popular histories of Berlin—helps illustrate the different political cultures of East and West. The GDR published a series of histories of nineteenth- and early-twentieth-century Berlin written by Annemarie Lange.[22] They are written in a lively style and filled with witty anecdotes about rich and poor, the famous and the obscure. They present a grand narrative that integrates the history of Bismarck and the Kaiser with that of factory workers and the corner pub. Though filled with stories of suffering and political repression, their tone is relentlessly optimistic. They offer clearly identifiable heroes—the right kind of socialists and revolutionaries—and villains, and the eventual triumph of the former is not in doubt. West German histories of Berlin written for a similarly broad audience are narrowly focused on either diplomacy and politics or artists and intellectuals; books about neighborhoods and popular culture, of which there are many, usually lack any larger context of politics or historical development. Although the Lange books were widely distributed in West as well as East Berlin, Westerners found it difficult to see history as a story of progress or triumph.

In barely perceptible ways, the West saw the East as an exciting, exotic, disturbing political culture. Westerners object to falsifications of history in the Eastern monuments, and they accuse the monuments of honoring immoral causes, but the nature of their message is disturbing in a more general way. Westerners, but especially West Germans, sense that this kind of historical confidence leads to Auschwitz and the Gulag. Yet it arouses a certain envy as well—at least on the part of architects and urban planners. Philip Johnson, who harbored fascist sympathies in the 1930s, presumably sensed the fulfillment of an architect's dream when he saw Stalinallee and concluded, "Here is a culture with architectural ambitions." He lamented that the postwar West—and united Berlin in the 1990s—had nothing comparable to offer.[23]

When unification came in 1990, the monuments that remained in East Berlin told a story that Westerners found either meaningless or false. Their essential foreignness, from the point of view of Western intellectuals, is explained by Annette Tietenberg, one of the organizers of the Initiative Politische Denkmäler, commenting on the fight over the Lenin monument:

> The naiveté of their claim to meaning and power makes the monuments of the GDR so fascinating. Where else does the direct, frank representation of power appear so openly? The simplicity of the semiotic system eludes all postmodern and deconstructivist models. This art is neither self-referential nor ambiguous. Only those who still believe in objectivity and truth, who are entirely free of doubt, need defend themselves against Lenin statues. For

all others, the Lenin monument was a relic of times gone by.[24]

There are, of course, people in the West who claim to believe in objectivity and truth. They tend to be the same conservatives whose bitter anticommunism was fueled by a conviction that they had a better idea. They hated the Lenin monument as a threat to their principles and to their victory in the Cold War.

We can only guess at how long the GDR monuments will remain controversial presences. In the future they may, like baroque palaces, be admired as products of a bygone era. For the same reason, hatred for Communist dictatorship may not translate into hatred for the monuments it left behind. Cities everywhere are filled with monuments that do not express the views of the current government or the current population. A new regime—as the united Berlin government is, at least in the East—can choose to demolish monuments as a symbolic act, or it can let them fade into the cityscape along with the nineteenth-century statues that now only catch the attention of pigeons. GDR monuments that are not demolished soon may become invisible, or they may, like the Victory Column, become Berlin landmarks.

The Politics of Street Names

The process of naming brings order and meaning, but it also brings power, as has been clear since Adam. So it is not surprising that names would also be the object of power struggles in Berlin. Street names are among the most obvious elements of a city's historical identity. Compared with more tangible elements of the urban landscape, they can be changed easily and cheaply, which makes them tempting targets for politicians eager to make a symbolic gesture. But symbolic gestures divide Berliners more than they unite them, so decisions about street names arouse their deep suspicions about one another.

The GDR used the power of naming in many ways, renaming schools, for example, and even entire cities, notably Chemnitz, which became Karl-Marx-Stadt (and is now Chemnitz again). It also left its mark on the street map of East Berlin. In 1950 the government renamed a great number of streets whose names were deemed "militaristic, fascist, or antidemocratic"; a second wave of renaming followed in the 1970s. As with monuments, here too reunification brought demands to remove all traces of the Communist state. The wish to forget the past motivated East Berliners to write to their new city government and ask that all these names be changed back, "so that we are not continuously and painfully reminded of the forty lost years," in one citizen's words. To leave the names would be to acknowledge the legitimacy of the Communist regime, which deserves no such honor, argued another. And a third wrote: "With the return address Leninallee one is, even outside Berlin, still perpetually recognizable as an East Berliner—and who wants that?"[25] Leninallee has indeed been renamed in the meantime, but the change has not necessarily made the letter writer indistinguishable from a West Berliner.

Christian Democrats from West Berlin also demanded that all the GDR's name changes simply be rescinded. Conservatives argued that if there is no longer an Adolf-Hitler-Platz, there should be no Wilhelm-Pieck-Strasse. This was the position of a Christian Democratic member of the Lichtenberg district council as he argued to restore the prewar names of eight streets named after antifascists: "Communists or fascists, in the end they're the same."[26] Opponents (who won the vote) threatened to sue him for defamation.

Whatever the GDR's motives, many of those it had honored with street names still enjoyed public sympathy. Like the GDR's monuments, its street names typically honored antifascists (most but not all of them Communists), with smaller numbers of streets named after figures associated with the early workers' movement and, in later years, deceased GDR politicians (many of whom were also honored as opponents of the Nazi regime). The names of Communists were bound to be controversial after 1989, but what about the architect Bruno Taut or the German-Jewish writers Heinrich Heine and Kurt Tucholsky? Or early socialists like August Bebel and Ferdinand Lassalle, honored by Western Social Democrats as well as Eastern Communists? Proposals to remove their names from street signs had little chance of success.

By 1991, the idea of automatically revoking all GDR names was dead, but the Christian Democrats still hoped to put through a long list of name changes all at once. Unfortunately for them, the power to name streets lay with the city's twenty-three district councils, and the increasingly unhappy East Berliners blocked many of the proposed changes. Christian Democratic leaders then demanded that the districts be stripped of their control over street names, leading Easterners to ask: Who are the supporters of democracy here? Subway stations, usually named after streets or squares, were a different matter. They were in the hands of the municipal transit authority, which changed the names of several stations to remove references to streets that West Berlin leaders considered an embarrassment.

The Christian Democrats' list of names to be changed grouped GDR leaders with concentration camp victims as well as Marx and Engels. It succeeded in uniting against it a broad coalition of Easterners and Westerners, prompting the government to put the issue on the back burner. In September 1993, municipal authorities turned the matter over to an independent commission similar to the one that had looked at monuments. Six months later, the commission issued a set of recommendations guided by the principle "that the second German democracy has no reason to honor politicians who actively contributed to the destruction of the first German democracy. The same goes for politicians who, after 1933, opposed one totalitarian dictatorship, that of the National Socialists, in order to replace it with another totalitarian dictatorship, that of the Communists."[27] Consequently, the commission recommended removing several prominent Communists from the city map, while sparing others who died too soon to aid Hitler or Ulbricht, notably Karl Marx, Rosa Luxemburg, and Karl Liebknecht.

By this time, the easy decisions had already been made. On the one hand, most non-Communists honored by the GDR were off the hook. On the other hand, the individual districts had removed from the map the names of slain border guards, minor GDR politicians, and foreign Communists such as Ho Chi Minh, Klement Gottwald, Jacques Duclos, and even François-Noel Babeuf. They restored some old names, especially very old ones, but they gave many streets new names: after GDR opposition figures, anti-Nazis who had not been honored by the GDR, or such suitably uncontroversial figures as Mark Twain and Vincent van Gogh.

The controversial streets before the commission were those named after anti-Nazi Communists. It sought a middle ground and managed to give offense on both sides. The left united above all against its recommendation to change Clara-Zetkin-Strasse back to Dorotheenstrasse, after the Great Elector's wife. Zetkin (1857–1933), who was Jewish, spent four decades as a Social Democrat and became an internationally recognized feminist, but after 1919 she joined the Communist Party and denounced the Weimar Republic. The commission declared that the street leading from eastern Berlin to the Reichstag must not be named after an opponent of parliamentary democracy. Leftists and feminists organized marches in protest. The threat to Zetkin and other idols of the left redounded to the benefit of the ex-Communist PDS, which emerged as eastern Berlin's strongest party in 1994 elections by appealing to the separate identity of misunderstood Ossis.

To the frustration of some commission members, the government had restricted its purview to the former East Berlin, effectively limiting its purge to *leftist* opponents of Weimar democracy. Leftists pointed to the case of Paul von Hindenburg, the president who appointed Hitler chancellor in 1933. The Active Museum, practicing its belief that history should be discussed rather than manipulated, mounted an explanatory plaque next to a street sign on West Berlin's Hindenburgdamm. The district of Steglitz responded by removing the plaque and sending the organization a bill for the cost of doing so. The West was not entirely immune to the spirit of change after 1989: Schöneberg and Wilmersdorf restored the names of Jews that the Nazis had removed; and in 1991, the Tiergarten district removed the name of General Alfred von Schlieffen, chief of the general staff at the turn of the century, and replaced it with that of the nineteenth-century writer and social reformer Bettina von Arnim. Those who objected to honoring Prussian militarism could cheer the demise of Schlieffen. Despite longstanding complaints, however, nothing was done about a group of sixteen streets near Tempelhof airport, all of which had been renamed in 1936 after World War I pilots. The most famous of these men was Manfred von Richthofen, the "Red Baron," celebrated for having shot down eighty-one enemy planes. The man responsible for the street names was the new air force chief, Hermann Göring, a fellow pilot who had assumed command of Richthofen's squadron after the latter's death. During the late 1940s, proposals to rename these streets came to nothing. Instead, in 1957 the district named yet another street after a World War I pilot, Ernst Udet, a man who had later risen to a high position in Göring's air force.

The commission in 1994 did not satisfy conservatives either. It recommended that new street names honor prominent Weimar democrats not yet represented on the city map. Justice for the Weimar Republic, however, was clearly not the main goal of the senator for transportation, the Christian Democrat Herwig Haase, when he decreed several name changes in 1995. The commission's most outspoken member, the historian Heinrich August Winkler, charged that in Haase's zeal to remove Communist names from the national capital, he chose "an affirmation of German greatness" over the "cultivation of democratic traditions."[28] Haase honored only one Weimar democrat: Hans-Beimler-Strasse would become Otto-Braun-Strasse, after the Prussian premier from 1920 to 1932. Like Beimler, Artur Becker was a Communist who had died defending an elected government in the Spanish Civil War; Haase wanted to return Artur-Becker-Strasse to its previous name, Kniprode-Strasse, after a fourteenth-century Teutonic knight known for his wars against Lithuania.

It is difficult to revive historical German street names without raising delicate foreign-policy issues. In the case of Dimitroffstrasse, named after Georgi Dimitroff, hero of the 1933 Reichstag fire trial and later head of the Comintern and of Communist Bulgaria, Haase decreed a return to the old name of Danziger Strasse, one of many streets named after formerly German cities now in Poland (and now known by their Polish names). The GDR had officially acknowledged the loss of this eastern territory in 1950; the Federal Republic did so in 1990. Citizens of Gdansk might not see the distinction between the desire to restore a traditional street name and a desire to regain the city once known as Danzig. When Haase changed the name of Wilhelm-Pieck-Strasse in 1994, he had more cautiously declined to restore the previous names of the street's two segments, which had honored Germany's annexation of the French provinces Alsace and Lorraine in 1871. Luckily an even older name for that street was available: Tor-Strasse (Gate Street), recalling the old city wall and gates it had replaced in the nineteenth century. Did French sensibilities weigh more heavily than Polish ones? More likely, Haase had an ear for the sensibilities of nationalist voters still bitter over the loss of Germany's eastern territories. In any case, Russian sensibilities apparently mattered. On the fiftieth anniversary of the Soviet conquest of Berlin, Haase wanted to rename Bersarinplatz, which honored the first Soviet commandant of occupied Berlin, General Nikolai Bersarin. Before his death in a motorcycle accident in June 1945, Bersarin had become a surprisingly popular figure, credited with vigorous efforts to feed the starving Berliners. Indeed, the non-Communist government of Greater Berlin had named the square after him in 1946, before the division of the city; and even East Berlin never honored any other Red Army commander with a street. Faced with protests from Berliners and from the Russian embassy, Mayor Diepgen overruled Haase.

The cases of Danzig and Alsace-Lorraine remind us that the naming of streets was a political act long before Berlin was divided. Names of medieval provenance—the street of the bakers or the Franciscans, or a six-hundred-year-old "New Market"—are venerable enough to be quaint and beloved. The West also kept most street names from the monarchist era: Bismarck, Moltke, and Roon, the triumvirate credited with German unification in 1871, grace a late-nineteenth-century quarter in nearly every West German city. The GDR, as noted, chose to disenfranchise these and other "militarists." After 1990, East and West did not see eye to eye over the name of Wilhelmstrasse—as the West Berlin segment of the street had always been known. Few people spoke out in favor of keeping the name Otto-Grotewohl-Strasse, as the East Berlin part of the street had been called since the death of the GDR's first prime minister in 1964. But some East Berliners questioned whether the weight of tradition was sufficient to justify restoring the original name, which honored the militarist King Friedrich Wilhelm I. In 1991 the district council of Mitte voted instead to call it Toleranzstrasse. The city government was not prepared to tolerate such originality. It simply overruled the district council in 1993 and restored the name Wilhelmstrasse.

More ill will arose just around the corner, as the municipal parliament prepared to move into the building of the former Prussian House of Deputies. Christian Democrats, led by parliament president Hanna-Renate Laurien, found it intolerable that the parliament stood on a street named after a Communist and "Soviet agent." To return Niederkirchnerstrasse to its previous name was out of the question, however, since the name "Prinz-Albrecht-Strasse" had come to be synonymous with "Gestapo." Most supporters of the "Topography of Terror" exhibit across the street thought that the renaming of the street after a Communist resistance fighter should be accepted as a historical fact. The leftist parties in the parliament mustered a bare majority in favor of keeping Niederkirchnerstrasse 5 as the parliament's address. The unhappy Christian Democrats and Free Democrats simply left the street name off their letterheads.

During the Weimar years, the Berlin city government had discussed the possibility of systematic renaming of streets, but in fact made few changes. The Third Reich was more active, honoring Hitler, Göring, and Horst Wessel—and after the war both East and West Berlin quickly removed the obviously Nazi street names. After 1990, the idea of simply wiping out the GDR's street names became more complicated when decisions had to be made about which previous name to restore and which period to return to. No one favored the Nazi names; to what previous era, then, might the clock be turned back?

Like his colleagues in charge of city planning, Haase seemed more comfortable reviving pre-1918 traditions than those of the Weimar Republic. Or else he wanted to rally his party's nationalist right wing, which had defined itself for decades by its anticommunism, and which had no great love for Weimar's Social Democrats. The name changes prompted Berlin's Social Democratic leader Walter Momper to observe in 1992 that the Christian Democrats "apparently feel the need to defeat Communism anew every day."[29] In the East, polls, petitions, and protests showed that not only former Communists resented what they saw as another example of Wessi arrogance at the expense of their streets and their history. The effort, the cost, and the divisiveness produced by the name changes also struck many Easterners as pointless. Were not these purely symbolic acts a diversion from Berlin's real problems?

Street names can be ephemeral, rootless, and inoffensive in a way that buildings and monuments perhaps cannot. Like sculptures and buildings, however, names contribute to the myths that constitute a collective identity. In that identity, or the lack of it, lies the source of reunified Berlin's difficulties with names. In hindsight, the unshakeable polarities that accompanied division and the Cold War may appear as comforting as they were uncomfortable, even in Berlin. Freedom and unity make it harder to agree on the proper names, the proper heroes, and the proper symbols to attach to buildings, streets, monuments, and the institutions of civic life.

Above all I want to make this city a representative of the German nation. This transcends any individual. We are all ephemeral beings. The city, however, as capital of the German Reich, must exist and must truly exist for the future.[1]

—Hitler, speech in Berlin, August 2, 1938

Berlin must be the true center of Europe, a capital that for everybody shall be *the* capital.[2]

—Hitler, table talk, September 25, 1941

Berlin is the place where we will see whether the Germans succeed in finding the way from the tragedy of division to a new identity.[3]

—Hans Stimmann, Berlin city building director, 1991

If the historical form of the city is to provide the standard, which of the many Berlin pasts is meant? Baroque or classical Berlin, Berlin from the time of unification or the chaotic Twenties, to say nothing of the insane building plans of the Nazi years?[4]

—Peter Schneider, 1993

Six

Capital of the New Germany

The Neue Wache

Tourists wandering down Unter den Linden in East Berlin did not always take notice of the massive and sooty facades of the opera, the university, or the arsenal, but they could be counted on to gather around a small stone building housing the "Memorial to the Victims of Fascism and Militarism." Their attention was drawn to it by the pair of East German soldiers standing guard outside. But it was the changing of the guard that drew crowds: camera shutters clicked when the soldiers goose-stepped into position. This East Berlin equivalent of Buckingham Palace puzzled many foreigners. Many of us have come to think of the goose step as the very embodiment of German militarism; how could one honor its victims by goose-stepping? Surely, some tourists thought, this was a bizarre ritual parody of militarism intended to exorcise the demons of the past.

On a typical Berlin autumn day in 1993—that is, in a cold rain—a large crowd gathered at the same building. Chancellor Helmut Kohl and a phalanx of German officials solemnly dedicated the new "Central Memorial to the Victims of War and Tyranny." Public remembrance is always difficult in Germany, and on this occasion chanting protesters did their best to spoil Kohl's day. They objected to Kohl's presence, to the form and purpose of his memorial, and to its location. The fact that the unified Federal Republic was the fourth consecutive regime to use the same building as a national memorial made the site burdened, not venerable.

The building in question is the Neue Wache (New Guardhouse), the first major commission given to Karl Friedrich Schinkel. Despite its small size, it is often ranked among his finest works. In the heart of royal Berlin, Schinkel fashioned a building of modest purpose into a model of restrained German neoclassicism. A portico of Greek Doric columns fronts a carefully proportioned, nearly cubical building inspired by Roman military architecture (fig. 53). Completed in 1818, it served for a century to house the soldiers assigned to guard the king.

The end of the monarchy in 1918 robbed the building of its original purpose, but it remained a prominent architectural monument. The Weimar Republic decided to turn the guardhouse into a memorial to the dead of World War I, choosing an austere design by Heinrich Tessenow for the building's interior. Tessenow's memorial, completed in 1931, offered a modern, abstract counterpart to Schinkel's classical simplicity. Through a circular opening in the roof, light (and rain) fell on a black stone block and a silver wreath. Bare stone walls surrounded that simple memorial, which stood alone at the center of the building's interior. The design was apparently acceptable to Nazi leaders as well: they kept the memorial essentially unchanged.

During the 1950s, the GDR restored the bomb-damaged building, rededicating it in 1960 as the "Memorial to the Victims of Fascism and Militarism," and posting their honor guard outside. In 1969 the interior was redesigned; its new centerpiece was a glass block with an eternal flame. Stones set in the floor marked the graves of an Unknown Soldier and an Unknown Resistance Fighter. Also set in the floor were urns containing earth from concentration camps and World War II battlefields.

In 1990, with the disbanding of the East German army, the goose-stepping guards were withdrawn and the memorial closed. What would be the fate of the building? Unlike many endless Berlin debates, this one did not drag on indecisively, thanks to the personal intervention of Chancellor Kohl. Kohl wanted a "worthy common memorial for the victims of both world wars, tyranny, racial persecution, resistance, expulsion, division, and terrorism."[5] Such a central state memorial would be the place for leaders and foreign dignitaries to lay wreaths on appropriate occasions. A single wreath-laying at the Neue Wache could take the place of ceremonial visits to a long list of memorial sites: Plötzensee, the Bendlerblock, Wannsee, Stasi headquarters, the new Wall memorial, and nearby concentration camps, as well as

53
The Neue Wache

memorials to soldiers, civilian victims of wartime bombing, Germans expelled from the former eastern provinces annexed by Poland and Russia, and the businessmen and officials assassinated by the radical Red Army Faction since the 1970s. All of these kinds and groups of victims were henceforth to be honored at the Neue Wache. Kohl wanted to create a single category of victims as an expression of national unity. His desire to build an identity out of their common status as victims "of war and tyranny" speaks volumes about the state of German national identity. The many objections to his project for the Neue Wache also reveal how fractured that identity remains.

Helmut Kohl has been a remarkably successful politician with a gift for the symbolic gesture that comforts the electorate and infuriates intellectuals inside and outside Germany. He has consistently kept his distance from commemorations of Germany's dark side, including the crimes of the Nazi past as well as, for example, a memorial service for Turks murdered by neo-Nazis in 1993. His decision to establish a national memorial at the Neue Wache and his choices for its design represent his most decisive intervention in the planning of the new national capital. The desire of Kohl—and of many conservative intellectuals—to honor national traditions drew them to a building distinguished by Schinkel's and Tessenow's architecture. This heritage anchored the building in the honorable German past; the intervening six decades, not so honorable, were the time of victims, whom a memorial could honor in the name of a Germany that now stood proudly as a unified democracy.

What was objectionable in this vision of a nation united in mourning? Plenty, it seems. Kohl's way of honoring victims had already created a furor eight years before, when he persuaded President Ronald Reagan to accompany him to a German military cemetery in the town of Bitburg. The graves he asked Reagan to honor were of soldiers who had fought against U.S. troops in World War II; a few were members of the Waffen-SS. The Bitburg visit became a public-relations disaster for Reagan, since he refused to embarrass Kohl by canceling it, despite protests from American war veterans and from Jewish groups. Under American pressure, however, the day's itinerary for May 5, 1985, was expanded to include a visit to the Bergen-Belsen concentration camp. Through their remembrance, Kohl and Reagan linked, and effectively equated, two groups of victims: concentration camp prisoners and German soldiers.

This implied equality of victims raised the biggest objection to the new memorial at the Neue Wache as well. Kohl (and Reagan) spoke for many German families, and some veterans elsewhere as well, in mourning all young soldiers who died in battle, whatever the motivations of their commanders. But this personal, seemingly unpolitical understanding of victimhood did not sit well with those who were more critically disposed toward German history. A national memorial is different from an individual act of mourning, observed Thomas Lutz of the Topography of Terror Foundation: it promotes "social recognition and beyond that an attempt to endow the nation with a sense of purpose."[6] And Kohl's formula of "war and tyranny," according to his critics, equated soldiers fighting for Hitler with Jews herded into gas chambers. He honored SS concentration camp guards along with the inmates they killed. Was Roland Freisler, the sadistic chief judge of the Volksgerichtshof, who died in a bombing raid in February 1945, a victim just like the many courageous resisters he sentenced to death? "German murderers are not victims!" chanted the demonstrators.

In the face of the protests, Kohl held fast to his plans but made one concession: the addition of a bronze plaque next to the building's entrance naming groups of victims being honored. Nazi officials and SS men were of course not among them. Kohl apparently acted to ensure that Ignaz Bubis, chairman of the Central Council of Jews in Germany, would attend the dedication. Bubis, though not thrilled with the compromise, agreed to it. On the other hand, the chairman of Berlin's main Jewish organization, Jerzy Kanal, refused to attend the ceremony, as did Berlin's senator for cultural affairs, Ulrich Roloff-Momin.

Kohl's vision of a community of victims appalled those Germans who were uncomfortable with their national identity. Germans who wanted to empathize with anti-Nazi resisters, deserters, and non-German Jews, drew back from a memorial that suggested their bonds with men and women—even their own parents or grandparents—who had cheered Hitler or fought in his war of conquest and extermination. They recognized that Kohl's plans for the Neue Wache reflected the desire, often expressed by him and his advisers, to treat Germany as a "normal" nation. None of the alternative models of identity proposed by antinationalist intellectuals has found much emotional resonance—allegiance to Europe, for example, or to democracy or international human rights. But the nation remains anathema to them.

Amid all the dispute about which victims to honor, the fact that victimhood was the touchstone of identity did not attract much criticism. Kohl's opponents tended to be people eager to express their solidarity with victims—victims they identified as non-German: Jewish victims of the Nazis, Turkish victims of neo-Nazi attacks, American Indians, and (in a case that raises fascinating and disturbing questions about the psychology of guilt) Palestinian victims of Israeli policies. Images of a nation of heroes seem to have died with the GDR. Instead of a national Heroes' Day, which the Third Reich had celebrated, since 1952 the Federal Republic has had a National Day of Mourning; in 1993 the memorial at the Neue Wache was dedicated on that day.

What victims have in common is a lack of responsibility for their fate. Thus Kohl's memorial might seem to commemorate German innocence, even in the face of the Third Reich. The historian Reinhart Koselleck argued that Kohl treated the Third Reich as an outside force that left victims in its wake: "Are war and tyranny a kind of traffic accident, then? No one wanted it? Everyone is a victim?"[7] As an alternative to the undifferentiated recognition of all victims, Koselleck proposed a different dedication. He was inspired by President Richard von Weizsäcker's celebrated 1985 speech commemorating the fortieth anniversary of Germany's defeat, in which Weizsäcker reviewed all the groups of victims and how they died. Koselleck's suggested summary: "To the Dead: Fallen, Murdered, Gassed, Died, Missing."[8] This dedication would honor the equality of all in death without putting the dead in the service of a national cause. Many intellectuals praised this compromise, but Koselleck's and Weizsäcker's morbid version of German history held no appeal for Kohl.

Just as the purpose of a national memorial was controversial, so was its location in a building stamped by military tradition. The Neue Wache was built in celebration of the Prussian army's victory over Napoleon, renovated to honor those who died for the fatherland in World War I, used by the Nazis for militarist rituals, and appropriated by the GDR for its goose-stepping ceremonies. Indeed, here was a surprising case of continuity with GDR tradition. The inclusion in the GDR's memorial of earth from concentration camps and battlefields (which still remains under the stone floor) suggested the equality of soldiers and camp prisoners as victims of "fascism and militarism." The Federal Republic's inclusive formula, "war and tyranny," is arguably not very different.

The ongoing debate about appropriate forms for public remembrance carried over to the design of the memorial. The decision to restore most elements of Tessenow's design was widely praised, but many artists were offended that their generation's work was spurned in favor of a design from 1930. No active provocation or unconventional "countermonument" was considered for the Neue Wache. Kohl personally approved not only the restoration of Tessenow's design but also the major deviation from it. Instead of Tessenow's granite block and silver wreath, the centerpiece of the new memorial is an enlarged bronze version of a Pietà modeled by Käthe Kollwitz in 1937. The sculptures and drawings of Kollwitz (1867–1945) are unusual among those of twentieth-century artists for their popularity both inside and outside artistic circles. Kollwitz was also honored in both East and West Germany; East Berlin gave the name Kollwitzstrasse to the street on which she had lived. She was a pacifist whose son died in World War I, and her sculpture of a mother mourning a dead son vividly expresses the horrors of war. The original statue, however, is only fifteen inches high. The sculptor Hermann Haacke was commissioned to make a copy four times as tall (fig. 54). Artists condemned this "blow-up" as a falsification of Kollwitz's work. Other critics questioned

54
Enlarged version of Käthe Kollwitz's Pietà in the Neue Wache

whether an expression of private grief should be transformed into a public monument.

Kohl had rejected designs for the memorial that conveyed a message of "hopelessness"; Kollwitz's statue embodied "indestructible humanity" instead.[9] Some of Kohl's critics probably preferred a message of hopelessness; others asked *how* the statue expressed hope. Koselleck argued that a national symbol of hope in the form of a Pietà—based on depictions of Mary mourning Jesus—must inevitably symbolize the Christian message of salvation. Thus the memorial represents "the very rupture that divides Christians from Jews. Or should the (surviving) Jews be obliged to recognize the dead son as their savior?" And not only Jews were implicitly excluded from the memorial; so were the women who died in World War II. The portrayal of a mother mourning her dead son was an appropriate memorial for World War I, when most of those who died were soldiers, but after a second war in which millions of women were themselves killed in bombing, mass executions, and gas chambers, "the surviving mother cannot be the central figure of our central memorial."[10]

Thus it was not merely a matter of taste to object to Kohl's choice of an artist trained in the nineteenth century and of a work that arguably reflected a turn-of-the-century style. The enlarged version of the statue creates an archetypal image of "mother earth, mother homeland, mother nation" that "honors the necessity of suffering and sacrifice," argued Kathrin Hoffmann-

Curtius, an art historian. In short, the memorial revived a nineteenth-century nationalist image by "using the image of a suffering mother to promote national unity."[11] Hoffmann-Curtius, and many others, reacted with alarm to any act that might revive German national pride. Kohl's memorial, if it did not affirm national identity, at least sent a message of hope in the name of Germany. His opponents wanted an active confrontation with the past, not a traditional monument suitable for gazing and for laying wreaths. Their kind of memorial would teach or admonish, not affirm anything, and certainly not affirm the legitimacy of German national pride.

From Bonn to Berlin

Other nations have national memorials that serve to affirm their historical identity and continued resilience. With the Neue Wache, Helmut Kohl wanted Germany to have the same thing. Instead it became—at least at first—another symbol of the division between those Germans who shared Kohl's desire for "normality" and those who thought Germany could not or should not become a "normal" nation.

Other nations also have capital cities that serve symbolic as well as practical purposes. The question of Germany's capital stirred another debate about national identity and urban form. Bonn or Berlin? Technically, the question of Germany's capital had long been settled. When the new West German state decided in 1949 to govern from Bonn, it underlined the provisional nature of the state and its seat of government by declaring that Berlin would resume its position as the German capital once the nation had been reunified. What was chosen in 1991 was therefore the seat of government, not the capital, but nearly everyone on both sides saw the decision as an opportunity either to revise or reaffirm the symbolic declaration of 1949.

After forty years, many people no longer considered Bonn a provisional capital and saw no reason to abandon it. They clashed with Berlin's supporters in a vigorous national debate that culminated in a Bundestag vote on the future seat of government. Parochial interests naturally spoke up for each side; the greater size of Berlin was balanced by the fact that Bonn was located in Germany's most populous state, North Rhine–Westphalia. Each side could invoke many symbols to argue that their city was the appropriate synecdoche for the new Germany. Bonn's supporters presented their city as the representative of a successful democracy, in contrast to Berlin, which had served as the capital of a monarchy, a failed democracy, and two dictatorships. Bonn, moreover, represented Germany's integration into the West, through its membership in NATO and the European Community. A move to Berlin, as near to Poland as Bonn was to Belgium, suggested a reorientation of Germany toward central or eastern Europe. Some Germans urged this constructive response to the disappearance of the Iron Curtain; for others, it bespoke an ominous return to Germany's claims to Continental hegemony. Berlin advocates' strongest response to these worries was the argument that West Germany needed to acknowledge that the addition of seventeen million East Germans had changed their state. Whereas Bonn was the capital of West Germany, Berlin alone had straddled the division of Germany and thus was the best place to heal the wounds of division.

Bonn, the provisional and provincial capital, effectively symbolized both the federal nature of the Federal Republic and the modest authority claimed by a liberal state. Its glass and steel government buildings scattered along the bank of the Rhine embody the postwar architecture and planning that claimed to be antiauthoritarian, unhierarchical, and democratic. Berlin, by contrast, might appear to embody centralization and authoritarian grandeur. For their part, Berliners were not alone in seeing Bonn as an isolated place of smug bureaucrats. Supporters of Berlin argued that Germany should be governed from its most diverse and cosmopolitan city, its repository of traditionally urban virtues like tolerance, experimentation, and irreverence.

The result of the Bundestag's vote on June 20, 1991, remained in doubt until the last minute. Berlin won by 338 to 320. The vote settled the symbolic battle but not the practical one. When would the government actually move? Would all of it move at once, or indeed would all of it move? Into what quarters? What would it all cost? Years would pass without any certain answers to these questions. Berliners suspected Bonn's powerful supporters of sabotaging the move. But the scale of construction required to turn the divided city into the capital of mighty Germany presented a formidable task to a government already committed to the even larger job of rebuilding eastern Germany.

The task of reattaching the city's two halves and building the new capital has occupied armies of developers, architects, planners, and critics in the 1990s. They flocked to Berlin from all over the world to offer their own distinctive talents. But in Berlin they cannot avoid the simultaneous identity crises of architecture, cities, and the nation. Amid the city's fragile and contested urban traditions, the prospect of so much that is new raises fears of losing whatever historical identity remains. The result has been a fierce battle to define the urban traditions of Berlin relevant to its rebuilding in the 1990s.

That the government would occupy the center of Berlin was never in doubt. Despite unwelcome reminders that the Nazi and Communist regimes had governed from here, the federal authorities wanted to claim the space of the Prussian kings, the German emperors, and the Weimar democrats. Each of the Bonn ministries duly requested massive amounts of office space in the city center, and most specified that only new buildings would fit their needs. Early in the process, Bonn therefore declared that several major buildings would have to be demolished: Göring's aviation ministry, the Nazi Reichsbank, and the GDR buildings around the royal palace's former site. But Bonn quickly learned that Berlin's historically significant buildings were not so easily disposed of, even when their significance was negative. In the face of opposition from all political parties in Berlin, the demolition plans were canceled or deferred. Some Bonn ministries would have to make themselves at home in Third Reich and GDR buildings.

The question, then, was how to fit one large federal government into the existing buildings and open spaces of central Berlin. The old city center had belonged to East Berlin and much of it had long been neglected, but during the 1980s the GDR had devoted considerable resources to its redevelopment. Workers and building materials from the entire country were diverted to Berlin so that the capital might stand up to comparison with West Berlin on the city's 750th anniversary. Most of the historic buildings still in ruins were finally restored, for example, the twin eighteenth-century churches that flank Schinkel's theater on Gendarmenmarkt. Renovation was accompanied by new construction to revive major inner-city streets, most notably Friedrichstrasse. Some of the new commercial buildings there were unfinished in 1989, and they have been torn down to make way for new, Western buildings. Amid a housing shortage, however, the new apartment buildings in the Nikolai Quarter and atop

Hitler's bunker must remain. In the 1990s, the center of East Berlin needs many changes, but it presents architects and planners with a messy urban fabric rather than a tabula rasa.

More space was available just to the west, where the Wall had stood. This included Potsdamer Platz, which had never been a center of government. As we have seen, it was designated to become an enormous complex of private offices and shops. The area just to its west is taken up by West Berlin's only major inner-city project before the 1980s, the "Kulturforum" that includes Mies van der Rohe's New National Gallery and Hans Scharoun's Philharmonic Hall and State Library. Elsewhere both government and private capital in West Berlin had long avoided building in the shadow of the Wall; its removal opened large tracts for development.

The new center of government will lie north of Potsdamer Platz, beyond the Brandenburg Gate. North and west of the Reichstag, a large area marked by a wide arc of the Spree River had long stood nearly empty after it was cleared by the combined efforts of Speer's demolition crews, Allied bombers, and postwar rubble clearance. Bonn and Berlin chose this site for the central organs of parliamentary government: the Bundestag, the Bundesrat (the upper house, representing the sixteen states), and the chancellery. Among the several international design competitions in the new capital, the one for the "Spree Arc" attracted the most attention, perhaps because it offered designers the most vacant land and hence the most freedom. From 835 entries, the jury was able to pick a clear winner, that of the Berlin architect Axel Schultes. Schultes's design succeeded in making an unmistakable urban statement: it lined up the new buildings in an east-west band across the open space of the Spree arc, connecting the old Friedrichstadt, on its eastern side, with the built-up West Berlin neighborhood of Moabit. It thus combined a neat symbol of reunification with a rigorous urban form for the government buildings (fig. 55).

Berlin greeted Schultes's plan with a rare chorus of praise. Most of the objections came from Bonn, a fact that further stiffened support for it in Berlin. Many Bonn officials preferred other designs that proposed dispersing the government buildings in the open space of the Spree arc, thus offering a less monumental effect, more like Bonn's government quarter. But the Berlin faction endorsed Schultes's more formal design that clearly sepa-

55
Model of Axel Schultes's plan for the Spree Arc government quarter. At upper right is the Reichstag (with a proposed new roof); behind it is the former East Berlin. Brandenburg Gate is at far right. Courtesy of German Information Center.

rated urban density from green space, rather than interspersing them. Berlin did not want another Hansa Quarter or another Bonn. The argument over Schultes's design, like that over Berlin as capital, thus reflected differing views of the connection between politics and architecture in Berlin's past. Detractors thought that a massive ensemble of buildings was an authoritarian gesture recalling Hitler or Ulbricht. Supporters found the design above all *urban* and accessible, and therefore democratic.

Critical Reconstruction

The Berlin government had insisted that the guidelines for the "Spree Arc" competition require a "city-compatible" mixture of functions. In other words, government was not to be isolated from commerce, culture, and residence, as it was in Bonn—a demand that Schultes's plan fulfilled at both ends of his east-west band and also along the banks of the Spree arc to the north. The goal was diversity, which became the watchword of Berlin urban planning in the 1990s. The roots of this policy lay in the 1980s, when the International Building Exhibition (IBA) had changed official policy toward inner-city districts near the Wall. IBA was a multiyear project of urban redevelopment, lavishly funded in the days when West Berlin was still the subsidized showcase of the West. It brought prominent architects to Berlin to design new apartment buildings that complemented their nineteenth-century neighborhoods. It also devoted resources to the renovation of old buildings and thus gave official approval to the rediscovery of the Mietskaserne (see chapter 3). IBA, in short, turned the efforts of city planners and architects to understanding and preserving the existing, functioning city. The clearest shift away from established planning practice was the embrace of urban mixture, as planners sought to bring apartments, entertainment, shopping, and workplaces into close proximity, as they had been in nineteenth-century urban neighborhoods.

As it faced the task of placing ministries in the city center, the Berlin government continued to insist on diversity. After the Spree arc, the most important competition addressed the Spree island where medieval Cölln had stood—that is, the site of the vanished royal palace and of the GDR's main government buildings. Despite international attention and 1,105 entries, the winning design was doomed to join the long line of unbuilt Berlin prizewinners, since no one seemed capable of making a final decision about the preservation or demolition of the Palace of the Republic and other existing buildings. But the competition guidelines set the pattern for the integration of government functions in the city. Foreign minister Klaus Kinkel wanted to take over the palace's site; Berlin agreed on the condition that a conference center and a public library be located there as well. City leaders sought this mixture of functions because they feared that a city center full of nothing but bureaucrats' offices would be as lifeless as an American downtown.

In 1993, Berlin's long-serving mayor, Eberhard Diepgen, conjured up a more hopeful picture of the city's future:

> It is a summer day at the turn of the century. The new square between the Lustgarten, foreign ministry, and city library has the character and charm of a cityscape like those we know from old black and white photographs. On park benches and chairs of a sidewalk café sit casually dressed students from the nearby Humboldt University. They drink espresso and leaf through a book from the library. Elegantly dressed visitors and officials of the foreign office saunter by. Visitors from all over the world look for free tables in the restaurant or buy international newspapers. An ideal place for rest and escape after a long stroll down Unter den Linden. . .[12]

Diepgen's vision captures the image of urban life envisioned by many of Berlin's civic leaders: diversity of occupations and activities, bustling street life, strolling and sitting. Though projected into the future, it is an attempt to recover an image from the past—as is explicit in Diepgen's reference to old photographs. Among Berlin's many pasts, the one sought here is indeed the age of black and white photography: the boom decades before and after 1900.

This model of urban life—which is by no means unique to Berlin—envisions a limited kind of diversity, one best captured by black and white photographs or film: memory in the form of pictures without the noises or smells. It is a memory of the 1920s without Nazis, Communists, and overwhelming poverty. It represents the point of view of the "flaneur," the bourgeois stroller, an urban type memorably defined by Walter Benjamin. Benjamin located the flaneur in the nineteenth-century Paris of Charles Baudelaire, but also in his own 1920s Berlin. As Benjamin recognized, the flaneur's view of urban spectacle, essential to the creation of modern art, was that of an outsider, a tourist in his own teeming city. The flaneur (a distinctly male figure, as feminist scholars have pointed out) sought temporary refuge from the responsibilities of his own existence, and found it in the public space of the city street.[13]

The appeal of Diepgen's image is a measure of the late-twentieth-century bourgeoisie's discontent with its cities—again, a sentiment not peculiar to Berlin. Here the crisis of modern architecture and urban planning coincides with the crisis of national identity. Advocates of a backward-looking urban form seek to restore lost roots in community and place. Meanwhile, German conservatives who want to restore a healthy national pride also look back to the age of black and white photography before 1918. In their genesis, these are two largely distinct tendencies: the impetus for urban restoration came from leftists who believed that the old neighborhoods of Mietskasernen nurtured the anti-authoritarian countercultures of West Berlin's Kreuzberg and East Berlin's Prenzlauer Berg. Emotional attachments to the old city created common ground between leftists with wistful memories of the 1960s and conservatives like the publisher Wolf Jobst Siedler and the Christian Democratic politician Diepgen. They agreed that some combination of Nazism, Communism, capitalism, and modernism had destroyed the city, and that only a more remote past could offer a model for its restoration. Urban and architectural forms do not automatically carry a particular political connotation. The unpredictable politics of urban form makes debates about the city more interesting than the repetitive polemics typical of German discussions of national identity. This unpredictability can heighten the nastiness—everyone can accuse everyone else of being a Nazi—but it can also generate practical results and workable compromises.

The 1890s or 1920s cannot be restored, except as a stage set for tourists. How can urban planning recapture the lost "character and charm" desired by Diepgen and many others? After all, it is found almost exclusively in quarters that took form before 1914, such as Kreuzberg and the Kurfürstendamm. Berlin's answer has been "critical reconstruction," the controversial set of planning guidelines intended to ensure that the sum of Berlin's many construction projects is a lively and liveable city.

Critical reconstruction grew out of long-simmering discontent with postwar urban development. It aimed to undo the errors of the previous half-century. The architectural historian Dieter Hoffmann-Axthelm, the leading theorist of critical reconstruction, argued that "in spite of all destruction Berlin is an extant city, shaped by history. We do not need to invent a new city, certainly not the metropolis of the third millennium."[14] The challenge was, rather, to understand and restore Berlin's identity. Hoffmann-Axthelm was among other things a theorist of the Kreuzberg counterculture of the 1970s and 1980s. He located Berlin's essence in the eighteenth-century block structure of Friedrichstadt and the dense pattern of five-story courtyard buildings that covered those and newer blocks at the end of the nineteenth century. Along with Siedler, he argued that this structure was essentially intact in 1945, despite substantial damage by Speer's crews and Allied bombers. Siedler and Hoffmann-Axthelm blamed the process of postwar reconstruction for destroying it: the massive scale of projects in both the capitalist West and the communist East wiped out not only salvageable buildings, but entire streets, blocks, and neighborhoods, creating desolate stretches of highways, parking lots, and monotonous tower blocks in place of lively streets.

This is a critique of urban modernism widely shared in Berlin and in the rest of the world. On the contested historical terrain of Berlin, however, any whiff of nostalgia arouses deep suspicion.

So too, then, did Berlin's solution. Critical reconstruction became the policy of Hans Stimmann, the Social Democratic planner who served as city building director from 1991 to 1996. He issued planning guidelines for the inner city that restored the outlines of old streets and squares and required new buildings to conform to the old blocks. Height limits—seventy-two feet for the eaves, a hundred feet for the set-back peak of a roof—followed nineteenth-century building codes. The newly rebuilt blocks are supposed to be divided into individual buildings with identifiable entrances, rules intended to prevent long and forbidding facades that generate no activity on the street.

As a practical matter, these guidelines struck many critics as a hopelessly romantic attempt to turn back the clock. For Hoffmann-Axthelm, a reduction in urban scale to the eighteenth- or nineteenth-century parcel is the necessary first step to restoring diversity in urban neighborhoods and flexibility in their development. This vision is at odds with the contemporary scale of commerce, capital investment, real estate development, and private as well as public bureaucracies. In fact, Stimmann's substantial powers did not extend to the most basic decisions about real estate investment; the Treuhand, trustee of East German property, insisted on selling its land quickly, in large parcels and to large developers. As critical reconstruction took form, Hoffmann-Axthelm himself feared that it was degenerating into mere street decoration, a facade that disguised the continued impoverishment of urban life.

Stimmann's guidelines explicitly sought a Berlin unified by Prussian classical order and by streets lined with masonry buildings. In seizing upon the tradition of Prussian neoclassicism, Stimmann sought to invoke the authority of the great Schinkel, who became his model of architectural simplicity and restraint. He was certainly correct in seeing Schinkel's influence on the turn-of-the-century city of Mietskasernen whose scale he wanted to restore, as well as on Peter Behrens and the other early modernist architects whose style he put forth as a model. Just as nineteenth-century Germans quoted Goethe to clinch any argument, however, twentieth-century Berlin architects are all Schinkel's heirs: Mies van der Rohe, Speer, and the builders of Stalinallee. For better or worse, Schinkel's protean architecture has inspired nearly everything that has come since.

Against Stimmann's attempt to claim Schinkel as an ally in

support of urban restoration, the architectural historian Tilmann Buddensieg argued convincingly that in his time Schinkel strove to shatter the uniformity of eighteenth-century Berlin.[15] In other words, the style now held up as the conservative norm was in its time radically innovative. Schinkel's genius thus can be seen as part of a Berlin tradition diametrically opposed to the spirit of critical reconstruction. Throughout the past century, it has been a commonplace to identify Berlin with continuous change, destruction, renewal, and experimentation. Again and again one hears Karl Scheffler's 1910 description of Berlin condemned "forever to become and never to be." For Daniel Libeskind, architect of the city's new Jewish Museum, Berlin is "a fascinating montage of conflicting histories, scales, forms and spaces." Complaining that Stimmann's rules "are transforming the fascinating diversity of the city into banal uniformity," he moved his practice from Berlin to Los Angeles.[16]

Fueling the nasty polemics was the fact that a great deal was at stake here: not just ideas, but enormous investments, lucrative commissions, and the sizeable egos of architects and architectural critics. It is nonetheless revealing how each side laid claim to history. Stimmann, although not a political conservative, proclaimed that he wanted to recover Berlin's lost traditions. Libeskind, admirer of Berlin's legacy of innovation, replied that "Stimmann's approach simply erases the last fifty years of Berlin's history. He seeks a more carefree age."[17] Other critics pointed out that critical reconstruction's version of Berlin's history excluded every facet of East German architecture and planning, leading them to conclude that it represented yet another German attempt to deny the past—in this case, the decades of division and the very existence of the GDR.

In its selective appropriation of tradition, the new Berlin will make a statement about German national identity, although it might not be one intended by the city's planners. The English architect Richard Rogers, who worked briefly on the redesign of Potsdamer Platz, saw one such unintentional statement. He wondered why Berlin's planning process was "much too bound to the past" and obsessed with the period around 1900. Comparing German and French design competitions, he observed that the latter are all about art and about "making a monument to the glory of France," whereas the Germans, especially in Berlin, shrink from such ambitions.[18] Rogers clearly had Stimmann's guidelines in mind, but even stronger evidence supporting his point was furnished by Stimmann's conservative opponents, who proposed to restore the exact prewar appearance, not only of the royal palace, but also of Pariser Platz and parts of Unter den Linden. (In fact, Stimmann was ousted in 1996 by Christian Democrats who sought a more uncritical reconstruction of Berlin.) Rogers implies that Germany's national timidity has forced Berlin into a sterile search for historical roots.

Also in 1993, however, Vittorio Magnago Lampugnani blamed the same lack of historical confidence for the opposite architectural result. In a polemical article, Lampugnani, director of the German Architecture Museum in Frankfurt, charged that fear of the past has condemned German architecture to disorder by banishing all convention and tradition. Anyone who builds solid, sensible buildings with traditional materials like stone and wood, according to Lampugnani, is labeled a Nazi.[19] A perusal of the furious response to Lampugnani in German architectural journals during 1994 reveals that he was not wholly wrong. Lampugnani invited criticism, however, when he asserted that Germany needed to return to a tradition of sound, conservative architecture it had maintained until 1945. Like the builders of Stalinallee, Lampugnani sought to reclaim architectural traditions from the Nazis. But his angriest critics, such as Daniel Libeskind, saw the same denial of modernity in Lampugnani's prescriptions, Stimmann's rules, and Speer's architecture, whether in the "authoritarian and repressive edicts," the recycling of pillared facades and other classical details, or the use of granite to create the illusion of permanence.[20]

Germany has been called the first postmodern nation and the first postnational society. Those labels refer to the tendency of German intellectuals to reject any unselfconscious German identity and to insist on questioning its nature and genesis. As they well know, however, their questions attract attention only because national identity still matters and must be fought, promoted, or reformed, according to one's beliefs about it. German architecture and urban design cannot escape the crisis of German national identity. All cities' buildings display their cultural traditions, but the sandy soil of the German capital conceals the traces of a history so fiercely contested that no site, however vacant, is safe from controversy. Each proposal for construction, demolition, preservation, or renovation ignites a battle over symbols of

Berlin and of Germany. None of the pieces of the new Berlin will present an unambiguous statement about Berlin's tradition or meaning, but most will nevertheless be attacked for doing so. Berlin faces the impossible task of reconciling the parochial and the cosmopolitan, expressions of pride and of humility, the demand to look forward and the appeal never to forget. A building or monument might be able to display the wounds of Berlin's past, but it can do little to heal or even hide them. Politicians and architects who want to put to rest the ghosts of Berlin are probably doomed to failure.

Chronology of Berlin's History

c. 1200 Settlements of Berlin and Cölln founded on opposite banks of the Spree River; both are granted town charters in the following years.

1237 Oldest known document mentioning Cölln.

1244 Oldest known document mentioning Berlin.

1307 Berlin and Cölln form a joint government.

1415 Burgrave Friedrich VI of the house of Hohenzollern is named Elector Friedrich I of Brandenburg.

1442 Elector Friedrich II dissolves the joint government of Berlin-Cölln, revokes many of the towns' privileges, and compels Cölln to give him land on its northern edge for the construction of a palace.

1447–48 Citizens of Berlin and Cölln revolt unsuccessfully against the elector.

1451 Friedrich II moves into the palace in Cölln, where he resides part-time.

1486 The new elector, Johann, resides full-time in the Cölln palace.

1538–40 A new, expanded palace is built.

1539 Berlin and Cölln adopt the Lutheran liturgy.

1618–48 During the Thirty Years' War, armies repeatedly march through Berlin-Cölln, demanding money and food supplies and spreading disease. Population falls from twelve thousand to six thousand.

1640–88 Reign of Elector Friedrich Wilhelm, the "Great Elector."

1647 Friedrich Wilhelm establishes a tree-lined boulevard linking the palace with the Tiergarten, the royal game park; the street will become known as Unter den Linden.

1658–83 Large fortification walls are built around the area of Berlin, Cölln, and a strip of land on the edge of Cölln, which in 1662 is granted a charter as the town of Friedrichswerder.

1664 After years of conflict between Lutherans and Calvinists, the elector issues an edict of religious toleration.

1674 A fourth town, Dorotheenstadt, is established on the north side of Unter den Linden.

1685 King Louis XIV of France revokes the Edict of Nantes, which had granted freedom of worship to the Protestant Huguenots. Encouraged by Friedrich Wilhelm, six thousand of them come to Berlin in the following years.

1688–1713 Reign of Elector Friedrich III.

1688 A fifth town, Friedrichstadt, is established south of Unter den Linden.

1695 Construction begins on the arsenal (Zeughaus) on Unter den Linden and on the queen's palace west of town, which will become known as Charlottenburg.

1698 The baroque reconstruction and expansion of the elector's palace begins.

1701 In the city of Königsberg, Elector Friedrich III crowns himself Friedrich I, King in Prussia.

1709 The five towns Berlin, Cölln, Friedrichswerder, Dorotheenstadt, and Friedrichstadt are legally united into a single city.

1713–40 Reign of King Friedrich Wilhelm I, the "soldier king."

1734 Work begins on a new town wall, enclosing a vastly expanded area.

1740–86 Reign of King Friedrich II, "Frederick the Great."

1786–97 Reign of King Friedrich Wilhelm II.

1788–91 Construction of the new Brandenburg Gate.

1797–1840 Reign of King Friedrich Wilhelm III.

1806 Napoleon's troops defeat the Prussian army; the king flees from Berlin, which is then occupied by Napoleon and his army. Napoleon has the quadriga removed from the Brandenburg Gate and shipped to Paris.

1810 Founding of Berlin's university.

1812 Friedrich Wilhelm allies himself with Napoleon in the latter's invasion of Russia.

1813 After Napoleon's defeat in Russia, Friedrich Wilhelm forms an alliance with Tsar Alexander I. Russian troops drive the French out of Berlin.

1814 After the occupation of Paris, the quadriga is returned to Berlin.

1814–15 The Congress of Vienna grants Prussia substantial new territories.

1817–18 Schinkel's Neue Wache (New Guardhouse) is built on Unter den Linden.

1823–30 Schinkel's museum (now known as the Old Museum) is built.

1838 Berlin's first rail line, to Potsdam, is opened.

1840–61 Reign of King Friedrich Wilhelm IV.

1841 Berlin's municipal boundaries are greatly expanded, especially to the north.

1848 Revolution breaks out in Berlin in March. At first the king agrees to demands for constitutional rights, but by the end of the year troops have restored his power.

1849 Friedrich Wilhelm refuses to accept the crown of a united Germany, offered to him by the National

Assembly, which has been meeting in Frankfurt. Efforts to unite Germany collapse.

1861–88 Reign of King Wilhelm I.

1861 Berlin annexes the suburbs of Wedding, Gesundbrunnen, and Moabit, and parts of Tempelhof and Schöneberg.

1862–66 Constitutional crisis in Prussia; deadlock between the liberal parliament, on the one hand, and the king, civil service, army, and the new prime minister, Otto von Bismarck, on the other.

1864 Prussia and Austria defeat Denmark in a brief war over the duchies of Schleswig and Holstein.

1866 Prussia defeats Austria in a brief war, leading to the Prussian parliament's capitulation to Bismarck and to the establishment in 1867 of the North German Confederation, with Berlin as its capital.

1867–69 Demolition of the city wall.

1867–71 Construction of a ring railroad around the edge of the city.

1870–71 Victorious war with France leads to the establishment of the German Empire (Deutsches Reich) under Prussian leadership; King Wilhelm I becomes the German emperor (Kaiser), Bismarck becomes imperial chancellor, and Berlin becomes the imperial capital. Reparations payments from France help to fuel an ongoing boom of commercial expansion.

1873 A financial crisis leads to a depression that lasts for several years. The Victory Column on Königsplatz is dedicated. The municipal government takes over the city's water supply system and begins a massive expansion; it also begins planning a municipal sewer system.

1877 The city's population reaches one million.

1878–90 The Social Democratic Party is outlawed in Germany.

1882 Opening of an east-west elevated railway through the city center. Founding of the Berlin Philharmonic Orchestra.

1888 The "Year of Three Emperors": After the death of ninety-year-old Wilhelm I, his son Friedrich III lives only three months; *his* son, Wilhelm II, then reigns until 1918.

1890 Bismarck, unable to get along with Wilhelm II, resigns.

1894 Completion of Reichstag building.

1902 Opening of the first stretch of what becomes Berlin's subway system.

1914–18 World War I. Starvation, strikes, and political tensions in Berlin.

1918 On the eve of Germany's military defeat, mutinies by sailors spark revolutionary uprisings across Germany at the beginning of November. On November 9, the emperor flees into exile. Moderate and radical socialists struggle for power.

1919 In January, an abortive Communist uprising is brutally suppressed by irregular troops; they capture and murder the Communist leaders Rosa Luxemburg and Karl Liebknecht. National elections, followed by a constitutional convention in Weimar, lead to the establishment of a German republic, usually known as the Weimar Republic. Its representatives are compelled to sign the Treaty of Versailles.

1920 In the "Kapp Putsch" in March, right-wing soldiers briefly seize control of Berlin, but are forced to flee after a general strike shuts down the city.
"Greater Berlin" is created in October when the city is merged with its suburbs and surrounding towns. The city's land area increases more than tenfold and its population doubles to nearly four million. The expanded city is divided into twenty administrative districts.

1923 Inflation becomes hyperinflation, leading to strikes and demonstrations. The mark declines to 4.2 trillion to the dollar before a currency reform in November.

1925 The Republic's first president, Friedrich Ebert, dies; the retired general Paul von Hindenburg, seventy-seven years old, is elected as his successor.

1929–32 Amid growing unemployment, political street violence increases, especially clashes between Communists and Nazis, both of whom find growing support.

1932 Hindenburg is reelected president, defeating the Nazi Party leader, Adolf Hitler; but in Reichstag elections, the Nazis become the largest party.

1933 Hindenburg appoints Hitler chancellor on January 30. The Nazis use the burning of the Reichstag on February 27 as a pretext for revoking civil liberties; the Weimar Republic gives way to a dictatorship. Political opponents of the Nazis, especially communists and socialists, are harassed, arrested, and killed. Systematic discrimination against Jews begins.

1936 Olympic Games held in Berlin.

1938 In a first stage of Hitler's and Speer's plans for rebuilding Berlin, the Victory Column, statues of Bismarck, Moltke, and Roon, and the statues of the Victory Boulevard are moved from Königsplatz to the Great Star in the Tiergarten. On November 9, "Kristallnacht," an orchestrated mob action attacks Jews and burns synagogues and Jewish-owned shops.

1939 German attack on Poland begins World War II.

1940 First British bombs fall on Berlin.

1942 Conference in the suburb of Wannsee establishes the procedures for the "final solution to the Jewish question."

1943–45 British and American bombing reduces much of the city to ruins.

1945 On April 30, Hitler commits suicide in his bunker; on May 2, Berlin surrenders to the Red Army, which occupies the city. In accordance with previous agreements, the Soviets later hand over control of twelve of the city's twenty districts: six to the Americans, four to the British, and two to the French. All four powers participate in the Allied Kommandatura that governs the city.

1946 Leaders of the Communists (KPD) and Social Democrats (SPD) merge their parties into the new Socialist Unity Party of Germany (SED). Opponents of the merger from the SPD refound their party in the Western sectors. In citywide elections, the SED receives 19.8 percent of the vote, versus 48.7 percent for the SPD, 22.2 percent for the Christian Democratic Union (CDU), and 9.3 percent for the Liberal Democrats (LDPD).

1947 Ernst Reuter (SPD) is elected mayor by the city council, but Soviet opposition prevents his installation in office.

1948 Four-power control of Germany breaks down in March when the Soviet representative withdraws from the Allied Control Council. In June, the Soviets close the road and rail corridors between Berlin and the Western zones of Germany, to which the Americans respond with a massive airlift of supplies to the city. The city government is also divided between the Soviet and Western sectors.

1949 The blockade and airlift end in May. The Federal Republic of Germany (West Germany) is founded, with its seat of government in Bonn. It claims Berlin as one of its states, but the Western allies place restrictions on the Bonn government's sovereignty in Berlin. The founding of the German Democratic Republic (GDR, or East Germany) follows in October. It declares Berlin to be its capital.

1950 Demolition of the ruins of the royal palace in East Berlin.

1953 On June 16 and 17, striking workers in Berlin and elsewhere in the GDR demand economic and political reforms. Amid violent confrontations with police, the regime appears to be in danger until Soviet troops and tanks crush the demonstrations.

1957–1966 Willy Brandt (SPD) is mayor of West Berlin.

1958 The Soviet leader, Nikita Khrushchev, demands that all troops be withdrawn from West Berlin, which would then become a "free city." Lengthy negotiations among the leading powers reach no results.

1961 Khrushchev renews his call for a "free city," spurring an unprecedented flood of refugees from East to West Berlin. On August 13, East German soldiers, police, and workers seal the border to West Berlin with what becomes known as the Berlin Wall.

1963 An agreement in December permits West Berliners to visit their East Berlin relatives for the first time since 1961.

1966–68 A growing student movement in West Berlin, protesting against the West German political system, the Vietnam War, and American imperialism, organizes demonstrations that lead to occasional violence.

1969 The new West German chancellor, Willy Brandt, seeks to open diplomatic contacts to the GDR and the Soviet Union.

1971 Erich Honecker replaces Walter Ulbricht as head of the SED and thus as the ruler of the GDR.

1972 The first four-power agreement on Berlin since 1948 eases tensions surrounding the city's status and opens the way for a gradual increase in contacts across the Wall.

1979–85 East Berlin designates its new satellite cities Marzahn, Hohenschönhausen, and Hellersdorf as separate districts within Berlin, the first changes in the twenty districts created in 1920.

1980 Squatters illegally take possession of many empty buildings in West Berlin, especially in Kreuzberg.

1981 Following elections, the SPD is ousted from the West Berlin government for the first time since 1955; Richard von Weizsäcker (CDU) becomes mayor.

1984 Weizsäcker is elected federal president; Eberhard Diepgen (CDU) replaces him as mayor.

1989 West Berlin elections in January lead to the creation of a new government, a coalition of SPD and the

Alternative List, Berlin's version of the Green Party; Walter Momper (SPD) becomes mayor.
In response to massive demonstrations in Leipzig, East Berlin, and elsewhere in the GDR, Honecker is removed from office and the Berlin Wall is opened on November 9.

1990 The four powers agree to permit the unification of Germany. On July 1, the West German deutschmark becomes the currency of the GDR as well. On October 3, the GDR ceases to exist and its territories join the Federal Republic, in which the reunified Berlin is now one of sixteen federal states.
After citywide elections in December, a CDU/SPD coalition forms a new city government; Diepgen returns as mayor.

1991 The Bundestag votes to move the seat of government from Bonn to Berlin.

1994 The last troops from the four powers are withdrawn from Berlin.

1995 Christo and Jeanne-Claude, his wife and partner, wrap the Reichstag in aluminum-coated fabric for two weeks; afterward work begins to renovate it as the Bundestag's new home.

Notes

One: Berlin Walls

1. Richard von Weizsäcker, quoted in Reinhard Rürup, ed., *Topographie des Terrors* (Berlin: Arenhövel, 1987), 205. Unless otherwise noted, the translations from German are my own.

2. Wim Wenders, foreword to first version of screenplay for *Wings of Desire,* reprinted in the publicity materials for the film. I am grateful to Christian Göldenboog for furnishing the citation.

3. Strobe Talbott, ed. and trans., *Khrushchev Remembers: The Last Testament* (Boston: Little, Brown, 1974), 501–4.

4. *New York Times,* April 30, 1993.

5. *New York Times,* Nov. 5, 1991.

6. Friedrich Nietzsche, "The Use and Disadvantage of History for Life" (1872).

7. This distinction between "intentional" and "unintentional" monuments was first made by the Austrian art historian Alois Riegl in *Der moderne Denkmalkultus* (1903), translated by Kurt W. Forster and Diane Ghirardo as "The Modern Cult of Monuments: Its Character and Its Origin," *Oppositions* 25 (fall 1982): 21–50.

8. The name meant simply "Checkpoint C" in U.S. armyspeak. The Russian writer Yevgeny Yevtushenko's assertion—in a poem—that it was "named in honor of a black soldier" is merely proof of a cultural gap that dwarfed the Wall.

9. Dieter Hoffmann-Axthelm and Ludovica Scarpa, *Berliner Mauern und Durchbrüche* (Berlin: Verlag Ästhetik und Kommunikation, 1987).

10. On the sense of confinement, see Paul Gleye, *Behind the Wall: An American in East Germany, 1988–89* (Carbondale: Southern Illinois University Press, 1991), 135–49.

11. On the shift from weakness to strength in Western rhetoric, see Michael S. Bruner, "Symbolic Uses of the Berlin Wall, 1961–1989," *Communication Quarterly* 37 (1989): 319–28.

12. For example, *Neues Deutschland,* Nov. 6 and Dec. 1, 1963; and see David Shears, *The Ugly Frontier* (London: Chatto and Windus, 1971), 11, 75–79; and Peter Wyden, *Wall: The Inside Story of Divided Berlin* (New York: Simon and Schuster, 1989), 566–68.

13. On the border guards, see *Neues Deutschland,* Nov. 30, 1985. Excerpts from schoolbooks are reprinted in Jürgen Petschull, *Die Mauer,* 2d ed. (Hamburg: Gruner und Jahr, 1989), 256–57, and Thomas Davey, *A Generation Divided: German Children and the Berlin Wall* (Durham: Duke University Press, 1987), 17–18.

14. *Neues Deutschland,* Sept. 10, 1963, and Aug. 13, 1966; *Tagesspiegel,* Sept. 11, 1990. Official versions of their deaths are disputed by Peter Boris, "Grenzsoldaten der DDR Mordopfer westlicher Banden?" *Deutschland Archiv* 22 (1989): 925–31.

15. Heiner Stachelhaus, *Joseph Beuys,* trans. David Britt (New York: Abbeville, 1991), 131.

16. Dietfried Müller-Hegemann, *Die Berliner Mauerkrankheit* (Herford: Nicolai, 1973), 6.

17. Ibid., 127–28.

18. In Lutz Rathenow and Harald Hauswald, *Ostberlin: Die andere Seite der Stadt in Texten und Bildern* (Munich: Piper, 1987), 154.

19. Peter Schneider, *The German Comedy: Scenes of Life after the Wall,* trans. Philip Boehm and Leigh Hafrey (New York: Farrar, Straus and Giroux, 1991), 13.

20. Jochim Stoltenberg, "Eine neue Zukunft," *Berliner Morgenpost,* June 14, 1990.

21. Peter Schneider, *Der Mauerspringer* (Darmstadt: Luchterhand, 1982), 102.

22. *Berliner Morgenpost,* August 13, 1991.

23. Sylvia Conradt and Kirsten Heckmann-Janz, *Reichstrümmerstadt: Leben in Berlin 1945–1961* (Darmstadt: Luchterhand, 1987), 206–7.

Two: Old Berlin

1. Letter reprinted in Hans Herzfeld, "Berlin als Kaiserstadt und Reichshauptstadt," in Friedrich-Meinecke-Institut, *Das Hauptstadtproblem in der Geschichte* (Tübingen: Niemeyer, 1952), 168.

2. Alfred Döblin, *Schicksalsreise,* quoted in Akademie der Künste, *Zur historischen Mitte Berlins* (Berlin: Akademie der Künste, 1992).

3. Friedrich Fürlinger, "City Planning in Divided Berlin," in *Berlin: Pivot of German Destiny,* ed. Charles B. Robson (Chapel Hill: University of North Carolina Press, 1960), 189.

4. See, for example, Günter Stahn, *Das Nikolaiviertel* (Berlin: Verlag für Bauwesen, 1991), 52.

5. Quoted in Bodo Rollka and Klaus-Dieter Wille, *Das Berliner Stadtschloss* (Berlin: Haude und Spener, 1987), 95.

6. Reprinted in Gerd-H. Zuchold, "Der Abriss des Berliner Schlosses," *Deutschland Archiv* 18 (1985): 192.

7. Ibid., 194.

8. Ibid., 186.

9. This discussion of the Hohenzollern palace and the Communist palace is confusing enough in any language, but more so in English than in German. In German, the word for a royal palace *(Schloss)* is entirely distinct from the name the East Germans gave to their parliament building: Palast der Republik. Perhaps this linguistic confusion hampered the proponents of rebuilding the royal palace in their attempt to gain foreign support. Appended to a brochure they issued in 1992 (Förderverein für die Ausstellung, *Die Bedeutung des Berliner Stadtschlosses für die Mitte Berlins—Eine Dokumentation* [Berlin: Förderverein, 1992]) are numerous letters of support solicited from prominent German scholars and cultural figures. Also included are three letters in English, all from prominent architects. Two of these—from Frank Gehry and Michael Wilford (partner of the late James Stirling)—oppose rebuilding the old palace. In the third, the American architect Robert Venturi comes out firmly against tearing down the royal palace!

10. Joachim Fest, "Plädoyer für den Wiederaufbau des Stadtschlosses," in *Das neue Berlin,* ed. Michael Mönninger (Frankfurt: Insel, 1991), 118.

11. Heinrich Moldenschardt, "Marx' und Engels' Schloss-Freiheit," in Akademie der Künste, *Zur historischen Mitte Berlins,* 25.

12. Peter Findeisen, "Anmerkungen, auch zum Thema Neubau des Berliner Schlosses," *Kritische Berichte* 22 (1994): 56.

13. *Frankfurter Rundschau,* April 10, 1993.

14. Friedrich Dieckmann, "Staatsräume im Innern Berlins: Ein Streifzug," *Architektur in Berlin: Jahrbuch 1992* (Hamburg: Junius, 1992), 32.

15. *Der Spiegel,* no. 51, Dec. 14, 1992, 206.

16. Wolf Jobst Siedler, "Das Schloss lag nicht in Berlin," in Förderverein Berliner Stadtschloss, *Das Schloss? Eine Ausstellung über die Mitte Berlins* (Berlin: Ernst und Sohn, 1993), 20.

17. *Frankfurter Allgemeine Zeitung,* March 19, 1993.

18. Fest, "Plädoyer," 110–11.

19. Rüdiger Schaper, in *Süddeutsche Zeitung,* Dec. 15, 1992.

20. Klaus Landowsky, quoted in *Tageszeitung,* Jan. 29, 1992.

21. *Tageszeitung,* Jan. 28, 1992.

22. Wolf Jobst Siedler, "Das Schloss lag nicht in Berlin—Berlin war das Schloss," in Förderverein, *Die Bedeutung des Berliner Stadtschlosses,* 11; Fest, "Plädoyer," 115; Boddien, quoted in *A3000,* no. 3 (1993): 14.

23. Michael S. Cullen and Uwe Kieling, *Das Brandenburger Tor: Geschichte eines deutschen Symbols* (Berlin: Argon, 1990), 108.

24. Jürgen Reiche, "Symbolgehalt und Bedeutungswandel eines politischen Monuments," in *Das Brandenburger Tor: Eine Monographie,* ed. Willmuth Arenhövel and Rolf Bothe (Berlin: Arenhövel, 1991), 304.

25. Peter Möbius and Helmut Trotnow, "Das Mauer-Komplott," *Die Zeit* (overseas ed.), Aug. 16, 1991.

26. Friedrich Morin, *Berlin und Potsdam im Jahre 1860* (reprint, Braunschweig: Archiv-Verlag, 1980), 16.

27. *Frankfurter Allgemeine Zeitung,* April 18, 1991.

28. Ulrike Krenzlin, "Eisernes Kreuz und Preussen-Adler: Ja oder Nein?" in *Hauptstadt Berlin—wohin mit der Mitte?* ed. Helmut Engel and Wolfgang Ribbe (Berlin: Akademie, 1993), 104–7.

Three: Metropolis

1. Dominique Laporte, *Christo* (New York: Pantheon, 1986), 83.

2. *Berlin für Kenner: Ein Bärenführer bei Tag und Nacht durch die deutsche Reichshauptstadt* (Berlin: Boll und Pickardt, 1912), quoted in Jürgen Schutte and Peter Sprengel, eds., *Die Berliner Moderne 1885–1914* (Stuttgart: Reclam, 1987), 97.

3. Sarah Kirsch, *Erdreich* (Stuttgart: Deutsche Verlags-Anstalt, 1982), 48.

4. Quoted in Michael Simmons, *Berlin: The Dispossessed City* (London: Hamish Hamilton, 1988), 74.

5. Quoted in Michael S. Cullen, *Der Reichstag: Die Geschichte eines Monuments* (Berlin: Frölich und Kaufmann, 1983), 33.

6. Ibid., 38.

7. Quoted in ibid., 32.

8. Ibid., 407.

9. *Wochenpost,* June 14, 1995.

10. Christo, 1977, quoted in *Christo—Projekte in der Stadt 1961–1981* (Cologne: Museum Ludwig, 1981), 95.

11. Quoted in Cullen, *Der Reichstag,* 7.

12. Bundestag debate reprinted in Michael S. Cullen and Wolfgang Volz, eds., *Christo–Jeanne-Claude: Der Reichstag "Dem Deutschen Volke"* (Bergisch Gladbach: Lübbe, 1995), 247.

13. Ibid., 249.

14. Ibid., 255.

15. *Berliner Zeitung,* June 24–25, 1995.

16. Brandt, 1977, quoted in *Christo—Projekte in der Stadt,* 95.

17. Bundestag debate, in Cullen and Volz, *Christo–Jeanne-Claude,* 227.

18. *Frankfurter Allgemeine Zeitung,* Feb. 26, 1994.

19. Goerd Peschken, "The Berlin 'Miethaus' and Renovation," in *Berlin: An Architectural Profile,* ed. Doug Clelland (London: AD Publications, 1983), 51.

20. *Berlin and Its Environs: Handbook for Travellers,* 6th ed. (Leipzig: Baedecker, 1923), 50.

21. Peter Gay, *Weimar Culture: The Outsider as Insider* (New York: Harper and Row, 1968).

22. Christopher Isherwood, preface to *The Berlin Stories* (New York: New Directions, 1954), x.

23. Peter Gay, "The Berlin-Jewish Spirit," in *Freud, Jews, and Other Germans* (New York: Oxford University Press, 1978), 171.

24. Harold Nicolson, "The Charm of Berlin," reprinted in *The Weimar*

Republic Sourcebook, ed. Anton Kaes, Martin Jay, and Edward Dimendberg (Berkeley: University of California Press, 1994), 425.

25. Gay, "The Berlin-Jewish Spirit," 170.

26. Harry Kessler, *Tagebücher 1918–1937* (Frankfurt: Insel, 1961), 108.

27. Karl Scheffler, *Berlin—ein Stadtschicksal* (reprint, Berlin: Fannei und Walz, 1989), 219.

28. Wilhelm Hausenstein, "Berliner Eindrücke," in *Hier schreibt Berlin,* ed. Herbert Günther (Berlin: Internationale Bibliothek, 1929), 391.

29. Quoted in Alan Balfour, *Berlin: The Politics of Order, 1737–1989* (New York: Rizzoli, 1990), 114. Columbus Haus should not be (but often is) confused with the SS's notorious Columbiahaus concentration camp, a different building.

30. Karl Scheffler's response in *Vossische Zeitung,* Aug. 29, 1920, reprinted in *Glänzender Asphalt: Berlin im Feuilleton der Weimarer Republik,* ed. Christian Jäger and Erhard Schütz (Berlin: Fannei und Walz, 1994), 119–20.

Four: Nazi Berlin

1. Adolf Hitler, *Mein Kampf* (New York: Reynal and Hitchcock, 1939), 363–64.

2. Quoted in Hilmar Hoffmann, *Mythos Olympia* (Berlin: Aufbau, 1993), 27.

3. Norman H. Baynes, ed., *The Speeches of Adolf Hitler, April 1922–August 1939* (London: Oxford University Press, 1942), 593–94.

4. Werner Jochmann, ed., *Adolf Hitler, Monologe im Führerhauptquartier 1941–1944: Die Aufzeichnungen Heinrich Heims* (Hamburg: Knaus, 1980), 101.

5. Julius Karl von Engelbrechten and Hans Volz, *Wir wandern durch das nationalsozialistische Berlin: Ein Führer durch die Gedenkstätten des Kampfes um die Reichshauptstadt* (Munich: Eher, 1937).

6. Adolf Hitler, speech of August 2, 1938, reprinted in Angela Schönberger, *Die Neue Reichskanzlei von Albert Speer* (Berlin: Mann, 1981), 177.

7. Albert Speer, *Inside the Third Reich,* trans. Richard and Clara Winston (New York: Avon, 1971), 151.

8. On Kernd'l's views: Alfred Kernd'l, *Zeugnisse der historischen Topographie auf dem Gelände der ehemaligen Reichskanzlei Berlin-Mitte* (Berlin: Archäologisches Landesamt, 1993); *Tageszeitung,* July 2, 1992, and April 13, 1995; *Berliner Zeitung,* July 27, 1992; *Der Spiegel,* no. 16, April 17, 1994, 56–60; and personal conversation, June 28, 1995.

9. Hitler, speech of August 2, 1938, reprinted in Schönberger, *Die Neue Reichskanzlei,* 178.

10. Hitler, speech of January 9, 1939, reprinted in ibid., 185.

11. Quoted in Hans J. Reichhardt and Wolfgang Schäche, *Von Berlin nach Germania: Über die Zerstörung der Reichshauptstadt durch Albert Speers Neugestaltungsplanungen* (Berlin: Landesarchiv, 1984), 77.

12. Elias Canetti, *The Conscience of Words,* trans. Joachim Neugroschel (New York: Seabury, 1979), 145–53.

13. Speer, *Inside the Third Reich,* 189.

14. Ibid., 93–94.

15. The story of the former Japanese embassy seems to be one of cross-cultural misunderstanding. German and Japanese officials agreed to restore it as a cultural center, German preservationists having pressed to keep the building. But when the Japanese determined that the building was beyond repair, they kept their end of the agreement by tearing it down and building a new structure identical to the old one.

16. Speer, *Inside the Third Reich,* 123–24; Wolfgang Schäche, "Das ehemalige Reichssportfeld in Berlin," *Bauwelt* 84 (1993): 930–37; Tilmann Buddensieg, "Olympia 1936—Olympia 2000," in *Berliner Labyrinth* (Berlin: Wagenbach, 1994), 95–110.

17. Quoted in Duff Hart-Davis, *Hitler's Games: The 1936 Olympics* (London: Century, 1986), 227.

18. Schäche, "Das ehemalige Reichssportfeld," 931; Hoffmann, *Mythos Olympia.*

19. Norbert Huse, "Bauten des 'Dritten Reiches,' " in *Verloren, gefährdet, geschützt: Baudenkmale in Berlin,* ed. Norbert Huse (Berlin: Argon, [1988]), 139, 143.

20. Quoted in Rürup, *Topographie des Terrors,* 14.

21. Quoted in Stefanie Endlich, "Gestapo-Gelände: Entwicklungen, Diskussionen, Meinungen, Forderungen, Perspektiven," in Akademie der Künste, *Zum Umgang mit dem Gestapo-Gelände* (Berlin: Akademie der Künste, 1989), 32.

22. "Missbrauchter 20. Juli," editorial, *Frankfurter Allgemeine Zeitung,* June 4, 1994.

23. *Frankfurter Allgemeine Zeitung,* June 10, 1994.

24. On Plötzensee, see John Czaplicka, "History, Aesthetics, and Contemporary Commemorative Practice in Berlin," *New German Critique* 65 (spring/summer 1995): 173–80.

25. Stefanie Endlich and Thomas Lutz, *Gedenken und Lernen an historischen Orten: Ein Wegweiser zu Gedenkstätten für die Opfer des Nationalsozialismus in Berlin* (Berlin: Edition Hentrich, 1995), 144–45.

26. Rürup, *Topographie des Terrors,* 187.

27. Quoted in Endlich, "Gestapo-Gelände," 53.

28. *Abschlussbericht der Fachkommission zur Erarbeitung von Vorschlägen für die künftige Nutzung des "Prinz-Albrecht-Geländes" ("Gestapo-Geländes") in Berlin-Kreuzberg* (Berlin, 1990).

29. Akademie der Künste, *Diskussion zum Umgang mit dem "Gestapo-Gelände"—Dokumentation* (Berlin: Akademie der Künste, 1986), 22.

30. Quoted in Frederick Baker, "The Berlin Wall: Production, Preservation, and Consumption of a Twentieth-Century Monument," *Antiquity* 67 (1993): 727.

31. Thomas Biller, Barbara Lauinger, and Wolfgang Schäche, "Entsteh-

ung und Entwicklung des Untersuchungsgebietes," in Bauausstellung Berlin, *Dokumentation zum Gelände des ehemaligen Prinz-Albrecht-Palais und seine Umgebung* (Berlin: Bauausstellung Berlin, 1983), 33.

32. Perspektive Berlin, *Ein Denkmal für die ermordeten Juden Europas: Dokumentation 1988–1995* (Berlin: Perspektive Berlin, 1995), 117.

33. Ibid., 88–102.

34. *This Week in Germany,* May 12, 1995, 6.

35. *Foyer: Magazin der Senatsverwaltung für Bau- und Wohnungswesen,* 4, no. 2 (June 1994): 26.

36. Quoted in Endlich, "Gestapo-Gelände," 37.

37. Wolfgang Nagel, senator for construction and housing, in *Frankfurter Rundschau,* April 30, 1994.

38. The term "countermonument" is from James E. Young, *The Texture of Memory: Holocaust Memorials and Meaning* (New Haven: Yale University Press, 1993), 27–48.

39. *Die Zeit,* May 18, 1989.

40. See Eike Geisel, "Die Asche ist der Stoff für das gute Gewissen," *Tagesspiegel,* Jan. 6, 1995; and Rafael Seligmann, "Genug bemitleidet," *Der Spiegel,* no. 3, Jan. 16, 1995, 162–63.

Five: Divided Berlin

1. Arthur Tedder, quoted in Michael Mönninger, "City Islands in a Metropolitan Sea," *Deutschland* (English ed.), no. 1 (Feb. 1996): 44.

2. Stephen Spender, *European Witness* (New York: Reynal and Hitchcock, 1946), 240.

3. Speech of Dec. 8, 1951, in Walter Ulbricht, *Zur Geschichte der deutschen Arbeiterbewegung: Aus Reden und Aufsätzen* (Berlin: Dietz, 1958), 299–300.

4. Rolf Schwedler, "Berlin und der internationale Städtebau," *Vorwärts,* Jan. 28, 1971, 27.

5. *Frankfurter Allgemeine Zeitung,* Sept. 17, 1994.

6. The Federal Republic acknowledged itself to be the *legal* successor of the Third Reich.

7. Quoted in Frank Werner, *Stadtplanung Berlin: Theorie und Realität* (Berlin: Kiepert, 1976), 138.

8. Rudolf Herrnstadt in *Neues Deutschland,* July 29, 1951, quoted in Johann Friedrich Geist and Klaus Kürvers, *Das Berliner Mietshaus 1945–1989* (Munich: Prestel, 1989), 332–33.

9. *Neues Deutschland,* March 14, 1951, reprinted in Andreas Schätzke, *Zwischen Bauhaus und Stalinallee: Architekturdiskussion im östlichen Deutschland 1945–1955* (Braunschweig: Vieweg, 1991), 136–37.

10. Reprinted in Geist and Kürvers, *Das Berliner Mietshaus,* 312–17.

11. *Die Stalinallee—die erste sozialistische Strasse der Hauptstadt Deutschlands Berlin* (Berlin: Deutsche Bauakademie, [1952]), 32.

12. Schwedler, "Berlin und der internationale Städtebau"; Friedrich Fürlinger, "City Planning in Divided Berlin," in *Berlin: Pivot of German*

Destiny, ed. Charles B. Robson (Chapel Hill: University of North Carolina Press, 1960), 186–89; Werner, *Stadtplanung Berlin,* 266–74; Alfred Schinz, *Berlin: Stadtschicksal und Städtebau* (Braunschweig: Westermann, 1964), 200–202.

13. Philip Johnson, "Berlins letzte Chance," *Tagesspiegel,* June 14, 1993.

14. Schwedler, "Berlin und der internationale Städtebau"; Geist and Kürvers, *Das Berliner Mietshaus,* 355–83.

15. *Bild,* Leipzig ed., Nov. 1, 1990.

16. *Berliner Zeitung,* Nov. 15, 1991.

17. *Berliner Zeitung,* Nov. 6, 1991.

18. *Die Zeit,* June 4, 1993.

19. *Tageszeitung,* Oct. 19, 1991.

20. *Bericht der Kommission zum Umgang mit den politischen Denkmälern der Nachkriegszeit im ehemaligen Ost-Berlin* (Berlin: Abgeordnetenhaus, 1993).

21. Rudolf Wassermann in *Die Welt,* Sept. 18, 1991; Hans-Peter Schwarz in *Die Welt,* Jan. 17, 1992.

22. Annemarie Lange, *Berlin zur Zeit Bebels und Bismarcks* (Berlin: Das Neue Berlin, 1959); Lange, *Das wilhelminische Berlin* (Berlin: Dietz, 1967).

23. Johnson, "Berlins letzte Chance."

24. Annette Tietenberg, "Marmor, Stein, und Eisen bricht," in *Demontage,* ed. Bernd Kramer (Berlin: Karin Kramer, 1992), 116.

25. Quoted in Annette Leo, "Spuren der DDR," in ibid., 61.

26. *Berliner Zeitung,* June 18, 1993.

27. Preamble to *Abschlussbericht der Unabhängigen Kommission zur Umbennung von Strassen* (Berlin: Senatsverwaltung für Verkehr und Betriebe, 1994).

28. *Tagesspiegel,* May 10, 1995.

29. *Berliner Zeitung,* Feb. 11, 1992.

Six: Capital of the New Germany

1. Reprinted in Schönberger, *Die neue Reichskanzlei von Albert Speer* (Berlin: Mann, 1981), 179.

2. Norman Cameron and R. H. Stevens, trans., *Hitler's Secret Conversations, 1941–1944* (New York: New American Library, 1961), 67.

3. Hans Stimmann, "Berliner Abkommen," *Bauwelt* 82 (1991): 2092.

4. Peter Schneider, "Um Himmels willen, nehmt euch Zeit," *Der Spiegel,* no. 21, May 24, 1993, 55.

5. Quoted in *Der Spiegel,* no. 40, Oct. 1, 1990, 276.

6. Thomas Lutz, "Widerstreitende Erinnerung in einem Denkmal vereint," in *Im Irrgarten deutscher Geschichte: Die Neue Wache, 1818–1993,* ed. Daniela Büchten and Anja Frey (Berlin: Aktives Museum, 1993), 53.

7. Reinhart Koselleck, "Stellen uns die Toten einen Termin?" in Akademie der Künste, *Streit um die Neue Wache* (Berlin: Akademie der Künste, 1993), 34.

8. Ibid.

9. Quoted in Stefan Lange, "Etappen eines Diskussionsverlaufs," in Büchten and Frey, *Im Irrgarten,* 48.

10. Koselleck, "Stellen uns die Toten einen Termin?" 31.

11. Kathrin Hoffmann-Curtius, "Ein Mutterbild für die Neue Wache in Berlin," in Büchten and Frey, *Im Irrgarten,* 31–32.

12. *Frankfurter Allgemeine Zeitung,* April 16, 1993.

13. Walter Benjamin, "Paris, Capital of the Nineteenth Century," in *Reflections,* trans. Edmund Jephcott (New York: Harcourt Brace Jovanovich, 1978), 146–62; Benjamin, "Die Wiederkehr des Flaneurs," in Franz Hessel, *Ein Flaneur in Berlin* (Berlin: Das Arsenal, 1984), 277–81.

14. Dieter Hoffmann-Axthelm, "Hinweise zur Entwicklung einer beschädigten Grossstadt," *Bauwelt* 82 (1991): 565.

15. Tilmann Buddensieg, "Von Schinkel zur Moderne—Berlin als Stadt des Wandels," in *Neue Berlinische Architektur: Eine Debatte,* ed. Annegret Burg (Berlin: Birkhäuser, 1994), 43–61.

16. Daniel Libeskind, "Deconstructing the Call to Order," in *Berlin,* ed. Alan Balfour (London: Academy Editions, 1995), 35–36.

17. *Berliner Zeitung,* April 29–30, 1995.

18. *Tageszeitung,* March 24, 1993.

19. Vittorio Magnago Lampugnani, "Die Provokation des Alltäglichen," *Der Spiegel,* no. 51, Dec. 20, 1993, 142–47.

20. Libeskind, "Deconstructing the Call to Order," 36.

Bibliography

Much of the enormous literature on Berlin is directly relevant to topics covered in this book, but it would be pointless to attempt a comprehensive listing here. Also indispensable for my work was Berlin's and Germany's daily and weekly press, as well as the voluminous official publications of the Berlin government and unpublished information and materials provided by individuals listed in the acknowledgments. In this bibliography I merely want to identify the most important works that address aspects of my topic, giving particular emphasis to those available in English (where possible) and to less specialized works.

On the use of monuments and memorials to define national and urban identity, see John R. Gillis, ed., *Commemorations: The Politics of National Identity* (Princeton: Princeton University Press, 1994); and M. Christine Boyer, *The City of Collective Memory* (Cambridge: MIT Press, 1994). On the German debate in the 1980s over the interpretation of the Nazi past, see *Forever in the Shadow of Hitler? Original Documents of the Historikerstreit, the Controversy Concerning the Singularity of the Holocaust,* trans. James Knowlton and Truett Cates (Atlantic Highlands, N.J.: Humanities Press, 1993); Charles Maier, *The Unmasterable Past: History, Holocaust, and German National Identity* (Cambridge: Harvard University Press, 1988); and Richard J. Evans, *In Hitler's Shadow: West German Historians and the Attempt to Escape from the Nazi Past* (New York: Pantheon, 1989). On Germany's recent identity crises, two journalists' books stand out: Anne McElvoy, *The Saddled Cow: East Germany's Life and Legacy* (London: Faber and Faber, 1992); and Marc Fisher, *After the Wall: Germany, the Germans, and the Burdens of History* (New York: Simon and Schuster, 1995). See also Peter Schneider, *The German Comedy: Scenes of Life after the Wall,* trans. Philip Boehm and Leigh Hafrey (New York: Farrar, Straus and Giroux, 1991); and John Borneman, *Belonging in the Two Berlins: Kin, State, Nation* (Cambridge: Cambridge University Press, 1992).

The best single book on the Wall is Peter Wyden, *Wall: The Inside Story of Divided Berlin* (New York: Simon and Schuster, 1989). Dieter Hoffmann-Axthelm and Ludovica Scarpa, *Berliner Mauern und Durchbrüche* (Berlin: Verlag Ästhetik und Kommunikation, 1987), put the Wall in the context of modern urban development. Also on the Wall: Frederick Baker, "The Berlin Wall: Production, Preservation, and Consumption of a Twentieth-Century Monument," *Antiquity* 67 (1993): 709–33; Mary Beth Stein, "Berlin/Berlin: The Wall in the Expressive Culture of a Divided City" (Ph.D. diss., Indiana University, 1993); and Alexis Karolides, "For the Stone Will Cry Out of the Wall" (M.Arch. thesis, Rice University, 1992). On the infrastructure of divided Berlin, see three articles by Richard L. Merritt: "Political Division and Municipal Services in Postwar Berlin," *Public Policy* 17 (1968): 165–98; "Infrastructural Changes in Berlin," *Annals of the Association of American Geographers* 63 (1973): 58–70; and "Postwar Berlin: Divided City," in *Berlin between Two Worlds,* ed. Ronald A. Francisco and Richard L. Merritt (Boulder: Westview, 1986), 153–75.

On the Hohenzollern legacy and the palace controversy: Robert R. Taylor, *Hohenzollern Berlin: Construction and Reconstruction* (Port Credit, Ont.: P. D. Meany, 1985); Förderverein Berliner Stadtschloss, *Das Schloss? Eine Ausstellung über die Mitte Berlins* (Berlin: Ernst und Sohn, 1993); Akademie der Künste, *Zur historischen Mitte Berlins* (Berlin: Akademie der Künste, 1992); *Kritische Berichte* 22, no. 1 (1994); and Karl Markus Michel, "Liebknechts Balkon," *Kursbuch* 112 (June 1993): 153–73. On the Brandenburg Gate, the voluminous literature includes Willmuth Arenhövel and Rolf Bothe, eds., *Das Brandenburger Tor: Eine Monographie* (Berlin: Arenhövel, 1991); Laurenz Demps, *Das Brandenburger Tor* (Berlin: Brandenburgisches Verlagshaus, 1991); and Michael S. Cullen and Uwe Kieling, *Das Brandenburger Tor: Geschichte eines deutschen Symbols* (Berlin: Argon, 1990).

On the Reichstag: Michael S. Cullen, *Der Reichstag: Parlament, Denkmal, Symbol* (Berlin: be.bra, 1995); Jacob Baal-Teshuva, ed., *Christo: The Reichstag and Urban Projects* (Munich: Prestel, 1993); Michael S. Cullen and Wolfgang Volz, eds., *Christo–Jeanne-Claude: Der Reichstag "Dem Deutschen Volke"* (Bergisch Gladbach: Lübbe, 1995); and Ansgar Klein et al., eds., *Kunst, Symbolik, und Politik: Die Reichstagsverhüllung als Denkanstoss* (Opladen: Leske und Budrich, 1995).

Major works on the Mietskaserne include Johann Friedrich Geist and Klaus Kürvers, *Das Berliner Mietshaus,* 3 vols. (Munich: Prestel, 1980–89); Harald Bodenschatz, *Platz frei für das neue Berlin!* (Berlin: Transit, 1987); Albert Gut, *Das Berliner Wohnhaus des 17. und 18. Jahrhunderts* (Berlin: Verlag für Bauwesen, 1984); and Julius Posener, *Berlin auf dem Wege zu einer neuen Architektur: Das Zeitalter Wilhelms II.* (Munich: Prestel, 1979). General introductions to Berlin modernity include Charles W. Haxthausen and Heidrun Suhr, eds., *Berlin: Culture and Metropolis* (Minneapolis: University of Minnesota Press, 1990); Peter Jelavich, *Berlin Cabaret* (Cambridge: Harvard University Press, 1993); Michael Bienert, *Die eingebildete Metropole: Berlin im Feuilleton der Weimarer Republik* (Stuttgart: Metzler, 1992); and two volumes on *Industriekultur* edited by Jochen Boberg, Tilman Fichter, and Eckart Gillen: *Exerzierfeld der Moderne* (Munich: Beck, 1984) on the nineteenth century, and *Die Metropole* (Munich: Beck, 1986) on the twentieth. A selection of primary texts is translated in Anton Kaes, Martin Jay, and Edward Dimendberg, eds., *The Weimar Republic Sourcebook* (Berkeley: University of California Press, 1994). On the architecture of Potsdamer Platz, see Alan Balfour, *Berlin: The Politics of Order, 1737–1989* (New York: Rizzoli, 1990).

On Hitler's chancellery, his plans for Berlin, and Nazi architecture, see Angela Schönberger, *Die neue Reichskanzlei von Albert Speer* (Berlin: Mann, 1981); the documents collected in Olaf Groehler, *Die neue Reichskanzlei: Das Ende* (Berlin: Brandenburgisches Verlagshaus, 1995); Stephen D. Helmer, *Hitler's Berlin: The Speer Plans for Reshaping the Central City* (Ann Arbor: UMI Research Press, 1985); Wolfgang Schäche, *Architektur und Städtebau in Berlin zwischen 1933–1945* (Berlin: Mann, 1991); Barbara Miller Lane, *Architecture and Politics in Germany, 1918–1945* (Cambridge: Harvard University Press, 1968); and Robert R. Taylor, *The Word in Stone: The Role of Architecture in the National Socialist Ideology* (Berkeley: University of California Press, 1974). On the emotive power of Nazi architecture, see Klaus Herding and Hans-Ernst Mittig, *Kunst und Alltag im NS-System: Albert Speers Berliner Strassenlaternen* (Giessen: Anabas, 1975); and Hans-Ernst Mittig, "NS-Architektur für uns," in *Architektur und Städtebau der 30er/40er Jahre,* ed. Werner Durth and Winfried Nerdinger (Bonn: Deutsches Nationalkomitee für Denkmalschutz, 1993). Tony Le Tissier, *Berlin Then and Now* (London: Battle of Britain Prints International, 1992), carefully compares old and new photographs to pinpoint the location of historic events.

Reinhard Rürup, ed., *Topography of Terror,* trans. Werner T. Angress (Berlin: Arenhövel, 1989), is the English translation of the exhibition catalog. On the debate surrounding it: Akademie der Künste, *Zum Umgang mit dem Gestapo-Gelände* (Berlin: Akademie der Künste, 1988); and *Der umschwiegene Ort* (Berlin: Neue Gesellschaft für bildende Kunst, n.d.). Works that place Berlin's problems with Holocaust remembrance in a wider context include James E. Young, *The Texture of Memory: Holocaust Memorials and Meaning* (New Haven: Yale University Press, 1993); Ian Buruma, *The Wages of Guilt: Memories of War in Germany and Japan* (New York: Farrar, Straus and Giroux, 1994); Jochen Spielmann, "Gedenken und Denkmal," in *Gedenken und Denkmal: Entwürfe zur Erinnerung an die Deportation und Vernichtung der jüdischen Bevölkerung Berlins* (Berlin: Berlinische Galerie, 1988), 7–46; and Stefanie Endlich, introduction to *Kunst im Raum—Denkmäler* (Berlin: Senatsverwaltung für Bau- und Wohnungswesen, 1994), 6–11. Jane Kramer examines the controversial Holocaust memorial in the *New Yorker,* Aug. 14, 1995, 48–65.

On Stalinallee and other aspects of postwar planning: Berlinische Galerie, *Hauptstadt Berlin: Internationaler städtebaulicher Wettbewerb 1957–58* (Berlin: Mann, 1990); Wolfgang Schäche and Wolfgang J. Streich, eds., *Stadtentwicklung Berlin nach 1945,* vol. 1 (Berlin: Institut für Regionalplanung der

Technischen Universität, 1985); and three articles by Simone Hain: "Berlin Ost: 'Im Westen wird man sich wundern,' " in *Neue Städte aus Ruinen,* ed. Klaus von Beyme et al. (Munich: Prestel, 1992), 32–57; "Reise nach Moskau: Wie Deutsche 'sozialistisch' bauen lernten," *Bauwelt* 83 (1992): 2546–58; and "Zwischen sowjetischer Europapolitik und linkem Nationalismus," in *Berlin—Hauptstadt der DDR 1949–1989,* ed. Bernd Wilczek (Baden-Baden: Elster, 1995), 33–50.

On GDR monuments, the best source is the exhibition catalog, *Erhalten—Zerstören—Verändern?* (Berlin: Aktives Museum, 1990), as well as Bernd Kramer, ed., *Demontage* (Berlin: Karin Kramer, 1992). Memorial plaques have been cataloged in two volumes by Martin Schönfeld: *Gedenktafeln in Ost-Berlin* (Berlin: Aktives Museum, 1991) and *Gedenktafeln in West-Berlin* (Berlin: Aktives Museum, 1993). GDR political symbolism is the topic of Maoz Azaryahu, *Von Wilhelmplatz zu Thälmannplatz: Politische Symbole im öffentlichen Leben der DDR,* trans. Kerstin Amrani and Alma Mandelbaum (Gerlingen: Bleicher, 1991); he focuses on one aspect in "Street Names and Political Identity: The Case of East Berlin," *Journal of Contemporary History* 21 (1986): 581–604.

On the Neue Wache, see Christoph Stölzl, ed., *Die Neue Wache Unter den Linden: Ein deutsches Denkmal im Wandel der Geschichte* (Berlin: Deutsches Historisches Museum, 1993); Akademie der Künste, *Streit um die Neue Wache* (Berlin: Akademie der Künste, 1993); and Daniela Büchten and Anja Frey, eds., *Im Irrgarten deutscher Geschichte: Die Neue Wache, 1818–1993* (Berlin: Aktives Museum, 1993).

The recent debates about Berlin architecture and planning have filled German architectural journals; some contributions are collected in Alan Balfour, ed., *Berlin* (London: Academy Editions, 1995); Gert Kähler, ed., *Einfach schwierig: Eine deutsche Architekturdebatte* (Braunschweig: Vieweg, 1995); Annegret Burg, ed., *Neue Berlinische Architektur: Eine Debatte* (Berlin: Birkhäuser, 1994); and Michael Mönninger, ed., *Das neue Berlin* (Frankfurt: Insel, 1991).

Index